Musicia

Eat Cakes

S

E I

C M

N I

E L

D A

I R

C I

N T

I I

O E

C O N N E C T I O N S

POP AND ROCK MUSICIANS' PRIVATE LIVES

PUBLIC DEATHS AND THE BITS IN BETWEEN

Musicians eat cakes" is a statement to indicate that the breed of creatures that compose, sing and play instruments are human and enjoy the occasional pastry just like those that listen to the sounds that they create.

Sting sang about 'Soul Cakes', The Darkness released an album called 'Hot Cakes' and embarked on a 2012 world tour called 'Let them Eat Cakes'. George Harrison once said, "All the world is birthday cake, so take a piece, but not too much".
There is an American cross genre band called 'Cake', a British mainly covers band called 'Eat Cake' and an electronic 4-piece band from London who go by the name 'Eat More Cake'.

However, as far as this publication is concerned, 'cakes' is an acronym for _Connections And Koincidences Equal Similarities_

This little book contains information about pop and rock musicians that have something in common other than musicality and although containing comprehensive content, has been casually put together so remember that an author has poetic licence to spell coincidences with a 'K' if it serves a purpose.

In these pages are a collection of circumstances that do not have to be read in any particular order but can be opened anywhere and scanned for a crumb of trivia or read in bite sized chunks of fact.

Chapters begin with quotes from songs appropriately referenced but song titles and names of albums are contained throughout as sub-sections and the reader can try and guess the writers / who had hits with / dates and any other related trivia – just for additional enjoyment or head scratching – answers at the end of the book.

So, have a nibble or finish it in one go and enjoy the separate ingredients that are OK on their own but are much more interesting when mixed together.

Any feedback is welcome, musicianseatcakes@btinternet.com providing that it is positive because if you wanted literal literature you should have ordered a main course rather than what goes best at coffee break -
a little slice of cake that even musicians eat.

INGREDIENTS

Appendix

PREFACE

There have been many interesting characters in the world of pop and rock music, some continuing to attract media attention while others have fallen by the wayside or shuffled off their mortal coil prematurely. This publication highlights connections from tenuous to tragic, coincidental to accidental in the lives and sometimes deaths of those who contributed to the soundtracks of our lives.

There are numerous in depth (auto) biographies of singers and musical players available, as well as lists, charts and quizzes. There have also been conspiracy theories, rumours and gossip surrounding the famous and infamous with readers often having difficulty separating fact from fiction.

This work highlights connections out with the studio, away from the musical collaborations and concentrates on relations, relationships and similarities in musicians' private lives.

Not all the wives, girl or boyfriends of featured artists are name checked, only those with musical connections or to others mentioned in the book. Similarly, not all family members are noted, only those with musical links.

Any reference to drugs, alcohol or the word 'groupie' is not made in a judgemental manner and many great musicians are not included because their stories do not connect to the themes discussed.

However, it is an easy read that does not bog the reader down with masses of information but tells enough about each of the characters to place them in context and the bibliography references further reading for those that wish to delve further into the backgrounds of the more enigmatic musicians mentioned.

It can be flicked through at leisure for interest, to select questions for trivia quizzes and as a reference for "whatever happened to 'oh what were they called'? "

Enjoy

Acknowledgements

Thanks to those who assisted with the content of this book all listed in the bibliography.

'For Emily, Whenever I May Find Her' * and all those who appreciate music, musicians, coincidences, connections, similarities, sarcasm, cynicism and humour.

*(a song by Paul Simon who said that Emily is not a person, the name is used to personify belief)

INTRODUCTION

When Harry Met Carey

In 1971, the song 'Without You' was number one in the music charts of the UK and Australia for 5 weeks, USA for 4, Ireland for 3 and 2 weeks at the top in New Zealand. The single made top 10 in Holland, Italy and South Africa and appeared in the top 50 of many others.

The singer of this version was credited as Nilsson and the writers were Pete Ham and Tom Evans.

Taking this information as a starting point, a number of connections and coincidences can be linked to highlight the theme for the remainder of this book.

Harry Edward Nilsson III's early life was chronicled in the autobiographical lyrics of his song, simply called '1941'.

"In 1941 the happy father had a son, in 1944 the father walked right out the door" - (i)

(Coincidently, history repeated itself thirty years later when Harry's second wife gave birth to his son

Zachary and Harry walked right out the door. The couple divorced and Nilsson was an absent father to Zak, although he remarried and had another six children).

Harry and one (half) sibling were raised by his mother while the third child was split from the rest of the family and raised elsewhere. Nilsson became interested in music from an early age, learned to play guitar and piano and began writing songs in the early 1960's. His first recordings were made in 1966 while he worked in a bank but quit to become a full time musician. At the launch of Apple, by the Beatles in 1968, John Lennon was asked who his favourite American artist was and he replied, Harry Nilsson. When Paul McCartney was asked to name his favourite American band, he gave the same answer. Nilsson had a vocal range beyond the average for a male voice and his break came when he recorded a song for the 1969 Movie 'Midnight Cowboy'. His own composition, 'I Guess The Lord Must Be In New York City' was rejected for the film but his version of the Fred Neil song 'Everybody's Talkin' was included and gained Harry Nilsson his first of two Grammy awards, the second being for 'Without You'.

Nilsson had further recognition as a writer of the Three Dog Night US hit 'One', well received album recordings and film and TV work including the children's short film 'The Point' but ironically for a songwriter, his biggest successes were with the two cover versions.

Pete Ham and Tom Evans were founding members of the UK Group – Badfinger, in 1969.

The band were signed to The Beatles' Apple record label, had 3 top 10 hits in the UK and USA with the Paul McCartney penned 'Come and Get It' followed by two Pete Ham compositions 'No Matter What' and 'Day After Day'. They had moderate album success, a few more singles that were minor hits, contributed to the soundtrack for the film The Magic Christian and were part of the backing band at the Concert for Bangla Desh in 1971. However, their achievements were eclipsed by Nilsson's cover version of the Ham / Evans song 'Without You'. Bad management, poor accounting decisions and internal fall outs between band members resulted in the original group disbanding in 1975.

This demise was unavoidable due to the tragic taking of his own life by Pete Ham.   Depressed and despondent, Ham hanged himself at the age of 27.

His 'Without You' co-writer Tom Evans continued with differing membership as Badfinger from 1978 until 1983 when tragically and coincidently, he also hanged himself.

After the major success of 'Without You', Harry Nilsson's career continued with more critical acclaim and criticism than public recognition and sales.
He ruptured his vocal chords during the infamous 'Pussycat' sessions with John Lennon and along with the ex-Beatle, his ex-colleague drummer Ringo Starr, ex-Monkee drummer Mickey Dolenz, and madcap Who drummer Keith Moon, the musicians were reported more for their drinking habits and behaviour than musical output.

Nilsson owned property in London, flat number 12, 9 Curzon Street near Mayfair.   When he wasn't staying there himself, he let friends have the use of it but tragedy struck in July 1974 when ex Mamas and Papas vocalist Cass Elliot was living there during her run of London Concert appearances.
Returning to the flat, exhausted after a show, Cass had a heart attack and died aged 32.
It was widely reported that she had choked to death on a ham sandwich but that is not the case.

Four years later, Nilsson's friend Keith Moon was living in the apartment and tragically died from an overdose of prescription drugs. Coincidently, Moon was also 32 years of age when he died and his death was in the same room where Mama Cass had passed away.

Devastated at the death of two friends in his house, Harry Nilsson sold the property and it was purchased by Moon's band mate from The Who, Pete Townsend.

In 1980, Harry was in the recording studio, coincidently writing a note to his friend John Lennon when he heard the news that the ex-Beatle had been shot dead.
Nilsson rarely appeared in public but this event spurred him on to become a spokesperson for the Coalition to Stop Gun Violence.

Harry Nilsson's health deteriorated and he had a massive heart attack in 1993, dying in January the following year at the age of 52.

The week following his death, Mariah Carey released her version of 'Without You' which became her biggest hit out with the USA where it reached number 3 in the charts, hitting the top spot in the UK, Austria, Germany, Holland, Ireland, Italy, New Zealand and Switzerland.

Mariah Carey, like Harry Nilsson was born in New York, was estranged from her father at the age of 3 and raised by her mother along with one sibling while the other (like Nilsson's experience) was split from the family and raised elsewhere.

She began singing from an early age and has a voice covering more than the standard octave range.

Therefore, from one song, two writers and two singers there are similarities, connections and coincidences in their life stories.

"But I guess that's just the way the story goes" - (ii)

Chapter 1

CHANGE PARTNERS

"Please then remember and don't get too close to one special one, he will take your defences and run. So we change partners, time to change partners, we must change partners, Again"   -   (iii)
Lyrics by Stephen Stills

The lifestyles of pop stars / rock musicians are not conducive to stable relationships due to the non-standard hours, requirement to travel, too little or too much money and the inevitable temptations.

Added to these practicalities are the often adventurous, experimental personalities of those involved and we have enough material to keep the gossip columnists busy for years, not to mention agony aunts, guidance counsellors and lawyers.

Then we have the more recent phenomenon of social media the content of which can influence relationships or at the very least spread rumours to the extent that no one knows what to believe.

You're The One That I Want

There are of course exceptions to the rule such as Rolling Stones drummer Charlie Watts who married his wife Shirley in 1964, Bee Gee Barry Gibb who wed Linda in 1970 and the shy 'asphalt businessman' Carl Thomas Dean who tied the knot with not so shy songstress Dolly Parton four years earlier. These marriages endured as did the thirty years and counting nuptials of Paul Hewson and Alison Stewart aka Mr and Mrs Bono but in many cases those striving for gold records with their bands rarely succeed in keeping the vows of their gold wedding bands and after playing together change tune and go solo.

One singer got married at the age of 16 to his pregnant girlfriend of the same age and they are still married more than 50 years later despite the reputation, rumours and admission by Tom Jones of his exploits with other women. Jones married his childhood sweetheart Linda in 1957, prior to his fame and they have remained husband and wife even although he confesses to have slept with up to 250 women a year at one point in his career.

Singer and songwriter Neil Sedaka sang that 'Breaking up is Hard to do' and has confirmed this by continuing to perform as a musician whilst remaining married to wife Leba for half a century.

However, the majority of pop / rock nuptials last considerably shorter, but the lives and in many cases, 'shared' loves of musicians offer similarities, on occasion coincidences and often connections. Perhaps it is inevitable that those who move in musical circles attract particular types of partners but it is surprising that even after failed relationships, the allure of musicians is too much for some and they continue romantic liaisons with others from the industry.

So much has been written about the lives and times of John, Paul, George and Ringo that most people think that they know all there is to know about the members of The Beatles.

In that case, it would be easy to answer the question, " Who, out of the 'fab four' married an English girl and following divorce, married someone from America ?"

The answer, coincidently, is all four Beatles.

John was first to get married, on 23 August 1962 when he wed Blackpool born, Cynthia Powell. The pair divorced in November 1968 by which time he had met Japanese born, but raised in the USA, Yoko Ono. Cynthia has since been married several times but the few years she spent with John as Mrs Lennon coincided with his rise to fame, through the 'Beatlemania' phase, first experiences with drugs and spiritual experimentation.

Such a rollercoaster life for newlyweds with a young child added to the pressures in the relationship and the couple's lives diverged. Cynthia has written about this part of her life and although many may have envied her position, she has always been candid in stating her perspective. Their split and John's subsequent life with Yoko Ono was played out in public as was his views on peace and universal love, but Cynthia's experience was of physical abuse and an absent father to their young son.

Ringo married Liverpudlian Maureen Cox in February 1965, separated in 1970, formally divorcing five years later. He got hitched to American Barbara Bach in April 1981.

George and Somerset born Pattie Boyd tied the knot in January 1966 and were divorced in the mid 1970's. In 1978, the guitarist married Mexican born but raised in the USA, Olivia Trinidad Arias.

Following his divorce from Hampshire born Heather Mills in 2008 Paul wed New Yorker Nancy Shevell in 2011.

Therefore, to an extent, their personal lives followed the same pattern, but their marital experiences were not altogether as harmonious as their musical collaborations.

Although Paul McCartney married an English girl followed by an American, he was of course married to an American initially, a union that lasted almost 30 years from 1969 until 1998 when Linda McCartney passed away as a result of breast cancer.

A much publicised romance with actress Jane Asher in the 1960's led to Paul moving in to the Asher's London home and the pair becoming engaged but the pressures of fame and the couple's busy work schedules resulted in the arrangement running its course and Jane and Paul separated.

Linda Eastman had a colourful past; brought up in the Scarsdale district of New York she attended Sarah Lawrence College before leaving to work in the Arts, previously married and with a daughter prior to meeting the Beatle who would become her husband. Linda was a rock photographer and had a reputation in music circles as a 'groupie' before hitching up with Macca. However, one report clarifies her status regarding musicians pre-McCartney, when Jefferson Airplane co-founder and lead singer Marty Balin ended up in bed with the photographer assigned to take pictures of his band. (1)

"She was a foxy chick and all of us were trying to make it with her and get close to her and everything. Somehow she ended up with me sleeping the night where I was, at my pad, but she left her bra and her panties on, you know, and I was making my moves, and she just turned me down. She says, 'I'm going to be with the biggest guy in the world' and then later she married Paul McCartney. She knew what she was headed for...she told me flat out... she had her sights set on somebody and that was that".

Author Howard Souness included this quote in his biography of Paul McCartney and despite Balin's statement, Souness claims that (2)

" Over the next two years Linda notched up approximately twenty lovers, most of whom were famous, including singers Tim Buckley and Jim Morrison".

Irrespective of their past experiences and the heartbreak that their nuptials caused to many McCartney fans, the marriage between Linda Eastman and James Paul McCartney was as successful as Paul's song writing. Paul adopted Linda's daughter Heather and had another three children Mary, Stella and James, with Linda. The Beatle's single from the era 'Get Back' is reportedly aimed at Paul McCartney's new wife's ex-husband Mel (real name Joseph / JoJo from Tucson Arizona) but although this is presumed by many to be the case, Paul maintained it was a fictional song.

After the Beatles, the couple along with one time Moody Blues' member Denny Laine, founded the band 'Wings'. As 'Wings' was just getting off the ground, another JoJo appeared in 1972 and the 'Get Back' phrase could well have been directed at her, even although it had been written a few years prior to their meeting. JoJo Patrie had been a model and

'groupie' who went on to marry Wings' guitarist Denny Laine but her presence created jealousy in the McCartney household. As Laine stated, (3) "She was basically trying to go through me to get to Paul" and he continued,
"I find it insulting that Linda looked on JoJo as a groupie. Linda was one of the biggest groupies on the face of the Earth if you want to put labels on people".

However, 'My Love', 'Mull of Kintyre', 'Live and Let Die' and the album 'Band on the Run' were all completed while Laine was a member of 'Wings' so the musicians rose above their personal differences to create together.

Linda went on to become an activist and entrepreneur in the vegetarian food business and Paul was devastated on the death of his soul mate in 1998 from the cancer she had been fighting for a few years and it was some time before the eligible widower was seen with a female companion in public.

Heather Mills was a controversial character who came to prominence as a charity worker following the amputation of her left leg below the knee as a result of being hit by a Police car in 1993. The ex-model was an inspiration to other disabled persons campaigning against landmines and other causes. However, there were inconsistencies and dubious allegations regarding her history and some erratic behaviour, suggestions of being a gold-digger and bad press put added pressure on the six year marriage of Heather and Paul. They were married in 2002 but separated by 2006, 3 years after the birth of their daughter Beatrice. A bitter divorce case was played out in public and the pair formally untied their knot in 2008.

Nancy Shevell was a successful business woman in her own right when she met Paul and the pair wed in 2011, in the same location, Marleybone Register Office, London, where Paul had married first wife Linda, 42 years previously. Nancy is a graduate from Arizona State, coincidently the same University that Linda had once attended.

Early in the Beatle's career, the group were marketed as 'four lads who shook the world' and appeared in all sorts of magazines, featured on various memorabilia and their individual personalities were portrayed as Ringo the happy fun guy, Paul cute, George the quiet one and cheeky chappie sarcastic John. The fact that John Lennon was a married man was kept under wraps during the Beatlemania phase and Cynthia and the couple's son Julian were rarely mentioned in the press.

Although The Beatles' story has been told and retold, before introducing anecdotes and facts about other musicians, the relationships of the 'fab four' and friends is worth retracing to highlight the similarities, connections and coincidences.

The Beatles formative musical direction was assisted and influenced by George Martin while the group's image and public personas were organised as far as he could control, by Manager Brian Epstein. It was suggested that Epstein felt intimidated by John Lennon's strong character but also recognised his individuality and the bachelor Manager attempted to have a relationship with Lennon whilst the pair were on holiday in Spain but was subjected to ridicule by the Beatle for his ludicrous attempt.

John Lennon first met Yoko Ono in late 1965 / early 1966, when the avant-garde conceptual artist put on a show and the outspoken singer / songwriter / guitarist handled an exhibit but it was not until 1968 that they became more of an item.

Prior to this, singer / songwriter Al Stewart met Yoko Ono when she was trying to raise £ 1000 to make a film and his experience can give an insight into her unique approach to art, when he asked what the intended film was about, Yoko replied, (4)
"Al, I want to make a film about people's bottoms``.
Undaunted, Al stomped up £ 100 for a 10% stake.
He was also the first to experience her original vocal compositions as Yoko confirmed,
"I did not have a set up like Al had then. So it was great that Al recorded me. He just pushed a few buttons and said go ahead so I started singing".

Until this time, the general public was not aware of the diminutive Japanese woman who would have a major effect on John Lennon, but although the following description was used to introduce Linda Eastman to the Beatle's story, it coincidently also applies to Yoko Ono.

"Brought up in the Scarsdale district of New York, she attended Sarah Lawrence College before leaving to work in the Arts, previously married and with a daughter prior to meeting the Beatle who would become her husband".

Therefore there are real similarities in the backgrounds of the woman that Paul McCartney married on 12 March 1969 and the woman that became the second wife of John Lennon just over a week later.

The events leading up to the Lennons' actual marriage were described in The Beatles' hit single 'The Ballad of John and Yoko' and their 'bed-ins', 'bag-ins' and other publicity events created controversial attention. Often ridiculed for the influence she had over her talented husband and blamed by some for the break – up of the most famous act in modern music, Yoko and John had one son together and despite a separation in the mid 1970's, they stayed together until John's untimely death in 1980.

During his split from Yoko, John had a relationship with May Pang. Although John referred to the time as his 'lost weekend' he was estranged from Yoko for about 18 months. Pang was later married and had two children with record producer Tony Visconti whose previous wife and mother of his other two children was the Welsh singer Mary Hopkin, another Apple label signing.

Yoko miscarried John's child in 1968 but their son Sean Taro Ono Lennon was born 7 Years later.

Richard Starkey was the last member to join the group when, in 1962, he replaced Pete Best as The Beatles' drummer. Nicknamed Ringo, he assumed the surname Starr and throughout the band's recordings, his token vocals were usually on the light-hearted songs like 'Yellow Submarine' and 'Octopus's Garden. Ringo and Maureen Cox had three children together, Zak, Jason and Lee and the couple divorced in 1975. Maureen later wed Isaac Tigrett, one of the co-founders of The Hard Rock Café and House of Blues, and the pair had a daughter Augusta. Maureen Starkey Tigrett died from leukaemia in December 1994, aged 48. In 1980, Ringo was in the movie 'Caveman' with actress and ex-Bond girl Barbara Bach and the following year, they were married.

Coincidently, 16 years previously, George Harrison had also met his wife to be on the set of a film. 20 year old Pattie Boyd was hired to play the part of a schoolgirl in The Beatle's first film, A Hard Day's Night in 1964. George asked her for a date and their relationship led to marriage 2 years later. Pattie took an interest in meditation, and the husband and wife were instrumental in the Beatles sojourn to Rishikesh in India at the invitation of the Maharishi Mahesh Yogi and they were accompanied by Pattie's sister Jenny and singer songwriter Donovan as well as Beach Boy Mike Love, jazz musician Paul Horn and others from outside the music industry. Many songs were written or inspired by that trip, including Donovan's 'Jennifer Juniper' (about Jenny Boyd), Lennon / McCartney's 'Dear Prudence' (about Mia Farrow's sister who was also in attendance) and 'Julia' (about John Lennon's mother). The lyrics to earlier Beatle's songs had been instigated by childhood memories of Liverpool, such as 'Penny Lane' and 'Strawberry Fields Forever' but increasingly some personal subjects were appearing. 'Hey Jude' was written for John Lennon's son Julian and George wrote 'Something' *for* his wife Pattie (a fact which Pattie confirmed in her autobiography, although George had previously denied that it was not expressly *about* her). Frank Sinatra, who was married to Mia Farrow at the time, described this song as the greatest love song of the past 50 years.

Although initially devoted to each other, cracks appeared in the Harrison's marriage and George had a fling with Ringo's wife Maureen. Pattie refers to this in her autobiography (5)

"The final straw was his affair with Maureen Starr......Then I found them locked into a bedroom at Friar Park.....Eventually he opened the door and said, 'Oh she's just a bit tired so she's lying down'......Maureen wasn't even prepared to be subtle.....she would turn up at Friar Park at midnight".

George had also become friendly with 'Cream' guitarist Eric Clapton and the two guitarists spent more time together when their respective bands split up and as George became more interested in Eastern religions, Eric became more interested in Mrs Harrison, writing the song 'Layla' for and about her. Eventually, Pattie moved in with Clapton, marrying him in 1979, however Faces and soon to be Rolling Stones guitarist Ronnie Wood added further intrigue to this chapter in the musicians' lives with revelations of his romantic involvement. Relating to himself and his then wife Krissie, he maintains, (6)
"George let her go (Pattie). But she wasn't going to be taken without me being her loving intermediary. That was around the same time that Krissie had a short fling with George. Remember, I'd pinched Krissie from Eric, and later, after Pattie and Eric split up, I had a lovely thing going with Pattie".

Musical chairs was becoming more common as the established musicians played together out with the confines of group membership structures but bed hopping and wife swapping was also not unusual.

Wood's first solo album was called 'I've Got my own Album to do' which is ironic considering many members of the Rolling Stones as well as George Harrison appear on it, but musically and personally many musicians and spouses at the time did get by with a little help from their friends.

George saw Olivia Arias when she was working in the Los Angeles office of his then record company and he asked her on a date, a romance which led to marriage in 1978, a son Dhani, born the same year and a marital partnership that lasted until George's death in 2001.

Pattie Boyd's sister Jenny, married Fleetwood Mac drummer Mick Fleetwood in 1970 and the couple had two daughters. They divorced in the mid 1970's but remarried and divorced again.

Therefore, for a time George Harrison and Mick Fleetwood were brothers in law through marriage.

Jenny had an affair with Bob Weston, one of Fleetwood Mac's guitarists resulting in him being ostracised and eventually fired from the group. She later married ex-King Crimson and session drummer Ian Wallace.

Fleetwood Mac in the 1970's was a musical soap opera, producing one of the best-selling albums ever in 'Rumours', which described the changing relationships between group members through songs such as 'You Make Loving Fun', 'Go Your Own Way',

Dreams' and 'Don't Stop'. In addition to Mick and Jenny's marital situation, Mick Fleetwood also had an affair with one of the group's writers and lead vocalists, Stevie Nicks. She was the long term girlfriend / partner of the band's guitarist / singer / writer Lindsey Buckingham.

Bassist John McVie was married to keyboardist / singer / songwriter Christine McVie but the couple went through a separation as Rumours was being made. Christine was seeing one of the band's lighting operators around this time and went on to have a relationship with Beach Boy drummer Dennis Wilson for a couple of years.

Stevie Nicks had a few liaisons with musicians, notably Eagles drummer Don Henley (by whom it was rumoured that she became pregnant, but did not bear a child). She was also romantically involved with one of the Eagles co-songwriters John David Souther and later claimed that her soul mate was Eagles' guitarist Joe Walsh.

Coincidently, bringing the connection back to The Beatles, in 2008 Joe Walsh married Marjorie Bach, Barbara's sister, making him Ringo Starr's brother in law through marriage.

Writing about marriage, relationship difficulties and affairs within a band setting proved successful for

Fleetwood Mac in the mid 1970's but ten years earlier, the same formulae were used by the Mamas and Papas. Husband and wife John and Michelle Phillips along with 'platonic' pair Cass Elliot and Denny Doherty had a successful string of harmonious songs in the mid 1960's such as 'Monday Monday' and 'Dedicated to the One I Love' but as relationships developed, lyrics reflected the changes. Michelle and Denny had an affair resulting in her expulsion from the group for a time, before being reinstated. Autobiographical lyrics of 'Creeque Alley' and 'I Saw Her Again Last Night' detail the personal situation within the quartet at the time.

Two acts that achieved success in the 1960's as married couples but by the following decade had gone their separate ways musically and personally were Ike & Tina Turner and Sonny and Cher. The heights of musical stardom achieved by both Tina Turner and Cher as solo artists eclipsed by far their previous successes alongside their ex-husbands.

In 1951 Ike Turner released a record called 'Rocket 88' which has been nominated as the first example of a Rock & Roll tune. He continued playing through the 1950's and in 1956 he met 16 year old Anna Mae Bullock who changed her name to Tina Turner and the pair married.

Although an accomplished guitarist, Ike was allegedly paid not to play on the Phil Spector epic 'River Deep Mountain High' in 1966. This recording catapulted the name Ike & Tina Turner into the pop charts although it was Tina's screeching vocals and Spector's wall of sound that were memorable.

On the back of this success, The Ike & Tina Turner Review continued touring with a changing number of singers as backing vocalists in The Ikettes. Their next major hits were a cover of John Fogerty's 'Proud Mary' and Tina's song about her hometown 'Nutbush City Limits' but unknown to the public the singer was suffering abuse at the hands of her domineering, cocaine addicted husband. By the mid-70's the couple had split professionally and personally and from Ike's perspective, the once accomplished guitarist and showman would lapse into relative obscurity with no more than a reputation as a drug dependent wife abuser.

On the other hand, Tina Turner's popularity was in the ascendency from her initial acting role as the Acid Queen in the Who's Tommy, she had a leading role in Mad Max beyond Thunderdome. Musically, a new generation witnessed 'Private dancer', 'What's Love Got to do with it', 'We Don't Need Another Hero' as well as duets with Bryan Adams 'It's Only Love' and Mick Jagger, her version of a Bond theme 'Goldeneye', 8 Grammy awards and major tours and live performances. When Ike Turner died in 2007, Tina claimed that she had not been in contact with him for 30 years and made preparations for her 50th anniversary tour.

During the existence of the Ike and Tina Turner Review, The Ikettes provided visual and vocal support to the husband and wife duo. A number of backing vocalists who once appeared in the line-up of Ikettes went on to provide vocals for other major acts – Vanetta Fields and Clydie King worked on 'Gimme Shelter' by The Rolling Stones, 'Wish You Were Here' by Pink Floyd and toured with Ray Charles as The Raylettes. Pat Arnold (PP) was prominent on The Small Faces Tin Soldier and solo work in the late 1960's and uniquely the first Caucasian Ikette was Bonnie O'Farrell. On leaving the 'Revue' she met singer Delaney Bramlett and the pair were married within a week. Delaney and Bonnie and Friends – with 'Friends including Eric Clapton and George Harrison recorded and toured for 5 years before splitting professionally and personally. During that time, Bonnie co-wrote with Leon Russell 'Superstar' a hit for The Carpenters and much covered by other artists and also had a daughter Bekka. The connections continued as Bekka Bramlett who is also a musician joined and became interim vocalist for Fleetwood Mac when Stevie Nicks took a sabbatical from the band. Bonnie later married another musician, 'outlaw country' songwriter and bassist Danny Sheridan.

Salvatore Bono was a 27 year old aspiring songwriter who was working in Phil Spector's recording studio when he met 16 year old Cherilyn Sarkisian. The pair recorded together as Caeser and Cleo but with no success, became romantically involved, got married, changed their name to Sonny and Cher and became a popular entertainment act.   Initial success with songs such as 'Baby Don't Go', 'The Beat Goes On' and the number one single 'I Got You Babe' led to high album sales, numerous television appearances and eventually their own television show, a mixture of music and humour.

Cher had the occasional solo hit with 'Bang Bang' and 'Gypsies Tramps and Thieves' but by the early 1970's the duo's popularity had waned and they went their separate ways musically and personally, divorcing in 1975.

While working with Phil Sector in 1966, Cher had sung backing to Tina Turner's lead vocal on 'River Deep Mountain High' and their lives had further similarities. Both were married to older men and began their musical careers in duos with their then husbands, both couples divorced in the early 1970's with the wives claiming abuse by their estranged partners, husbands musical careers stalled and like Tina Turner,

Cher's solo popularity dipped and then went into the realms of superstardom, as an actress and then again as a recording artist and live performer.

Cher had a child with Sonny (Chastity born 1969, changed gender and formally became Chaz in 2010) and a son Elijah with second husband musician Greg Allman whom she married 3 days after divorcing Sonny but also divorced after 2 years.
Cher and Greg recorded (Allman and Woman) and toured together during this time with little critical or commercial success.
Guitarist Les Dudek had played on Allman Brothers records and he also had a short lived and not altogether successful musical (Black Rose) and personal relationships with Cher. However, in the early 1980's Cher became more successful with her acting credits in 'Silkwood', 'Mask', 'Witches of Eastwick' and 'Moonstruck' for which she won Best Actress Academy Award. In parallel with movie success, Cher's album recordings from the second half of the 80's struck gold and single success 'I Found Someone', and 'If I Could Turn Back Time' leading into further hits in the 1990's with 'It's in His Kiss (shoop shoop song)' and her biggest hit to date 'Believe' in 1998.

However in that year, ex-musical and marital partner Sonny Bono was killed in a skiing accident when he hit a tree on the slopes. Since 'retiring' from music,

Bono had become a successful politician, as Mayor of Palm Springs from 1988-92 and election to the US House of Representatives in 1994. On his death, Bono's fourth wife Mary was elected to take his seat and coincidently his fatal accident occurred less than a week after the death from a similar skier tree collision of Michael Kennedy, son of the late Robert Kennedy from the political family dynasty.

As well as her many movie and musical accolades, Cher has courted controversy for her fashion, outspoken views, relationships and plastic surgery operations, but the contralto tones of the four letter single named Cher are instantly recognisable across generations of music buying public.

A lower key husband and wife band membership occurred during the hippie-era in the San Francisco outfit 'It's a Beautiful Day' with violin virtuoso David La Flamme and his then wife Linda on keyboards. Although not achieving major commercial success, they were popular for a few years, their best known number being 'White Bird'. Original drummer Val Fuentes and David La Flamme were still performing 40 years later with David's current wife also called Linda in the line-up.

From a beautiful day, to a 'Perfect Day' and the composer of that song, Lou Reed who emerged from

Andy Warhol's Exploding Plastic Inevitable 'Velvet Underground' experience to wider acceptance with 'Transformer' and 'Berlin' and the classic single 'Walk on the Wild Side'. Reed was in his mid-sixties when he married performance artist Laurie Anderson, just over 60 at the time, whose most commercial success was her hit single 'O Superman' in 1981.

Life on the road has been portrayed over the years in film, books and song as long journeys interspersed with impersonal hotel rooms and live performances. There are of course stories of parties, partaking of illegal substances, taking of illicit females (and on occasion males) as well as the infamous televisions being thrown out of windows into swimming pools. However, first-hand accounts can offer realism to some of the claims of musicians about their experiences and the effect the lifestyle can have on relationships.

Victoria Balfour interviewed a number of 'Rock Wives' in the mid 1980's for her book of the same name and some of the examples are anything but glamorous. She quotes Mick Jagger's ex Bianca, who called to decline the offer to be included in the expose but did indicate that, (7)
"So many of these women allow themselves to be destroyed in the adulation of the male gods. It's terrible. In the marriage, it's very hard for rock stars

to relate to anybody in a normal way, because other women become so available to them."

The temptation for musicians while away from their wives or girlfriends is echoed by Claudette Robinson who married writer, singer and record company executive Smokie Robinson back in 1959. She was a also a member of the Miracles, Smokie's backing group and witnessed females 'offering' themselves to band members, married or not. Claudette also discussed the rigours of touring which resulted in her case of 5 miscarriages leading to her quitting live performances at an attempt to maintain a family life. Smokie and Claudette Robinson were married for over 25 years although the relationship was not without problems due to the pressures and temptations of fame.   However it ended in tears as Smokie, the composer of the bittersweet 'Tears of a Clown' and 'Tracks of my Tears' did have extra-marital affairs.

Marilyn Wilson was interviewed by Victoria Balfour and reminisced of her time as wife of Beach Boy Brian Wilson from the mid-sixties until the late seventies, a period that saw the 'genius' at work and his retreat into mental illness, but her insight is also revealing in that the lifestyle of musicians on the road can be mirrored in their home lives. As Mrs Wilson, she became irate at the numbers of strangers and leeches who would hang around her house and blames the availability of drugs from these people for the demise of Brian's condition. She stated, (8)

"I had twenty, thirty people in my house every day. I had girls in my house knocking on his bedroom door. I didn't know who was who."

Another Beach Boy, Carl Wilson gained a famous singing father-in-law in 1987 when he married Gina, a daughter of the 'Little old Wine Drinker' himself, Dean Martin.

Having mentioned Donovan's connection with the Beatles, the Scottish singer / songwriter also has a connection to the Rolling Stones having dated a girl called Linda Lawrence, in the 1960's, Linda being the ex-girlfriend and mother of one of Brian Jones' children. Linda was another 'rock wife' featured in Balfour's book.

Brian Jones was one of the founding members of the Rolling Stones and in the early days of the band, his contributions can be heard on a variety of instruments such as marimba, sitar, harpsichord, mellotron, oboe, slide guitar and blues harmonica giving the band's music added style. Jones was also a fashion icon of the era but as the decade wore on, his involvement with drugs altered his already carefree personality and he became a liability to his fellow musicians. In June 1969, he was effectively fired from the band he co-founded and less than a month later Brian Jones was dead, aged 27.

As well as his musical legacy, Jones had fathered six children, all to different women, the youngest when he was 17 was only 14, and others were married. Linda Lawrence gave birth to Jones' fourth child in 1964 and a year later, he started his relationship with Italian actress and former model, Anita Pallenberg. In 1967, during a trip to Morocco, Pallenberg left the increasingly erratic behaviour of Rolling Stone guitarist Brian Jones and began a 13 year relationship with Rolling Stone guitarist Keith Richards. Although they never married, she gave birth to 3 children by Richards, Tara (who died) Dandelion (later called Angela) and Marlon.

There have been rumours, denials and more rumours surrounding this period of the Stones' history with Keith Richards claiming that Pallenberg had an affair with lead singer Mick Jagger and Jagger's ex-girlfriend Marianne Faithfull even claiming that Jagger and Brian Jones had a fling. There is also a story that Jagger wrote the song 'Angie' to appease Mrs. Bowie after she apparently caught the Stones' singer and her then husband David in a compromising position, but there is no proof that this occurred. Keith Richards is thought to have come up with the title of the song, possibly named after his daughter Angela or maybe just because it worked well with the melody but neither explanation nor denial can prevent rumours circulating once they have been suggested.

Much was made of David Bowie's androgynous image in the early seventies and his declaration that he was bi-sexual despite being married. While some welcomed such overt behaviour, others were sceptical, (9)

"This has led some gay critics, most notably John Gill in his provocative book 'Queer Noises', to brand Bowie as a closet homophobe who cynically manipulated his own sexuality in order to impress a straight rock critic".

As Bowie matured, he has tried to distance himself from some of the statements he made earlier in his career and regretted publicly announcing that he was bi-sexual. Some critics suggest that these statements were as much part of his act as the outrageous clothes and make up but ex-wife Angie maintains that the pair shared lovers, male and female. Victoria Balfour quotes from an interview Bowie gave to UK music paper Melody Maker back in 1972, (10)

"As a matter of fact, when he and his wife met, he recalled, 'We were both laying the same bloke'".

Balfour later states, (11)

"On the eve of their wedding, they spent the night with a mutual friend named Clare.   The next day – March 20, 1970 – the accommodating Clare was a witness at Angie and David's wedding".

The marriage ended before the decade ended and

despite anyone's opinion on Bowie's sexual preferences, he later got engaged to dancer Melissa Hurley but this romance ended and in 1992, ex-supermodel, actress and cosmetics entrepreneur Iman Abdulmajid became the new Mrs. David Bowie, a marriage that has endured for more than 20 years.

Prior to Keith Richards hooking up with Anita Pallenberg, he had been in a relationship with a girl called Linda Keith but she had left him to move to New York where she courted the charms of an upcoming guitarist called Jimmy James, soon to become Jimi Hendrix.   Linda was instrumental in bringing Hendrix to the attention of ex-Animals bassist Chas Chandler, who became his manager. Brian Jones and Linda Keith were then a couple for a short time, while Richards had a brief affair with Marianne Faithfull but did not pursue this romance as she was continuing her relationship with Mick Jagger.

Pausing for reflection, although the many relationships can seem confusing, it is not difficult to recognise connections.

Brian Jones ex-girlfriend Linda Lawrence had maintained her friendship off and on with Donovan and although the troubadour had other relationships and was also the father of two children (one of whom, actress Ione Skye was married for a time to Beastie Boy Adam Horovitz), the pair resumed their romance and married in 1970 having another two children together. Donovan and Linda's marriage has lasted more than 40 years.

Mick Jagger and singer Marianne Faithful were very much a couple of the sixties scene through music, films, drug busts, fashion and lifestyle. Following the couple's break-up, Jagger fathered a child, a girl, with another singer Marsha Hunt, before actually tying the knot with Nicaraguan born Bianca De Macias with whom he had another daughter. When this marriage ended, the Stones frontman seduced Texan Jerry Hall from another lead singer, Bryan Ferry from the group Roxy Music.

Hall and Jagger lived together for some time and had a daughter and a son prior to marrying in a Hindu beach ceremony in 1990 and having another son and daughter. The marriage was annulled in 1999.

Jagger has been romantically linked to many women, over the years and been the target for a number of paternity suits and he also features in the memoirs of some fans of musicians who took their admiration all the way to physical encounters, as groupies. A self-confessed 'Canyon Girl' Sally Parmer notes in her autobiographical memories – Blue Jean Baby – that she lost her virginity to Brian Jones but that a male acquaintance of hers had actually slept with Mick Jagger. These rumours about Jagger's sexuality are unsubstantiated but his exploits with females have many clamouring to admit the liaisons.

Famous Groupies

One of the most famous groupies was Pamela Des Barres who wrote of her experiences as Pamela Ann Miller in her tell all resume of her time in the music business – "I'm with the Band" -. Released in 1987, the book recounts events from the sixties and seventies when Pamela, as a nanny to Frank Zappa's children, then became a member of the GTO's from the Mothers of Invention / Captain Beefheart camp and with her musical connections reportedly enjoyed the company of Jimmy Page, Keith Moon, members of the Byrds, Jim Morrison and of course, Mick Jagger. Pamela was an actress for a time, married musician Michael Des Barres in 1977, divorced in 1991 and two years later released a further account of her lifestyle "Take Another Little Piece of my Heart : A Groupie Grows Up".

More recently in 2007, Pamela Des Barres produced yet another publication on the same theme with "Let's Spend the Night Together: Backstage Secrets of Rock Muses and Supergroupies". She has undertaken public readings from the book, assisted by other ex-groupie contributors and some of these are available on the internet.

The following exert is taken from one of those readings in which she claims (1A)
"In the 1960's, 'groupie' was just a word used to describe girls who wanted to hang out with groups,

but over the years it has slowly become a negative term". She maintains that
"We inspired the guys as much as we were inspired by them. It was very equal".
Des Barres' insight is interesting not only from the gossip or titillating perspectives but her take on where the lifestyle fits in relation to feminism. She says, "People often ask me whether I felt demeaned and I always say it was exactly the opposite of that: it was empowering. Any woman who gets out there, looks on stage and goes after someone who inspires her – that is the ultimate feminist act, surely? Some women like doctors, politicians, football stars – I like musicians, and I was always very focussed about who I wanted to be with. I consider myself a sexual pioneer. To me great sex is like touching God, and I was lucky enough to have experienced it to the hilt and wrote about it freely, openly and joyously, when not many other women had".
Des Barres is perhaps the most famous 'groupie' of her generation but she is not the only one who has written about her exploits.

Coincidently, not only was Zappa's children's nanny from a 'groupie' background, so too was their mother Gail who married Frank in 1967, and remained as a couple until Frank's death 26 years and four children later. Their offspring were anointed with 'artsy' appellations by the avant-garde adult Zappas. First born daughter was named 'Moon Unit, next came her

brother 'Dweezil', another brother 'Ahmet Rodan' and finally sister 'Diva'.   Like the character in Shel Silverstein's 'A Boy Named Sue', popularised by Johnny Cash, giving an 'awful' name can make a person strong and build character!   Gail Zappa recounts an episode from her daughter's sixth grade when a classmate said to her, (12)
"Why did your parents call you Moon"?
to which the youngster replied,
"Why did yours name you Debbie"?
In an interview their father Frank was reported as commenting
"that the kids did not like their names and it was always a problem for them growing up but they're going to find out if they haven't already that it's not the first part of the name that's going to give them trouble, it's the last".

Victoria Balfour confronted Mrs Zappa with the obvious – 'Gail has had to live with the fact that groupies do not consider a rock star with a wedding ring off limits' and received the response, (13)
"I was a groupie. That's how I know" and her husband's previous quotation on the subject was introduced to their conversation,
"Groupies....one of the most amazingly beautiful products of the sexual revolution"
and Gail's response was,
"I hate it a lot".

The American band Grand Funk Railroad sung about 'Sweet Connie' in their tongue in cheek autobiographical experience 'We're an American Band'. They were referring to Connie Hamzy a groupie who claims among her conquests members of the Who, Led Zeppelin, Bad Company, Doobie Brothers, Allman Brothers, ZZ Top and The Eagles. Perhaps surprisingly, Hamzy also mentions that she 'performed' with 'clean cut' Neil Diamond and 'cleaner cut' Richard Carpenter. Then again, they are musicians and then again they are human and then again it might not be true but then again 'Carpenters' did have a hit after all with the Leon Russell / Bonnie Bramlett song 'Superstar' which in its original incarnation was subtitled 'Groupie'.

In the late 1950's Tura Satana was an exotic dancer with an alter ego as 'Groupie' Miss Japan Beautiful who 'befriended' Elvis Presley and reportedly gave him 'dancing lessons'.

Catherine James began hanging out with musicians in the mid-1960's and became involved with Denny Laine who was in the early line-up of the Moody Blues, prior to going solo and then becoming a member of Wings with the McCartneys. James had Laine's child but the relationship did not last and she reportedly had a brief liaison with Mick Jagger and then Jimmy Page.

Led Zeppelin's Jimmy Page has been mentioned in the memoirs of a few famous groupies but in the early 1970's he was known to be involved with Lori Maddox, one of the 'LA girls of '72. Manager Peter Grant was said to have kept this secret and often arranged to smuggle Maddox into Page's rooms because at the start of their relationship she was only 14 years old. Later she supposedly had trysts with Iggy Pop, David Bowie and Keith Moon prior to leaving the lifestyle altogether.

Also 14 when she began on the groupie scene, was Sable Starr, nicknamed 'Queen of the Groupies', who claimed to have been involved with Robert Plant, Mick Jagger, Marc Bolan, David Bowie, Rod Stewart, Alice Cooper, Richard Hell, Iggy Pop and Johnny Thunders. She passed away from brain cancer in 2009 at the age of 51.

Friend and fellow groupie Lynn aka 'Queenie Glam' hung out with Lori Maddox and Sable Starr and the girls shared the list of celebrity musician 'conquests'.

Morgana Welch is another teenaged groupie involved with Led Zeppelin having had relationships with both Jean Paul Jones and Robert Plant as well as their buddy, 'Hats off to Roy' Harper. She has also written of her exploits in 'Hollywood Diaries' (in addition to publishing a vegetarian food book).

Whereas some ladies who were close to rock stars kept diaries for future reference when it came time to appear on talk shows or write about their exploits, one groupie had another way to recall her past liaisons. Cynthia Plaster Caster not only got up close and personal with musicians but she used her artistic skills to take plaster cast moulds of their penises. She has over 70 male exhibits and some female breasts taken from musicians over a 30 year period but the most famous cast was one of her earliest works of Jimi Hendrix. Although there were others involved in these activities, Cynthia is the best known and has been immortalised in the song by 'Kiss' named after her.

It may be surprising to know who first used the word groupie to describe 'girls who like to hang around with members of groups'. None other than the pop star with the boy next door image, Herman of the Hermits, smiling Peter Noone, that is, according to Cynthia's memory, but she does not have a plaster cast of any part of his anatomy as a memento, or if she does, there is a kind of hush all over the world preventing anyone finding out.

One groupie who prefers the title 'muse' rather than the derogatory connotations of the original term has had involvement with musicians since the age of 16 when she was the girlfriend of Barry Cowsill from the harmony singing family the Cowsills.

Bebe Buell was also said to have dated David Cassidy prior to co-habiting with record producer, songwriter and multi-instrumentalist Todd Rundgren during which time they both had other relationships.

In 1974, Buell was one of Playboy's Playmates of the Month and in 1977 she gave birth to daughter Liv, whose father was Aerosmith's lead singer Steve Tyler, who at the time was having a serious drug problem so Rundgren and Buell brought up the daughter as their own. When Liv was nine years old, she found out that Tyler was her biological father, Rundgren and Buell finally split with the former subsequently marrying one of his backing vocalists Michelle Gray.

Bebe Buell claims to have also dated David Bowie, Mick Jagger, Elvis Costello and Duran Duran's John Taylor. She married Coyote Shivers in 1992 but divorced a few years later and in 2002 married musician Jim Wallerstein from grunge band Das Damen.

A couple of years before Steve Tyler got together with Bebe Buell he moved in with 16 year old groupie Julia Holcomb and not long after she became pregnant. The couple agreed on abortion but many years later Holcomb broke her silence and admitted regret for having the abortion.

Most of the groupie reminiscences concern the heyday of Rock Gods era late sixties early seventies following the summer of love, dawning of the permissive society and the decadent pre-punk musicians and bands with limousines, private aircraft, stadium venues, high financial advances, powder trails and free sex.

In the modern 'groupie' scene an organised unit has emerged by the name of 'The Plastics' – an international sisterhood of like-minded individuals arranged in 'Chapters'.

The President of the Plastics is Lexa Vonn and they claim to be 'saving the world, one band at a time'.

Summer The FirstTime

Despite the headline grabbing activities of Rolling Stones' members' Jagger. Richards, Jones and Wood, it was the 'quiet one' Bill Wyman who received the most negative press.

When the Rolling Stones were first launched as a band in 1963, bass player Bill Wyman was into his fourth year of marriage, but like John Lennon's status in The Beatles, the existence of a wife was kept quiet. Their son Stephen was born the previous year but Bill and his wife Diane separated in the mid 1960's.

Wyman had a number of relationships over the years but, a couple of years short of his 50th birthday in 1984 he met Mandy Smith. Without being judgemental, the following quotes from his autobiography 'Stone Alone' sums up the story of Bill

Wyman's relationship with Mandy, from first seeing her (14)

"She took my breath away......I've got to meet that girl, got to talk to her....I was totally besotted with Mandy from the moment I saw her"   A couple of weeks later, at her mother's home, "I grabbed hold of her and gave her a big kiss. She was a woman at 13 and she certainly looked like the twenty year old I had originally believed her to have been. When I asked her mother if I could take Mandy out to dinner, I was told she had been going to clubs and pubs for a year and a half; there was no objection.   For two and a half years we were an incredibly well-kept secret"

The pair dated with her mother's consent but when the press caught wind of the story, (15)
"All hell broke loose.....It was a nightmare.....I didn't think I'd done her any harm, whatever her age.....I'd looked after Mandy and treated her honourably.....I simply wanted to be with her"

The bad press contributed to the couple splitting up for a time but, in 1989 the 53 year old musician married 19 year old Mandy Smith. Certain factions of the press continued to deride the couple's relationship and by 1991 they had separated. However, prior to their divorce in 1993, Wyman's son Stephen became engaged to Smith's mother.

Although Bill Wyman's relationship was initially kept secret from the media, when the press did get wind of an adult musician having liaisons with a minor, they hounded the pair and did not let go, like a dog with a bone. However, there have been blatant references to underage sex in a number of songs and little was reported about this for whatever reasons. It is possible that in some cases songs merely told fictional accounts but some lyrics are obviously biographical. Motorhead, Drive By Audio, Wishbone Ash, Nils Lofgren, Ted Nugent and Aerosmith all have songs called 'Jailbait' which is the slang term for girls below the age of consent.

The Led Zeppelin track 'Sick Again' is about teenage groupies and the Beastie Boys reference Zeppelin's guitarist's penchant for 'underage' girls in their song 'The New Style'.

Gary Pucket and the Union Gap had a major hit in 1968 singing about 'Young Girl' and a year later a song by Jane Birkin and Serge Gainsborough caused controversy due to its sexual overtones. However, 'Je t'aime ....moi non plus' was mild compared to a Gainsborough composition recorded with his 12 year old daughter in 1984 which reached number 2 in the French charts despite the strong innuendo in the lyrics of 'Lemon Incest'.

The story of Bill Wyman's initial relationship with the 13 year old resurrected a previous musician's scandal.

In 1958, Jerry Lee Lewis was a popular American rock and roll pianist with exciting hits like 'Whole Lotta Shaking Going On' and 'Great Balls of Fire'. Known affectionately as 'The Killer' he all but killed his career when the public heard he had married his cousin Myra Brown, who was 13 at the time. This was Lewis's third of seven marriages and the union lasted 13 years, during which time his record sales slumped and many agents refused to book him. In 1986, Myra Lewis told Victoria Balfour, (16)

"I felt guilty because they messed up his career. They just about destroyed his name for ten years – the best years of his life. Because he loved me."

Despite these thoughts about the man she left in 1970, Myra also gave an insight into Jerry Lee Lewis's dominant and in some cases abusive behaviour and said that the one thing she learned from the marriage was that she doesn't, (17)

"ever want to marry anyone famous ever again".

An age difference in the other direction was the case of Marvin Gaye's first wife, Anna Gordy, sister of Tamla Motown boss Berry Gordy. Anna was 41 when she wed 24 year old Gaye in 1964 and when it was found that she could not have children, Marvin had a son with her teenage niece and Anna adopted the boy as her own. In the early 1970's Gaye had another two children by another teenager, Janis Hunter, who he married in 1976, his first marriage formally annulled one year later and his second marriage formally over by 1981.

An even greater age gap exists between Rene Angelil and his famous wife. Angelil was a singer who achieved local success in his native Quebec, Canada in the early sixties and when he was 38 he met the 12 year old girl whom he would later marry.
She was a singer, also from Quebec, although she represented Switzerland in the Eurovision Song Contest in 1988. Angelil had become manager for the lady in question, Celine Dion and the couple were married in 1994 by which time she was established as a major star and on her way to becoming one of the most successful and popular singers ever with album sales in excess of 200 million.

Do it Again

There are plenty more relationship connections between musicians, in some cases involving more than one marriage.

Patsy Kensit is better known as an actress than a singer but in the eighties she fronted a band called 'Eighth Wonder' who had number one singles in Japan and Italy, a top 10 with 'I'm Not Scared' in the UK, France and Germany and some minor placings in the

US charts. However, her connection with musicians continued in her personal life having been married to Big Audio Dynamite's Dan Donovan, Simple Mind's Jim Kerr with whom she had a son and Liam Gallagher from the band Oasis with whom she had her second boy, all marriages ending in divorce.

Prior to marrying Patsy Kensit, Kerr was married to the Pretenders front woman Chrissie Hynde for 6 years from 1984 and the pair had a daughter, Hynde's second, her first child having been born the year before she wed Jim Kerr, the girl's father being Ray Davies from The Kinks.

Kensit's third marriage lasted from 1997 until 2000, but husband Liam Gallagher fathered a daughter in 1998 to wannabe singer songwriter Lisa Moorish and five years later Moorish gave birth to a son, the boy's father being another 'bad boy' of popular music, Pete Docherty.

In 2001, Liam Gallagher again became a father when Canadian Nicole Appleton from the girl-group 'All Saints' bore him another son. The couple married in 2008 but 10 years previous, Appleton had been engaged to former 'Take That' and soon to be solo star Robbie Williams. Nicole's older sister ex-All Saints member Natalie, also married a musician called Liam, in her case, Liam Howlett from The Prodigy.

In the case of Jack and Meg White of The White Stripes the rumour was that they were brother and sister but prior to achieving recognition as musicians, they were in fact married and although they parted matrimonially, they stayed together musically for a time but Jack's talent has taken him beyond the confines of the duo.

In 2005, Jack married model Karen Elson with Meg acting as maid of honour but six years later the couple held a divorce party, coincidently, the same year that he formally disbanded his partnership with Meg in the White Stripes. Between times, Jack White wrote and sang the theme for a James Bond movie, 'Another Way to Die' for Quantum of Solace, along with Alicia Keys and continued his musical journey.

Meg White had in 2009, married Jackson Smith the son of two other iconic musicians 'punk poet' Patti Smith and ex-MC5 guitarist, the late Fred 'Sonic' Smith.

Another duo that featured an ex-romantically involved couple who remained together professionally despite their personal relationship having ended was Dave Stewart and Annie Lennox. Initially as The Tourists and then globally as The Eurythmics, they achieved major success selling in excess of 75 million albums and although they ceased formally working with each other in the 1990's, Annie and Dave do appear together on occasion.

Dave Stewart has since collaborated and or produced major acts such as Mick Jagger, Tom Petty, Stevie Nicks and his ex-wife (from 1987-96), Siobhan Fahey , one third of Bananarama and half of Shakespears Sister.

Annie Lennox continues to have a successful career as writer and singer and having adopted a somewhat androgynous image and become a gay icon for many, she has been married three times.

The romantic antics of musicians have been of interest since the beginning of rock and roll especially when there is a connection to other famous names.

Back in 1968, Small Faces frontman Steve Marriot married model Jenny Rylance and soon after quit the band and moved to Humble Pie. The remaining members of the Small Faces joined with Ronnie Wood and Rod Stewart, the latter having recently broke up his relationship with Rylance. Jenny left Marriot in 1973 and the singer married twice more.

The majority of Rod Stewart's many publicised romances have been with models but one was an actress who can be heard on his hit single 'Tonight's the Night'. Swedish film star (and ex-Bond girl) Britt Ekland whispers in French at the end of the song. Before the pair's musical and personal involvement, Ekland had been married to eccentric British acting icon Peter Sellers with whom she had a daughter

(Sellers died of a heart attack in 1980 at the age of 54 and his son Michael, from his previous marriage and Ekland's stepson, also died from heart failure exactly 26 years to the day since his father passed away). Before she teamed up with Rod Stewart, Ekland had a son with record producer Lou Adler and following the break up with Stewart in the late 1970's, she was briefly engaged to Phil Lewis from the bands 'Girl' and 'LA Guns'. Lewis was more than 12 years younger than the Swede but when she married one time Stray Cats drummer Slim Jim Phantom in 1984, the age difference between the two was almost twenty years. The couple had a son and divorced after eight years of marriage.

Ian Paice and Jon Lord were both in the classic line-up of Deep Purple when the band was named 'In Rock'. As well as the original and reformed versions of Deep Purple, drummer Paice and keyboardist Lord featured in Paice, Ashton and Lord and the band Whitesnake but music is not the only connection they had. Jon Lord, who died in the summer of 2012, and Ian Paice were married to twin sisters Vicky and Jacky.

Together Again

In some cases, well known and / or famous musicians got together and formally became a couple.

One such musical showbiz marriage in 1972 was between an enigmatic songstress and an introverted singer songwriter with a troubled past.

Carly Simon was the daughter of publishing house co-founder of Simon and Schuster, Richard L Simon, and she initially played in a duo with sister Lucy before branching out on her own. Simon's first hit single in America, 'That's the Way I've Always Heard it Should Be' was followed by 'Anticipation' but in 1973, her global breakthrough took her to unanticipated attention.

'You're So Vain' was a well-crafted song but the lyrical content caught the imagination of the public who decided it was autobiographical and persistently guessed and asked the composer who the subject was. The list of possible suspects included musicians Mick Jagger, Kris Kristofferson, Cat Stevens, James Taylor, David Cassidy, David Bowie and Record mogul David Geffen as well as actors Warren Beatty and Nick Nolte. Carly could not understand the infatuation with 'who' was so vain but eventually entered into the spirit of the conundrum and over the years dropped hints. Mick Jagger had sung on the record and Warren Beatty reportedly telephoned the composer of the work to thank her for writing the song about him but there was no proof that it was either of them or the others mentioned but just prior to the record's release Carly Simon had married James Taylor and stated it was not about her new husband.

Carly revealed that the person's name contained an 'A' and an 'E', joking that "two vowels ain't bad" and then revealed that an 'R' also featured. If these hints were true, some names were ruled out but it still did not allow the subject to be identified.

Taking all rumours, hints and facts into consideration, the most likely possibility is that the song was inspired by a composite of more than one person, perhaps partly Warren Beatty and Mick Jagger and very likely ex-boyfriend guitar maker Daniel Armstrong and possibly A N Other.

Although this song has followed Simon throughout her career, she achieved further success recording a Bond theme ' Nobody Does it Better', releasing albums including children's material, jazz standards, contemporary opera, Christmas songs and standard songwriter material. Carly Simon contributed songs to a number of soundtracks including the hits 'Why' and 'Coming around Again' but her biggest achievement was her composition 'Let the River Run' which featured in the film Working Girl and won her a Grammy, a Golden Globe and an Oscar.
Whilst married to Taylor, the pair had a son Ben and daughter Sally, both of whom are musicians.
However, on the negative side, Carly rarely performs live due to nerves and stage fright, admitted to having a stammer and had to battle breast cancer in the late 1990's. Prior to marrying Taylor, she had a broken

engagement and following divorce from him she had another engagement to drummer Russell Kunkel who among others used to play for James Taylor. She then had a ten year marriage that also ended in divorce.

Like Simon, James Taylor was brought up in a well to do family, his father being a physician and assistant Professor of medicine. He developed an early interest in music and took up the cello then guitar. He also played with his musical siblings and when he met future guitarist Danny Kortchmar the pair started working together and the future looked positive. However, James suffered from depression and committed himself for psychological treatment. Unfortunately when he returned to music, James Taylor developed a drug addiction and just as his song 'Carolina on My Mind' was receiving positive reviews, he returned to the psychiatric hospital. A socially aware individual, James used his experience from his time in the mental institution as material for his next single 'Fire and Rain' and along with his many live appearances, the hard working troubadour was on the ladder of success.

James Taylor very quickly ascended that ladder with his next album release and his extremely popular version of friend Carole King's 'You've Got a Friend'. Now much sought after, Taylor starred with Beach Boy Dennis Wilson in the movie 'Two Lane Black Top', continued to record and tour and also married Carly Simon. Declining popularity, drug abuse and too much work took its toll on the celebrity musicians' marriage and after splitting in 1981, the couple divorced two years later and reportedly no longer communicate.

Taylor overcame addiction problems and due to a loyal following, his career received a boost and his popularity was re-established. He also married again, divorced again and remarried and in addition to Ben and Sally, has twin boys.

Among the many tributes and awards achieved by James Taylor are five Grammy wins and whilst married to Carly Simon, the pair featured on each other's material including duetting remakes of 'How Sweet it is (to be Loved by You)' and 'Mockingbird'.

Having mentioned session and touring drummer Russ Kunkell, he has played with many of rock music's A listers and featured on many albums recorded by Carly and James, Jackson Browne, Linda Ronstadt, Dan Fogelberg, Neil Diamond, Crosby Stills Nash and Young together and apart as well as producing numerous artists. On a personal level, he has been in relationships with other musicians and in addition to his engagement to Carly Simon, Kunkel was married to Leah Cohen who, as well as recording her own album, was the sister of 'Mama' Cass Elliot. When Cass died Russ and Leah raised her daughter as well as their own son.

In 1990, Russell Kunkell married fellow musician

Nicolette Larson who had previously been engaged to singer / songwriter Andrew Gold. Larson was best known for her work with Neil Young and her hit cover of his song 'Lotta Love' but features as backing vocalist on many US recordings including the Doobie Brothers, Van Halen and Dolly Parton.
The marriage with Kunkel lasted until Nicolette's death aged 45, in 1997.

Before the phenomenal success of her album 'Tapestry' in 1971, Carole King was not part of the LA set that she blended into 'like a natural woman'. Her first success came eleven years previously at the age of 18 when she helped co-write, along with new husband Gerry Gofffin, 'Will You Still Love Me Tomorrow' which was a number 1 for the Shirelles. Carole was also the inspiration for ex-boyfriend Neil Sedaka's hit 'Oh! Carol' and to which she responded with 'Oh Neil'.
The husband and wife writing partnership of Goffin and King were responsible for more than 20 hits for other artists including 'The Locomotion' for Little Eva and later Kylie Minogue, 'Going Back' for Dusty Springfield, also covered by The Byrds, 'Pleasant Valley Sunday' for the Monkees, 'Take Good Care of My Baby' for Bobby Vee and a proposed follow up for Vee for which Carole had the hit herself, 'It Might as well Rain Until September'. Goffin and King divorced in 1968 with Gerry suffering from mental health problems and Carole continued to write solo, 'You've

Got a Friend' a major hit for James Taylor, 'It's Too Late' which was another major hit for herself and Carole King's pedigree was established without the assistance of ex-husband.

The husband and wife writing team of Jeff Barry and Ellie Greenwich were contemporaries of Goffin and King. The couple were married for four years from 1962 and in that short time wrote the no.1 hit 'Do Wah Diddy Diddy' for Manfred Mann and along with Phil Spector, the pair were responsible for 'Chapel of Love' for The Dixie Cups, 'Be My Baby' and 'Baby I Love You' for the Ronettes, 'Then He Kissed Me' and 'Da Doo Ron Ron' for The Crystals and the Ike and Tina Turner breakthrough record, 'River Deep Mountain High'. Pressures of writing together put strain on their personal relationship and the marriage failed, but not before they had discovered a new singer / songwriter and introduced a young Neil Diamond into the business.

Yet another married couple writing partnership is Barry Mann and Cynthia Weil who wed in 1961 and have been composing hits ever since. Examples from the sixties are 'We Gotta Get Outta This Place' a hit for The Animals and in collaboration with Phil Spector 'You've Lost That Loving Feeling' the Righteous Brothers classic.

Mann and Weil wrote 'Here You Come Again' for Dolly Parton, 'I Just Can't Help Believing' for Elvis Presley and along with James Horner composed the Grammy winning song from 1986 'Somewhere Out There' used in the animated film 'An American Tale'. They are an award winning couple who continued their song writing and marital partnership over the half century with many beneficiaries from the Drifters to Hanson singing their compositions.

The most successful pop music song writing team of the fifties were an American married couple. Felice and Boudleaux Bryant composed 'Love Hurts', 'All I Have to do is Dream', 'Bye Bye Love' and 'Raining in my Heart'.

Also successful at that time was the man credited with inventing the solid body guitar, pioneer of audio effects experimentation and who was an early user of the technique sound on sound which he used effectively on his wife's vocals giving the married couple numerous hits throughout the fifties.
Les Paul married second wife Colleen Summers in 1949 and using her stage name Mary Ford the pair performed 'How High the Moon', 'Bye Bye Blue' and a catalogue of other guitar based songs featuring Mary's lead vocal harmonising with her own backing. They had their own radio and then television show with the theme tune being their number one hit 'Vaya Con Dios' but following their success, the couple divorced in 1964.

Nick Ashford and Valerie Simpson was another pair of successful performers and songwriters that were husband and wife. Ashford and Simpson wed in 1974 and as a singing act they had a few hits, their biggest being 10 years later with 'Solid as a Rock'. However, as songwriters, they were responsible for a number of classic Motown hits including 'Ain't Nothing Like the Real Thing', 'You're all I Need to Get By' and the popular 'Reach out and Touch'.

Moving from the pop / soul genre back to the 'California' scene of the late sixties / early seventies, a female singer songwriter that featured very much in this American environment was Canadian born Joni Mitchell. Albums 'For the Roses', 'Ladies of the Canyon' and 'Blue' typified the radio friendly era of poets with unique guitar tunings with an in-crowd of musicians guesting on each other's songs and reportedly guesting as each other's lovers. Joni was briefly married in the mid-sixties to troubadour Chuck Mitchell and her name was romantically and / or amicably linked to Crosby, Stills, Nash and Young as well as James Taylor. Certainly Graham Nash and Joni Mitchell were the 'hippie' couple at the time, inspiring each other's best work of the period. Mitchell progressed from the piano / acoustic material to jazz influenced musical structures but continued to display in her lyrics the enigmatic artistry she had always portrayed, making her arguably the best female pop/rock composer of the genre.

Joni Mitchell was married to record producer / bassist Larry Klein from 1982 until 1994 and the pair worked together during this period. Klein subsequently married Brazilian singer Luciana Souza in 2006 and Joni all but retired from the music business to concentrate on her first love, painting.

Yet another female singer with romantic links to Steven Stills and Graham Nash was Rita Coolidge. The inspiration for Leon Russell's (Joe Cocker hit) 'Delta Lady', Coolidge was receiving attention and had a couple of minor hits when she met singer /songwriter Kriss Kristofferson and the pair were married in 1973, going on to release successful duet albums and singles prior to divorcing in 1980.

Stephen Stills was married for six years to Veronique Sanson, one of France's most popular recording artists. With her signature 'vibrato' voice, Sanson has released more than two dozen albums and has twice won the Best Female Artist of the year in her native France and with Stills had a son Chris, also a musician. Outside France, Veronique Sanson is best known as the writer of 'Amoureuse' which has been covered by numerous artists and in the UK was a major hit for Pauline Mathews aka Kiki Dee, who had a few moderate hits of her own as well as her work with Elton John (and a relationship with Scottish born Davey Johnstone, Elton's guitarist).

Also in a relationship with a Scot was Bee Gee Maurice Gibb who was married to Scottish singer Lulu from 1969 until 1973. Although they were young when they married (19 and 20 respectively), both were seasoned professionals having experienced success at an early stage with hit records (including number 1's), television appearances and media recognition as well as the various trappings that success brings. Their work commitments, (his) drinking habits and emotional immaturity lead to an early divorce although the two remained friends. They had collaborated on a few tracks during their marriage, with Maurice estranged from his Bee Gee brothers for a time, he wrote with his wife's brother Billy Lawrie, but Lulu and Maurice appeared together on British television in 2002 singing 'First of May' on a Lulu tribute show only months before his untimely death.

Lorraine McIntosh provided the female vocals alongside Ricky Ross's lead singing on Scottish band Deacon Blue's first album 'Raintown' and its breakthrough single 'Dignity' in 1987 and the follow up long player 'When the World Knows your Name' in 1989. The following year, the couple were married and the band continued recording and playing live gigs although work on individual projects has resulted in lengthy periods between outputs of new material. Drummer Dougie Vipond pursued a career as a television sports presenter, Ross became a radio presenter and McIntosh a television actress but in

2004 keyboard player Graeme Kelling passed away. However, Deacon Blue continues to play as a group with the married couple at the helm.

Playing music together also progressed to marriage for another couple.

Prior to forming super trio The Police, Stewart Copeland had progressed from road manager with progressive band 'Curved Air' to being the group's drummer. Vocalist in Curved Air was Sonja Kristina and she and Copeland became an item and were married from 1982-91.

The musical legacy of Paul Simon is immeasurable from his early material with Art Garfunkel through the 'world music' which introduced the rhythms of South Africa and Brazil to a welcoming public and his iconic solo work. Melodic, rhythmic, lyrical, harmonious and various other descriptions could be used and lists of songs could be printed to highlight his contribution to the modern culture but two album titles sum up the quality and diversity of Simon's output 'Bridge Over Troubled Water' and 'Graceland'.

Paul Simon's first marriage lasted from 1969-75 and son Harper, also a musician resulted from that union. He was briefly wed to actress Carrie Fisher in the eighties but in 1992, Paul married musician Edie Brickell and the pair have three children. Brickell found fame along with her 'New Bohemians' in 1998 with their first album release 'Shooting Rubberbands at the Stars' and its popular single 'What I Am'. Although no longer a prodigious performer, Edie Brickell continues to play and formed the indie outfit 'The Heavy Circle' in 2008 along with stepson Harper Simon and she also plays as part of the loose conglomeration of established artists such as Andy Fairweather Low, Pino Palladino, Steve Gadd and others in 'The Gaddabouts'.

One of the world's most eligible bachelors in the early 1980's first took the plunge and got married at the age of 36. He was 'Born to Run', 'Born in the USA', he had been 'Blinded by the Light, was 'Dancing in the Dark' and 'Racing in the Street' but he emerged from the 'Tunnel of Love' and enjoyed the 'Human Touch'. Bruce Springsteen wed model Julianne Phillips 1985 but it was over three years later and soon after his working relationship with a singer / guitarist from his E Street Band was more personal. Patti Scialfa had joined the 'Boss's Band in 1984 and in 1991 she and Bruce got married and had three children. When domestic duties allow, Patti tours as an 'E Streeter' but she has also released three solo albums.

Another singer songwriter has released three albums and came out from the shadows as backing vocalist in her husband's touring band. Pegi Young married maverick musician Neil Young back in 1978 but has only emerged as a solo artist in the last few years as their children have now grown up.

Two influential 'American' singers were actually born in Germany and were romantically linked early in their musical careers. Cologne born Christa Paffgen had been a model and an actress (with a small role in La Dolce Vita among other films) before moving to New York and teaming up with Andy Warhol who included her in his movie 'Chelsea Girl.

Using the name 'Nico' she briefly sang with The Velvet Underground before embarking on a solo singing career. Around this time she met a young up and coming songwriter who was ten years her junior and the pair were an item for a short time with him providing three songs and playing guitar on her debut album.

Jackson Browne was born in Heidelberg in 1948 and has had a consistent musical career both critically and commercially since Nico, The Jackson 5, The Byrds and The Eagles showcased his song writing skills. The majority of his albums have made top 50 in both UK and USA and after more than 40 years on the road, Browne still has sell-out tours. He has been a political and environmental activist for many years and is the recipient of many honours for his work and music. Unfortunately Nico's career post early seventies was not successful and the sultry chanteuse never reached her potential due to heroin addiction.

There have been a number of 'country marriages' and relationships but unless they were surrounded by controversy or one or both of the artists had mainstream success, only diehard country music fans would be aware of the unions.

George Jones was married four times and Tammy Wynette had five husbands including Jones for a very stormy 6 years prior to D.I.V.O.R.C.E.

'Alternative' country singer /songwriter, actor, author, activist and controversial individual Steve Earle has had a colourful life including 3 Grammy wins, 7 marriages (twice to the same woman), had a number of his songs covered by other artists, many of his compositions used in films, been arrested, jailed and is a recovering heroin addict. In 2005, at the age of 50, Earle married for the seventh time to a fellow musician, Allison Moorer who had previously been nominated for an Oscar for her song 'A Soft Place to Fall' which featured in the film 'The Horse Whisperer' (in which she also had an acting role). Moorer and Earle were nominated for a Grammy for their duet 'Days Aren't Long Enough'.

'Outlaw' and 'Highwayman' Waylon Jennings was also married four times including to fellow Country singer Jessi Colter. Jennings was a popular live act but this was not reflected in record sales

In 1991, Clint Black and actress / singer Lisa Hartman exchanged vows, Tim McGraw and Faith Hill were married in 1996, Garth Brooks and Trisha Yearwood wed in 2005 and Roseanne Cash was married to Rodney Crowell for 13 years.

Nashville session guitarist Pat Bergeson married jazz singer Annie Sellick but prior to this, he was husband for four years to a bluegrass fiddler and vocalist who would become the most successful artist of the genre. Alison Krauss solo work, her duets with Robert Plant and as a member of the band Union Station have earned her 27 Grammy awards making her in 2012 the most awarded living musician.

Various musical and personal collaborations have taken place over the years and across styles of music.

A Cowsill married a Bangle in 2003 when John Cowsill wed Vicki Peterson and two Canadians became engaged in the autumn of 2012 when Nickleback frontman Chad Krueger began dating fellow singer Avril Lavigne and the couple swapped rings.

Two Cuban born nationals who moved to the United States got together romantically and married in 1978 by which time they had also begun playing together musically. By the mid-1980's this act was on its way to being the biggest selling Latin crossover act ever with album sales in excess of 100 million and numerous awards including 3 Grammys.

Singer Gloria Maria Milagrosa Fajardo Garcia De
Estefan and husband Emilio, leader of assorted
musicians going by the name of Miami Sound Machine
produced ballads and dance tunes tinged with the
samba beats of their Latin heritage and found a global
receptive audience.   From 'Dr Beat' and 'I Need your
Love' through to 'Anything for You' and 'Don't Wanna
Lose You', Gloria Estefan with support from Emilio
consistently released hits throughout the eighties. In
addition, she has appeared as an actress in films and
television, written children's books and with her
husband is involved in a number of business ventures.

American Gwen Stefani has achieved success as a
singer with the band 'No Doubt', singer / songwriter
as a solo performer, actress and fashion designer.
She is also the mother of two sons with British singer /
guitarist Gavin Rossdale, ex-Bush. Episodes from
Gavin's past have put pressure on the marriage, when
it was discovered that he had fathered a daughter in
the 1980's and also following an expose by singer Boy
George in his 1995 autobiography that his friend
Peter Robinson, better known as 'gay' singer 'Marilyn'
had previously been in a relationship with Rossdale.

Courtney Love has been an actress, artist, fronted the
controversial band 'Hole' as well as solo work but will
forever be associated in the eyes of music fans as the
wife of Kurt Cobain for two years prior to his suicide in

1994, and the mother of Cobain's daughter Francis Bean. Much of the negative press surrounding Love / Hole / Cobain stems from their involvement with drugs but aside from this, her questionable musical ability and singing style drew major criticism. Nevertheless, Courtney Love is still considered as an influential figure in the alternative rock scene.

One hit wonders, Ashton Gardner & Dyke were best known for their early 70's record 'Resurrection Shuffle' but drummer Ron Dyke had another reason to be remembered by music fans (especially pubescent boys) of the period. He married a band member who was not a singer, songwriter or musician but was an integral part of an innovative sounding group from the era. Stacia (Blake) was the 'interpretive dancer' with the 'Silver Machine' exponents 'Hawkwind'. At over six feet tall and busty, her often topless and sometimes nude appearances added the erotic to the exotic light shows of the 'Space Ritual' sound.

Mexican born guitar virtuoso Carlos Santana married Deborah King (whose father Saunders had a hit record, 'S K Blues', in 1942) and they had three children. The couple divorced after more than 30 years of marriage and at the end of 2010, Carlos married fellow musician Cindy Blackman who, as a jazz / rock percussionist has played with many of the modern era's jazz elite as well been the touring drummer for rocker Lenny Kravitz and Santana.

Keeping it in the family are French Canadian Regine Chassagne a multi-instrumentalist in the band Arcade Fire along with her American born husband Win Butler who is the band's main writer and vocalist.

Also, Scottish singer songwriter KT Tunstall married Luke Bullen the drummer in her band in 2008 and Irish songstress Imelda May wed her rockabilly guitarist Darrell Higham six years previous.

In 2003, Elvis married a jazz singer but this was obviously not The King, but Declan Patrick McManus aka Elvis Costello who wed Canadian musician Diana Krall. Costello began his musical journey during the punk era on the independent Stiff Records label with clever self- penned singles like 'Watching the Detectives' and progressed to mainstream labels with 'Oliver's Army', and deeper song such as 'Shipbuilding' and 'Every Day I Write the Book'. Elvis Costello has contributed to movie soundtracks, had hits with cover versions and his own material and collaborated with other musicians. One such collaboration with Irish band The Pogues resulted in his second marriage, having divorced the mother of his son in 1974, Costello was married to fellow musician, Pogues' bassist Caitlin O'Riordan for six years.
He wed Diana Krall in 2003 and the couple have twin boys.

Already an established and respected pianist and singer in the popular jazz genre, multi award winning Krall has had crossover recognition in mainstream music charts and after marrying Costello, the pair collaborated on material that had wider appeal.

The 'original' Elvis and his wife Priscilla Presley had one daughter. Lisa Marie Presley uses some of the income from her late father's estate in various charities but in addition to inheriting his wealth, she also followed in his musical footsteps to an extent. Her first two albums were US top ten and her third released in 2012 broke the top 50 and a few singles have charted in different countries.

She married for a fourth time to musician Michael Lockwood, currently a member of her touring band and the couple have twin girls. The best man at the wedding was her first husband Danny Keough with whom she had a daughter and a son.

Between those marriages, Presley was briefly wed to actor Nicholas Cage and had a very public relationship and short marriage to Michael Jackson.

Therefore the daughter of The King and The King of Pop were an item but sadly Lisa Marie's legendary father and legendary second husband both died prematurely trapped in the trappings of their mega-stardom.

Some, but not all, music from yesteryear has lasted the pace and despite going out of fashion has retained enough interest to survive amid the competition and distractions of alternative sounds. Similarly, a number of marriages and relationships have suffered over time but others have weathered the storms and still shine brightly.

Chapter 2

TEACH YOUR CHILDREN

"And you, of tender years, can't know the fears that your elders grew by, and so please help them with your youth, they seek the truth before they can die. Teach your parents well, their parent's hell will slowly go by, and feed them on your dreams, the one they picked the one you'll know by" - (iv) Graham Nash

The Young Ones

It is not unusual for children to join the family firm or take up the same career as one of their parents. In the case of musicians, a number of offspring have attempted to be recognised for their own talents irrespective of their heritage, some with more success than others.

In 1962, the instrumental tune 'Telstar' reached number one in the US charts and was the first record by a British group to do so (only 3 other solo acts had achieved this since World War II, Vera Lynn, Laurie London and Acker Bilk).
The Joe Meek produced single inspired by the space

race, was attributed to The Tornados who were Billy Fury's backing band.

Rhythm guitarist with The Tornados was George Bellamy whose son Matt was born in 1978 and went on to front the incredibly successful trio Muse. One of the major live show draws in the world during the noughties, the popularity of Muse can be measured in album sales, not singles.

Matt Bellamy is main composer, vocalist, keyboard player and guitarist, and features in numerous polls for his fretboard ability and appeal as a frontman and his star has risen higher than that of his 'Telstar' father.

Contemporary of the Tornados and Billy Fury, was singer Marty Wilde who was a regular on the late 1950's UK television shows 6.5 Special and Oh Boy and had a number of chart placings. Wilde also co-wrote hits for others (under an assumed name) including 'Ice in the Sun' by Status Quo, 'I'm a Tiger' by Lulu and The Casuals 1968 ballad 'Jesamine'. Having married a singer from The Vernons Girls, three of their four children have worked in the music industry and while Ricky has made a name for himself as a producer and his younger sister Roxanne is a backing vocalist for, among others, Kylie Minogue.

However, older sister Kim was a major star in the eighties and had a number of hits most of which were written by her father and brother. These included her first smash, 'Kids in America' but Kim Wilde's biggest US hit was the number one remake of 'You keep me Hanging on'. Kim took a break from music and became a successful gardener but has returned to recording and performing on occasion but is another example of a musician's offspring who surpassed the fame of her parents.

Another sixties musician, Tremeloes' bassist Chip Hawkes who sang on a number of the group's most popular tracks, had a son who also had a few minor hits and one top 10 in US / number 1 in UK with 'The One and Only' in 1991.
Chesney Hawkes looked for a time that he might have become a bigger star but his career did not progress after his initial success and in addition to appearances on 'reality' type TV shows, his musical output is minimal.

Brian Poole had been the original lead singer with The Tremeloes, from 1962 when they were signed to Decca in favour of The Beatles who were rejected, until he left the group in 1966. He fronted the singles 'Do You Love Me' and 'Someone Someone'.
Alisha's Attic was a duo consisting of two sisters who had two albums and 5 singles that made the UK top 20 in the second half of the nineties. Writers and singers Karen and Shelly are the daughters of Brian Poole. Since coming out of the Attic, the girls have continued writing in successful collaborations with

other artists.

Shelly married Ally McErlaine, guitarist from the band Texas.

Some established artists had children who made their way in music with a more low key approach, working for recognition and avoiding mention of or comparison to their famous parent(s).

Albert Hammond is known for singing his own songs 'It Never Rains in Southern California' and 'Free Electric Band' but as a songwriter he has co-written some of the best known hits from the last 40 years such as 'Air that I Breathe', 'When I Need You', 'To all the Girls I Loved Before', 'One Moment in Time' as well as novelty pop singles such as 'Gimme Dat Ding' , 'Little Arrows' and 'Freedom Come Freedom Go'. Albert Hammond's son Albert Hammond Jnr. is a solo recording artist and also guitarist with critically acclaimed and much awarded 'garage' band 'The Strokes'.

Another recording artist more famous as a songwriter than a performer is Robert Zimmerman aka Bob Dylan, and considering after a 50 year career he can still sell out large venues, it puts in perspective the legacy of his writing talents. Dylan's songbook is extensive and his own material covers many genres from Christian to country and flavours of most things in between. Examples of his written work that became hits for others include 'Tambourine Man', 'Blowing in the Wind', 'A Hard Rain's Gonna Fall', 'This Wheel's on Fire', 'Mighty Quinn', 'If Not For You' and 'Knocking on Heaven's Door'.

Possibly the greatest lyricist of the pop / rock movement, Dylan is a multi-award winner including Grammy, Oscar and Golden Globe and his work has been analysed, criticised, plagiarised and lionised. One of Bob Dylan's sons, Jakob, fronts the Grammy award winning band The Wallflowers and has also embarked on a solo career, releasing a couple of albums.

Contemporary and also much lauded singer and songwriter Paul Simon enjoyed major success with singing partner Art Garfunkel as well as immense popularity as a solo act and a performer who was instrumental in popularising cross culture music. The man who brought us the 'Sound of Silence' was 'Still Crazy After all these Years' and had a 'Mother and Child Reunion' has a son Harper, from his first marriage.

Harper Simon wrote and produced his first eponymous album and formed the ensemble The Heavy Circles with his stepmother Edie Brickell.

Art Garfunkel's son James has recorded a little but is not overtly following a musical path.

Simon and Garfunkel have had global success especially in English speaking countries and Paul Simon extended his popularity into Africa and South America when he embraced local rhythms and worked with 'world' musicians.

Another global star is Julio Iglesias.
Iglesias is of Spanish descent and was once a goalkeeper for a Real Madrid team but following a car crash in which he damaged his spine he moved to the UK to complete his studies and subsequently settled in Miami, USA.
As a singer and recording artist, Iglesias is in the top 20 of best-selling musical acts ever, having released in excess of 75 albums sung in more than a dozen different languages, which is a far cry from his humble fourth place as Spain's 1970 Eurovision entry. The English speaking world is familiar with his versions of 'Begin the Beguine' and his duet with Willie Nelson, 'To all the Girls I've Loved Before' but his numerous recordings sell particularly well in areas that share the language of the songs. He has three children from his first marriage, five from his second and interestingly Iglesias' father fathered another two children at the age of 89, giving the sexagenarian singer two half siblings.
Julio Iglesias Jnr. was a successful model but tried to

make a career in music with limited success unlike younger brother Enrique who emulated his father by conquering the Spanish language recording market and crossing over into mainstream the English market.

Enrique Iglesias breakthrough came in 2001 with his second English language album 'Escape' featuring the global hit single 'Hero' and he has maintained his heroic popularity over the years.

A unique father and daughter 'act' reignited the career of a female singer, years after her father's death.

Mellow voiced crooner Nat King Cole died in 1965 leaving his dulcet toned recordings as his legacy as well as a vast catalogue of jazz material. Daughter Natalie was only 15 at the time of his death and made a career for herself as an R&B singer winning two Grammys in 1975 before a lull in popularity. Having avoided recording her late father's material a reworking of his two best known songs 'Unforgettable' and 'When I Fall in Love' with his daughter's added vocals resulted in strong sales for these 'manufactured' duets assisting with a resurgence of Natalie's musical popularity.

Two families of harmony vocalists produced another generation of successful singers.

Mama Michelle Phillips and then husband Papa John Phillips epitomised the hippy lifestyle of the 'summer of love' as they harmonised their way to musical success with 'Monday Monday', 'California Dreaming', 'Dedicated to the One I Love' and many other melodious songs. In 1968 their daughter Chynna was born.

Also born that year was Carnie Wilson whose parents were ex-Honey's vocalist Marilyn and her then husband, legendary Beach Boy writer, singer, arranger Brian Wilson. The following year, Carnie's sister Wendy was born and the siblings became childhood friends with Chynna Phillips.

Perhaps it was inevitable that the trio of friends who were surrounded by music, musicians and all things musical throughout their formative years would eventually form a vocal group. This they did in 1990 releasing the debut album simply called Wilson Phillips which sold remarkably well as did a string of singles that hit the top in the USA. The trio split following the release of their second album with Chynna releasing a solo album and the Wilsons recording together before the three reunited in 2004 and recorded together again.

Various offspring from The Beatles' camp have pursued music in the illustrious footsteps of their Fab four fathers.

With drummer Ringo as a father and drummer Keith Moon as a godfather, Zak Starkey appeared destined to sit behind a kit. However, his father discouraged this as a possible career, nevertheless, percussion prevailed for the young 'Starr'. Having cut his teeth in teenage bands, performing in pubs Zak progressed to drumming for major acts and has worked with many including Paul Weller, Red Hot Chilli Peppers and Johnny Marr as well as being recognised as an official member of both The Who and Oasis.
More musical connections, Ringo's daughter Lee had triplets with partner Jay Mehler guitarist from Kasabian.

George Harrison's only child Dhani is a guitarist and singer with his band 'Thenewno2' and also recorded in a side project with Ben Harper and Joseph Arthur as 'Fistful of Mercy'.

Of the many McCartney children, only son James is pursuing music having released a couple of EP's and played on some of his parent's recordings.

John Lennon's son Julian, from his first marriage, is the only Beatle offspring to have been in the charts in his own right. His first album and single of the same name 'Valotte' was a hit in 1984 as was the single

'Two Late for Goodbyes'. Another single 'Saltwater' sold well in a few countries, topping the charts in Australia and to date Julian has released five albums.

Julian's half-brother Sean, born to Yoko Ono, has released three solo albums, a number of collaborative works, played as session musician and toured extensively.

Similarly, some of the children of the Brothers Gibb have avoided a musical life whereas others have embraced the hereditary Bee Gee musicality. Maurice Gibb's children Adam and Samantha were in the band Luna Park but Adam was not keen on playing live and moved away from performing while Samantha Gibb and the Cartel continue to play and record.
Robin's son Spencer released material under the banner '54 Seconds' as well as recent solo work, while his half-brother Robin John worked with his late father on the classical piece 'Requiem for Titanic'.
Barry's son Steven played with Nikki Siix and was guitarist with heavy metal band 'Crowbar' but is no longer with them, his younger brother Travis worked on videos for the band while another brother Ashley is writing songs for his father.

Further musical and personal collaborations produced eclectic music from one generation to the next beginning in Canada.

Known to a more modern music audience as the writer of the much covered 'Hallelujah' Leonard Cohen, from Quebec, has a history as a poet, author and composer of deep and on occasion depressing songs. A favourite with the bedsit brigade in the 1960's 'Suzanne', 'Famous Blue Raincoat', 'Bird on the Wire', 'So Long Marianne' and 'Hey, that's no way to Say Goodbye' are just some of the titles, the lyrics of which show Cohen's literary ability and observational qualities. His basic instrumental accompaniment and deep vocal personalised his style and casual listeners often missed his subtle humour. Many of Cohen's songs are inspired by the women in his life and despite numerous relationships he never married but did have two children with his partner Suzanne Elrod in the early seventies. Adam Cohen is singer / guitarist with band the Low Millions and his sister Lorca is a photographer / videographer.

Also from Quebec, contemporary folk duo Kate and Anna McGarrigle came to prominence in the mid 1970's and maintained a strong fan base supported by the many artists who covered their songs. The sisters continued performing up until the untimely death of Kate at the age of 63 in 2010. Kate married singer songwriter Louden Wainwright III in 1971 and the pair separated in 1976, divorcing two years later but the union produced daughter Martha and son Rufus.

Louden Wainwright III, wore his heart on his sleeve and his humour in the listeners' face. He has made more than twenty studio albums and a number of live releases with his breakthrough coming in the early seventies with the humorous metaphorical song 'Dead Skunk (in the Middle of the Road)'. Perhaps it is inevitable that children from diverse musical backgrounds and estranged parents would make careers in music but their first mention in the industry was on their father's songs 'Pretty Little Martha' and 'Rufus is a Tit Man'.

Martha Wainwright has recorded her own material, collaborated with established acts and received critical acclaim for her performances, not least her interpretation of the songs of legendary French chanteuse Edith Piaf.

Older brother Rufus is also a critically acclaimed musician who has written and recorded introspective material but in addition has composed opera, set Shakespeare to music, performed the Judy Garland songbook and even written for ballet.
Rufus is openly gay and is in a formal relationship with partner Jorn Weisbrodt, however he describes himself as a complete libertarian and in 2011 became father to a daughter, noting that Jorn was 'Deputy Dad'.
The mother of the girl, named Viva Katherine

Wainwright Cohen, is Lorca Cohen, daughter of Leonard.

Therefore, the child Viva has two grandfathers, who with their acoustic guitars and word power entertained a generation of music lovers, one with almost spiritual reverence and the other with irreverence.

Rufus and Martha Wainwright have both toured and recorded with fellow musician Teddy Thomson, who has released five albums since 2000 with positive reviews, his fourth release 'A Piece of What You Need' reaching the UK top 10.
Teddy is the son of acclaimed guitarist Richard Thomson who has had a successful, if low key career as a songwriter, solo artist, session musician and alumni of folk cult Fairport Convention of which he was one of the original members at the age of 18.
In the 1970's Richard and his then wife Linda released a few albums that have retrospectively been given favourable mention in the music press such as 1974's 'I Want to See the Bright Lights Tonight' and their final release when the marriage broke up, 'Shoot Out the Lights.
Linda Thomson is Teddy's mother and he encouraged her out of retirement after she quit the music business following the inability to sing because of spasmodic dysphonia.
Teddy's sister Kamilla is also a singer and various

permutations of the Thomsons, Wainwrights and McGarrigles have guested at each other's shows.

Although the eclectic sounds continued from the various mixes of styles and genres the geography of the music also moves around with many of these working musicians performing in any number of countries.

Meet on the Ledge

However, the next family groupings are firmly ensconced in the traditional British folk scene.

Prior to marrying Richard Thomson, Linda was in a brief relationship with renowned folk guitarist Martin Carthy, who has played with various Fairport Conventioners and been a member of both The Albion Band and Steeleye Span.
Carthy married Norma Waterson from the traditional English folk music family group The Watersons and continued the movement with the collaborative Waterson:Carthy. Their daughter Eliza, as well as playing with her parent's group, is an award winning singer/guitarist/fiddler in her own right and has released many solo albums and collaborations including work with contemporary musicians including Paul Weller, Roger McGuinn and Billy Bragg. Eliza

Carthy also played at a tribute concert to singer songwriter Kirstie MacColl who was tragically killed.

Kirstie is forever linked to The Pogues festive version of 'Fairytale in New York' on which she sings the refrain to Shaun McGowan's taunting lyrics but in addition she sang the excellent Billy Bragg cover 'New England, wrote the Tracy Ullman smash 'They Don't Know' and co-wrote the humorous 'There's a Guy Works Down the Chip Shop Swears He's Elvis'.
Kirstie McColl was married to record producer Steve Lillywhite and she often collaborated with the artists he was producing.
One collaboration produced her most successful US release 'Walking Down Madison'. This single was co-written by Johnny Marr who also suggested the tongue in cheek album title paraphrased from a Jimi Hendrix release, 'Electric Landlady'. Her final UK chart placing was the 1995 'best of - Galore', but sadly five years later Kirstie McColl was killed at the age of 41.

On holiday in Mexico with her two sons, Kirstie was struck by a powerboat and died instantly. The family were swimming in the 'safe zone' when the speeding craft entered giving McColl time to push her boys to safety but too late for her own life. There was much controversy after the tragic event with allegations of a cover up and an innocent man apparently being paid to take the blame. A 'justice for Kirsty' campaign was launched and it exposed the Mexican authorities' ineptitude in its handling of the case.

Kirsty McColl's, like all musicians' legacy is in the recorded work but a simple park bench situated in a park in London's Soho Square provides a focal point for her fans and inscribed on the bench are Kirstie's lyrics

"One Day I'll Be Waiting There, No Empty Bench in Soho Square".

Kirstie McColl's father, Ewan was a renowned folk musician who was known in the drama world for his acting and was infamous in the political world of the 1940 / 50's for his Communist beliefs and protest songs. He also caused controversy when he blatantly courted American Peggy Seeger while he was still married to Kirstie's mother.

Seeger was the sister and half-sister respectively of established folk singers Mike Seeger and Pete Seeger. In 1959, a very pregnant Peggy took part in a 'marriage of convenience' to Scottish folk-singer Alex Campbell, a friend of Ewan McColl's so that she could get a visa to stay in the UK and be with McColl, the father of her pending child. McColl and Seeger were eventually married years later.

As well as the hundreds of folk songs that came out of these arrangements, Ewan McColl wrote a song for Seeger in the late fifties that was recorded by Roberta Flack in 1972, winning both the singer and writer a Grammy award.

Featured in the Clint Eastwood film 'Play Misty for

Me', McColl's song 'The First Time Ever I Saw Your Face' was a major hit for Flack but the composer dismissed this and all other cover versions, criticising even an Elvis Presley rendition.

Nevertheless, this links the traditional folk world with the pop/rock genre both musically and musician bloodline.
Ewan McColl's grandson, Kirstie McColl's son Jamie, is a member of the indie band 'Bombay Bicycle Club'. The group have released three albums with their debut making the top 50 and the next two reaching the top 10.

The Ian Campbell Folk Group (not related to Alex Campbell) had various members throughout its existence from 1956 until 1978 but always centered around Ian Campbell and his sister Lorna. Influential on the folk circuit, the Ian Campbell Folk Group made the UK Top 50 in 1965 with their version of Bob Dylan's 'The Times They Are a Changing'.

The times certainly changed because the year the group disbanded, Ian's sons formed a pop / reggie band which went on to sell in excess of 70 million records and became a force to be reckoned with in the pop charts.

Guitarist Robin Campbell and younger brother Ali on vocals helped create the Birmingham multi-cultural band UB40 achieving hits on both sides of the Atlantic, mainly with reggiefied versions of pop covers. UB40 were very successful for a time but bad financial management saw the outfit declaring bankruptcy. When Ali resigned from the group in 2008, his brother and Robin's twin, Duncan took over as lead singer.

The Campbells are an example of a family with music crossing the generations but a different style of music was performed by each.

Before leaving the more traditional folk sound, it must be acknowledged that much of today's pop / rock music grew out of the legacy of traditional blues, swing and localised folk and country sounds. One of the most inspirational writers from the American Great Depression era was Woody Guthrie.

This man was the inspiration for Bob Dylan, Bruce Springsteen, Bono and many more artists. Guthrie's legacy is in the library of songs he left behind when he passed away in 1967, many of which were kept alive by the above named Pete Seeger who continued to perform them as the writer's health deteriorated. Two years after his father passed away, Arlo Guthrie appeared at the Woodstock Festival where he sang his own composition 'Coming into Los Angeles' but his most famous work is the epic 'Alice's Restaurant' a talking blues style song that lasts almost 20 minutes, although Arlo often extended it in concert. He also starred in a film based on the song but his early promise as a writer / singer / actor did not lead to great commercial success, despite a hit single with Steve Goodman's 'City of New Orleans', although he maintains somewhat of a cult following and by including versions of some of his father's best loved numbers in his live sets, has also been responsible for continuing the Guthrie legacy.

Wasn't Born to Follow

One musician's offspring not only followed in his father's footsteps but retraced them. Keyboard wizard Rick Wakeman is a solo recording artist, author, television personality (grumpy old man) and the ivory tinkler that can be heard on Cat Steven's 'Morning has Broken' and David Bowie's 'Life on Mars' but he was also a member of two successful bands. Initially in the folk / rock outfit The Strawbs, Wakeman joined the band for two albums before leaving to join the progressive band 'Yes'.

The Strawbs early material had featured Sandy Denny on vocals but she left and moved on to Fairport Convention. Dave Cousins was the mainstay of The Strawbs and when Wakeman joined, so too did Richard Hudson and John Ford who stayed through the group's biggest success with 'Lay Down' and 'Part of the Union'.

The pair then left and had hits under the original moniker 'Hudson Ford'.

Meanwhile Wakeman had moved to the creative force that had begun to get noticed with the release of The Yes Album and contributed to the arguably the band's most successful and creative period. With dramatically arty album covers and symphonic rock, 'Fragile', 'Close to the Edge' and 'Tales from Topographic Oceans' vaulted 'Yes' into the major league.

Rick Wakeman, still only in his twenties simultaneously worked on solo material creating the dramatic concept albums 'The Six Wives of Henry VIII', 'Journey to the Centre of the Earth' and 'The Myths and Legends of King Arthur and the Knights of the Round Table'.

In addition to an erratic personal life, workaholic Wakeman also staged extravagant performances of his works, including an 'on ice' spectacular so perhaps it is no surprise that before the age of 30 he suffered three heart attacks.

There were various permutations of 'Yes' members' reunions but in 2008 Wakeman keyboard skills again featured on a 'Yes' tour and tracks on a new album, 'Fly from Here' but surprisingly it was not Rick, but his son Oliver Wakeman who played with this version of his father's old band.

Coincidently Oliver's next musical stint was as keyboardist for a tour and album by a reformed Strawbs, so history repeated itself and then history repeated itself again.

Oliver Wakeman has also recorded a number of solo projects and collaborations as has Adam Wakeman, another of Rick's sons. Adam and Rick have recorded together and Adam became a member of Ozzy Osborne's band.

Although the band 'Yes' were one of the most popular progressive outfits around in the seventies, their popularity was overshadowed by fellow English musicians in a group named Led Zeppelin.

When drummer John Bonham died in 1980 so too did the band Led Zeppelin, as the remaining members decided that without the powerhouse behind his kit they would no longer perform under the Zeppelin banner.

However, in 2007, Page, Plant, Jones and Bonham were onstage together for a tribute concert playing the Led Zeppelin favourites to an appreciative audience. The drummer reprising the percussive sound of his father was Jason Bonham. The quartet had previously played together at Atlantic Records 40th anniversary concert in 1988 and two years later at Jason's wedding. Drummer Jason Bonham has also played as a member of Foreigner and with Joe Bonamassa.

English singer songwriter Roy Harper has had a lengthy critically acclaimed career as a singer songwriter and can count as fans many of rock's illustrious players. Harper is often cited as an inspiration for Jethro Tull, Led Zeppelin who sang the tribute 'Hats off to (Roy) Harper' on the band's 'Album III' and also Pink Floyd for whom Harper sang the lead vocal on 'Have a Cigar'. However, he did not match this prestige with commercial success and a similar fate has thus far followed son Nick Harper, popular but not yet successful.

Another influential singer, song writing guitarist Stephen Stills has five children, having been married three times, and two of them, son Chris and daughter Jennifer are in the music business. Chris has released two solo albums and played with a number of established acts and Jen has contributed to a film soundtrack and backed others on tour and record.

James Raymond was adopted as a child and knew nothing of his biological parents until in his thirties, married and with his own child on the way, the gifted keyboard player researched his past.
The woman who gave him up for adoption now lived in Australia but as a young single parent in the early sixties, she had realised that was the best option to give the child the chance of a better future. The natural father was at the time of the pregnancy, a

young carefree would be musician. James got to meet this man who was about to undergo a liver transplant and they found they had much in common, not least a love of music. David Crosby survived the transplant and when he recuperated was able to add to his already successful band experiences with The Byrds and Crosby, Stills, Nash & Young, the new acronym CPR, which was Crosby (along with guitarist Jeff Pevar) and his new found musical and filial friend, James Raymond. In addition to touring and recording together in CPR, James became a member of his 'absent' father's famous touring band for Crosby, Stills and Nash.

When Crosby had left (was fired from) The Byrds in 1967, he discovered a young singer called Joni Mitchell and produced her first album. Joni progressed from that friendship to 'date' a few musicians notably a well-documented relationship through his and her songs with Crosby's colleague Graham Nash. Prior to this, as a teenager Joni Mitchell had given birth to daughter and gave her up for adoption.
Coincidently, in a similar situation to Crosby and Raymond, Joni and her daughter were reunited 32 years later.

A famous father maintained his popularity into his later years which then allowed him to share success with his daughter.

Frank Sinatra made his name as an actor and singer in the 1940's but despite troughs in his career and alleged links to the Mafia, he re-emerged in the popular music era recording his best known work such as 'My Way' and 'New York New York'.
In 1966, Sinatra hit number one on both sides of the Atlantic with his version of 'Strangers in the Night' and in the same year his daughter Nancy achieved the same with 'These Boots were made for Walking'. Her boots had also followed in pater's footsteps with Nancy having a musical and acting career as well.

The following year, Frank and Nancy Sinatra became the first father / daughter duet to reach the top of the charts with their recording of 'Something Stupid'.

Another actor and singer emerging from the 1950's was Pat Boone who had a number of hits, including reaching the top, mainly with cover versions of R&B material. Boone also toured and recorded with his wife and four daughters, reaching the top 30 twice in the mid 1970's. However, the family act was eclipsed by the debut single in 1977 by one of the daughters, Debbie, when 'You Light up my Life' became the biggest hit of the decade, spending 10 weeks at number 1 in the US charts.

Subsequently most of Debbie's recordings were either country style or Christian music.

Billy Ray Cyrus is also a country singer who has moved towards Christian recordings. Although he has had a number of contemporary country music hits, he is forever tainted with the image of his global crossover success 'Achy Breaky Heart' which was responsible for popularising the 'line dancing' craze.

Billy Ray's fame was overshadowed by that of his daughter 'Destiny Hope' aka Miley Cyrus and her alter ego 'Miley Ray Stewart' from the fictional Disney programme 'Hannah Montana'. Before the age of 20, Miley Cyrus had starred in hit television shows, movies, successful tours as a musician with vast single and album sales and had worldwide exposure as a major celebrity. Her popularity assisted her father's career and he too joined the Hannah Montana bandwagon.

The final father and daughter musicians span not only musical genres but continents and cultures.

Renowned sitar player Ravi Shankar passed on his skills on the traditional Indian instrument to his daughter Anoushka who is a Grammy nominee and has been widely recognised for her contribution to world music, crossing the genres whilst retaining the classic sound of the sitar. One particular collaboration was with Grammy award winner Norah Jones who happens to be her half-sister, Ravi Shankar being both girls father.

Lullaby

As well as the children of a number of musicians following in their illustrious footsteps, there are a few musicians who are connected in more tragic circumstances in that their lives have been touched by the sad loss of a child.

Some have kept their personal grief away from the media while others have used their musicianship as a catharsis and composed tributes to their loss.

Joe Walsh wrote a "Song for Emma", a heart wrenching ode to his 3 year old daughter who was killed by a drunk driver. He also had a subtle memorial built for her, the story of which resulted in another song dedication, as explained by Stevie Nicks in the liner notes on her 'Timespace' album (a)

"(After meeting Joe Walsh) I remember thinking, I can never be far from this person again... he is my soul. He seemed to be in a lot of pain, though hid it well. But finally, a few days later, (we were in Denver), he rented a jeep and drove me up into the snow covered hills of Colorado...for about two hours...He wouldn't tell me where we were going, but he did tell me a story of a little daughter that he had lost. To Joe, she was more than a child...she was three and a half...and she could relate to him.

I guess I had been complaining about a lot of things going on on the road, and he decided to make me aware how unimportant my problems were, if they were compared to worse sorrows. So he told me that he had taken his little girl to this magic park whenever he could, and the only thing she EVER complained about was that she was too little to reach up to the drinking fountain.

As we drove up to this beautiful park, (it was snowing a little bit), he came around to open my door and help me down, and when I looked up and saw the park...his baby's park, and I burst into tears saying "You built a drinking fountain here for her...didn't you ?" I was right, under a huge beautiful hanging tree, was a tiny silver drinking fountain...I left Joe to get to it, and on it, it said, "dedicated to HER and all others who were too small to get a drink."

So he wrote a song for her, (Emma's Song), and I wrote a song for him..."This is your song...I said...to the people, but it was Joe's song. Thank you Joe, for the most committed song I ever wrote...But more than that, thank you for inspiring me in so many ways. Nothing in my life ever seems as dark anymore since we took that drive.

The song referred to is Stevie Nicks' composition, "Has Anyone Ever Written Anything for You."

Another musician lost his son as a result of a drunk driver. Ted Turner, one of the original guitarists from the English group Wishbone Ash was in America in the early 1990's when his 11 year old son Christopher (Kipp) was killed by a drunk driver in Arizona.
The driver of the car left the scene but was traced from a serial number found on a piece of glass from his Rolls Royce headlight.
Following a campaign by the family, the State law was changed, Kipp's Law, which increased the penalty for those who flee the scene of such a crime.

Two musician's families were dogged with bad luck including the deaths of children.

The inspirational protest singer Woody Guthrie suffered for years and eventually died at age 55 from Huntington's Disease a genetic condition that had claimed his mother and later two of his daughters at 41. His 23 year old son Bill was killed and daughter Lorinna who had since been adopted was 19 when she died, both in car accidents.
Guthrie's father had been badly burned when Woody was younger and when he was seven years old his sister was killed by a fire. A tragic coincidence occurred in 1947 when Woody Guthrie's 4 year old daughter Cathy was also killed in a house fire.

Singer Jackie Wilson was shot twice but survived, although one of the assaults resulted in the loss of one of his kidneys. However, Wilson suffered a greater loss when his 16 year old son Jack jnr. was not so lucky and was killed by a firearm.

Three young children of musicians were the victims of drowning.

In 1963, singer Sam Cooke's 18 month old son drowned in a swimming pool, the following year, Cooke himself was shot dead.

Jerry Lee Lewis's son was 3 years old when he drowned.

Status Quo guitarist Rick Parfitt's 2 year old daughter Heidi drowned in a swimming pool in 1980 and the family campaigned for additional safety around pools.

The 21 year old daughter of dramatic singer Shirley Bassey was found dead in an English river in 1985. There was speculation that Samantha Novak's death could have been suicide or something more suspicious but it appears to have been an accident.

Further tragedies blighted the private lives of performers who prefer to keep their offstage lives private.

On Valentine's Day in 1996, the artist Prince whose personal life is surrounded by secrecy married Mayte Garcia, a dancer in his New Power Generation. Towards the end of the year, she gave birth to Prince Rogers Nelson's son. Sadly, the Boy Gregory was born with a rare defect known as Pfeiffer Syndrome type 2 which resulted in pressure on the brain and he unfortunately died shortly after birth.   The couple divorced four years later.

In 1977, the band Led Zeppelin was touring North America when singer Robert Plant was contacted to be told that his 6 year old son Karac Pendragon was seriously ill. Another telephone call two hours later gave the devastating news that he was dead.
The child had contracted a virus, his condition deteriorated rapidly and he actually died in the ambulance on the way to hospital.
The band's tour was immediately cancelled and Plant became reclusive for a time, later writing the song 'All My Love' for the final Zeppelin studio album, as his tribute.

Losing a child at any age, in any circumstances is tragic and the fact that a parent is a famous rock star does nothing to diminish the emotional distress.

In 1976, Rolling Stone Keith Richards long term girlfriend Anita Pallenberg gave birth to their son Tara, but another tragedy ensued when at the age of only 10 weeks, Tara died in his cot from Sudden Infant Death Syndrome.

Although Keith Richards rarely spoke of his loss, he understood the impact of a father losing a child and was one of the first to contact Eric Clapton to console the guitarist on the tragic death of his 4 year old son Conor, following his fall from the 49th floor of a New York building in 1991.   Clapton wrote the emotional song 'Tears in Heaven' in respect of his loss.

Clapton's erstwhile Cream colleague Jack Bruce's son Joe died from an asthma attack in 1997.   Although no longer a child at aged 28, the loss of an offspring was no less devastating for the Scottish musician and age is no barrier to grief when a parent outlives a child.

30 year old Ann Lise-Lotte Casper died following a car crash in New York State in 1998.   She was the daughter of ABBA's Anni-Frid Lynstad.

Three singers lost their teenage children in different circumstances.

Actor and singer John Travolta's eldest of three children died while the family were on holiday in the Bahamas in 2009. Jett Travolta often had seizures, the final one being fatal a couple of months before the boy turned 17.

Eli, the 18 year old son of Rick Danko bass player and vocalist with 'The Band' choked to death following a college party in 1989.

Marie Osmond gave birth to 3 children and adopted a further five, one of whom Michael, committed suicide at the age of 19 by jumping from the 18th floor of an apartment block.

Having started this tragically sad list with the terrible death of a 3 year old girl, the final name is that of a 4 year old girl who had no chance of survival in her short life.

Motley Crue vocalist Vince Neil set up the Skylar Neil Memorial Fund which has raised millions of dollars for children's charities. The rock singer did this in honour of his daughter Skylar who succumbed to cancer at just 4 years old.

One artist retained his dignity throughout a life laced with tragic events.

Roy Orbison did not cultivate an image but the instantly recognisable died black hair, black clothing and dark glasses along with his emotional and powerful yet vulnerable vocals set him apart from the 'trendy' artists of the early sixties. His initial writing success 'Claudette' was written for his first girlfriend whom he married in 1957. It was covered by the Everly Brothers but it was his own renditions of self-penned material that gave Orbison his first taste of stardom with 'Only The Lonely', 'Its Over', 'Running Scared' and 'Pretty Woman'. He toured with The Beatles, The Rolling Stones and The Beach Boys but at the height of his fame tragic events destroyed the dream.

Roy and Claudette had two boys but the couple divorced in 1965 due to her infidelity, only to re-marry and have another son. Keen motorcyclists, Roy broke his foot when he fell from his bike but worse was to come as Claudette was killed when a vehicle crashed into her motorbike.

Orbison continued to tour to support his family but while he was in the UK in 1968, his Tennessee home burned down, killing his 6 and 10 year old sons.

As music trends changed, Orbison's style lost its popularity, he remarried, had another two sons and although his hits dried up, other artists kept his songs alive with live performances and sales. 'Blue Bayou' was covered by Linda Ronstadt and 'Crying' by Don

Maclean as well as material championed by Bruce Springsteen maintained his royalties.

Born with poor eyesight that required corrective vision spectacles, having suffered from jaundice as a child, duodenal ulcers in the 1960's, Orbison's health deteriorated in the 1970's and he required a triple heart bypass.

A resurgent career in the late 1980's saw the Big 'O' working with Bono and his U2 sidekick The Edge, who wrote 'She's a Mystery to Me' for him. Jeff Lynne produced Roy's final solo album 'Mystery Girl' and co-wrote with Tom Petty, the hit single 'You Got It'. The pair, along with Roy, Bob Dylan and George Harrison formed the successful Traveling Wilburys. This new found popularity was tragically cut short when 'Lefty Wilbury' (Orbison), suffered a fatal heart attack on 6 December 1988. Although Roy Orbison seemed to have been around since the beginnings of rock and roll and throughout the many fickle fashions of the music business, he was in fact only 52 when he died.

In 1993, the Orbison family home again burned down but fortunately, unlike the 1968 disaster, there were no deaths or injuries on this occasion but coincidently, following the first tragedy, Orbison's property had been bought by a musician friend. Neighbour Johnny Cash had purchased the burned out buildings and planted an orchard in their place. When Johnny Cash died, his property was also bought by a musician.

Bee Gee Barry Gibb intended to renovate Cash's old home but unfortunately and coincidently, during the refurbishment, yet another fire destroyed the structural legacy of Johnny Cash and his wife June Carter.

A more sinister connection to homes being devastated by fire occurred in 1987 when Orbison's friend and colleague, who had also recorded with and produced Johnny Cash had his home burned down. In this instance, musician Tom Petty and members of his family were asleep in the house when it was deliberately set on fire in an arson attack. Although the building was wrecked and most of his possessions were destroyed, everyone escaped unhurt from the flames.

Roy Orbison's second wife Barbara had been acting as his manager in the final years of his career and life, and as his widow, she continued to oversee his business affairs including tributes and re-released material. Barbara Orbison continued with her many charitable works although she too became ill and died as a result of pancreatic cancer in 2011, aged 61. Coincidently, the date of her death was 6 December, exactly 23 years to the day since Roy passed away.

Chapter 3

BROTHERS AND SISTERS

"Brothers and sisters, brothers and sisters unite, it's the time of your lives, it's the time of your lives, breakdown, breakdown, got to spread love around, got to spread love around"(v)

Coldplay – Berryman, Buckland, Champion, Martin – Universal Music Publishing Group

Join Together

There have been many musical acts containing siblings, some harmonious, others with more than a hint of rivalry, physical altercations and break-ups.

A few group nomenclatures suggest family connections but the members did not share birth names and were not related.

In the 1960's, The Walker Brothers topped the UK charts and the good looking Americans featured in teen magazines.   John, Scott and Gary assumed the surname Walker but were in fact John Maus, Scott Engel and Gary Leeds. Initially John was the lead vocalist but the deep baritone voice of Scott was to the fore on the hits 'Make It Easy on Yourself', 'The Sun Ain't Gonna Shine Anymore' and 'My Ship Is Coming In.   Disenchanted with the pop star image, Scott Walker moved away from the commercial ballads and recorded solo work with a more theatrical artistic sound which sold reasonably well but did not achieve the same popularity, before a further Walker Brothers reunion hit in the 1970's with a cover of the Tom Rush song 'No Regrets'.   Scott became more reclusive through choice while John and Gary's short career success faded.

Similarly, The Righteous Brothers were not brothers but were made up of the baritone voice of Bill Medley and the tenor and falsetto vocal of Bobby Hatfield combining as The Righteous Brothers to score a major hit in 1966 with the Phil Spector produced epic 'You've Lost That Lovin' Feeling'.

The duo had a few other hit placings, mainly in the USA but did not have another major success until their version of 'Unchained Melody' was featured in the hit film 'Ghost' which resurrected interest and Greatest Hits packages were sold on the back of the single's success. Although Unchained Melody is credited to the Righteous Brothers, it is in fact sung solely by Bobby Hatfield, however Bill Medley scored a major hit with a song from another popular film when his duet with Jennifer Warnes of ' I've Had The Time Of My Life' from the 'Dirty Dancing' soundtrack hit the top in many countries ?

Moving from the 1960's into the '70's The Flying Burrito Brothers and The Doobie Brothers were American groups with various members, none of whom were related.
The 'Burritos' were ostensibly an offshoot from The Byrds and featured Chris Hillman, Chris Ethridge and Gram Parsons as well as pedal steel virtuoso 'Sneeky Pete' Kleinow. Many stellar country and bluegrass musicians assisted in the line-ups of this short lived but incredibly influential early incarnation of country rock, complete with signature outlandish 'Nudie' suits.
The initial success of the non-sibling Doobie Brothers was feel-good pop/rock harmony guitar driven sound of original member Tom Johnson's vocal and song writing skills on 'Listen to the Music', 'China Grove' and 'Long Train Running'.   The band's more soulful sound for their subsequent career was when they recruited vocalist Michael MacDonald and further hits followed, 'Takin it to the Streets' and 'What a Fool Believes'.
The name Doobie Brothers came from the slang word 'doobie' meaning a joint.

The similar appearance and monikers of the leather jacketed Ramones gave the impression of brothers but in fact Dee Dee, Joey, Johnny and Tommy Ramone were actually Douglas Colvin, Jeffry Hyman, John Cummings and Thomas Elderyi. When drummer Elderyi moved from live performances to concentrate on studio work, his replacement Marc Bell assumed the name Marky Ramone.

The Ramones legacy is that they are considered the first punk band and whether first or not, they were certainly there at the beginning of the punk movement with their fast paced, little over 2 minute pop excitement such as 'Sheena is a Punk Rocker' and 'Rockaway Beach'. A later, Phil Spector production of the Ronettes hit 'Baby I Love You' gave the non-brothers their highest UK chart placing in 1980 and as sales dwindled over the years, The Ramones called it a day 16 years later.

The Blues Brothers were not siblings and not initially a musical act in the traditional sense, but the image they portrayed was and still is impersonated, mimicked and parodied by many amateur and some professional acts.
The 'original – Blues Brothers Show Band and Revue' was a musical interlude on the American television show in 1978 featuring actor comedians Dan Akroyd and John Belushi. Both were Blues enthusiasts and the image of the band's frontmen Elwood Blues (Akroyd) and Jake Blues (Belushi) with their suits, ties,

hats and dark glasses caught on with the public. The music was not played for laughs and the soulful / R&B sound was provided by top notch musicians from Saturday Night Live's house band supplemented with players from the calibre of Booker T and the MG's. The act released its first album 'Briefcase Full of Blues' in 1978 and it reached the top in the USA. Included in the liner notes was a fictional explanation of how Elwood and Jake became blood brothers by cutting their fingers on a guitar string once used by blues guitar legend Elmore James. A successful film and live appearances augured well for the 'band' but the potential was not realised as John Belushi died in 1982 of an accidental overdose. Further incarnations of the Blues Brothers act performed over the years with John's brother James Belushi and actor John Goodman performing alongside Akroyd, who expanded his interest in the genre with his involvement in the House of Blues nightclub franchise.

The Funk Brothers was the name given to the group of session musicians who played on most of the Motown hits that came out of 'the motor city', Detroit. These include the majority of records by The Supremes, The Four Tops, classic tracks such as 'I Heard it Through the Grapevine' by Marvin Gaye, 'Dancing in the Street' by Martha Reeves and the Vandellas and Mary Wells 'My Guy'.

Many backroom musicians featured on Motown records but the National Academy of Recording Arts and Sciences recognises 13 individuals as officially designated Funk Brothers.

So there we have a few acts all giving the impression that they were bands of brothers but they were in fact strands of others.

There are also a few examples of male dominated groups including the word 'sister(s)' in their name.

Sisters of Mercy is the name of a Leonard Cohen song and was also used as a band name for the output of Andrew Eldritch and various other musicians over a 30 year period since the early 1980's. Initially a drummer and singer, Eldritch replaced himself with electronic percussion which was christened 'Doktor Avalanche'. Over the years the drum machine was upgraded and musicians replaced and although Sisters of Mercy released three albums, they have ceased to record since 1993 due to a dispute with the record company. Andrew and the Doktor also recorded as The Sisterhood but despite the band names, the machine and the singer were not sisters.

Twisted Sister came to prominence as the MTV era dawned and the American rockers have had various styles attributed to them from glam to punk but what they have never had in their line-up is sisters or indeed females. The most stable membership of Dee Snider, Jay Jay French, Eddie Ojeda, AJ Pero and Mark Mendoza took a 10 year hiatus but reformed in 1997 and still perform. Best known songs are 'I Wanna Rock' and 'We're Not Gonna Take it' and the established image of the band lived up to the Twisted Sister moniker as members partially dressed in women's clothing with badly applied make-up, on purpose giving them a freaky drag appearance.

More recently The Scissor Sisters have brightened up the charts with their brand of electro / glam rock / pop. Members use double entendre names consistent with the group's image and Jake Shears, Ana Matronic, Del Marquis, Babydaddy and Randy Real are obviously not related sisters. The name actually came from a phrase used by lesbians to denote a sexual position and the band members met through the New York gay scene.

There have also been a few acts with names suggesting same age as well as same family, but the members were not twins.

The music press often mentions the Glimmer Twins but this is not referring to an actual act with this appellation, it is a nom de plume for the joint talents of Jagger and Richards. Mick and Keith used the title on occasion as producers of Rolling Stones and other artists' material.

In the 1980's Alannah Currie, Tom Bailey and Joe Leeway took the name The Thomson Twins into the charts on a number of occasions with 'We are Detective', 'Lies', 'Doctor Doctor', 'Love on your Side', 'You Take me Up' and their biggest hit 'Hold me Now'. The trio were far from being twins but took the name from characters in 'Herges Tin Tin' cartoon publication. Leeway left in 1986 and Bailey and Currie continued for a few years as The Thomson Twins with lesser success and although not related, they eventually became so by marrying. The husband and wife had two children and moved to New Zealand, the birthplace of Currie, and continued writing, mainly for others.
One notable success was their song 'I Want that Man' which was a hit for Debbie Harry.
Now divorced, the pair again reside in the UK and Currie has remarried to musician Jimmy Cauty. With his artistic background, Cauty was a leading light in the 'acid-house / ambient' sounds via involvement in KLF, The Orb and as one of The Timelords behind the novelty hit 'Doctorin the Tardis'.
However, the name Jimmy Cauty became infamous

along with Bill Drummond in 1994 when the pair were filmed on a Scottish island setting fire to and totally destroying £ 1 million in notes.

Tom Bailey has also remarried and still makes music.

Another trio used the nomenclature 'twins' as part of the group's name. Before evolving into two bands, 'Cuban Heels' and 'Simple Minds' Scotland's wonderfully named but short lived punk band 'Johnny and the Self-Abusers' had a song called 'The Cocteau Twins' and this is the name adopted by fellow Scots Robin Guthrie, Elizabeth Fraser and Will Heggie (replaced in 1983 by Simon Raymonde). The sound produced by the Cocteau Twins was mystical and ethereal with layered guitars by Guthrie and the 'mouth music' of Liz Fraser who often sang in a way that made the lyrics indiscernible. The Cocteau Twins made nine albums, the most commercially successful being 'Heaven and Las Vegas' released in 1990. For a time Fraser and Guthrie were a couple and had a daughter but both relationship and band split up around 1997. Individually ex members are still involved in music.

Aphex Twin is one of the many aliases of the critically acclaimed electronic / ambient / techno / house / synthesiser musician Richard D James. He has permission from Aphex Systems Ltd to use the prefix and added twin in memory of his brother who died at birth.

Two of Us

In a few cases, at the time of their birth musicians were twins but their siblings died immediately or shortly after, leaving them to be raised without the family member with whom they shared a womb.

Some reports maintain that Justin Timberlake had a birth twin but this is not the case. He did have a sister Laura Katherine who died minutes after her birth but Justin was in his teens at the time.

Jamiroqui frontman Jay Kay's identical twin brother died a few weeks after birth.

However, the first 'superstar' of the rock/pop era, Elvis Aaron Presley had a twin, Jesse Garon Presley who died at birth and had he lived, the life and career of the 'King' and the impact he had on the rise of rock 'n' roll could well have been different.

Another performer born a twin but whose sibling died at birth was the flamboyant showman pianist and one time highest paid entertainer in the world, Liberace.

The first actual twin duo to have a number one record in the UK (reaching the top 10 in their native USA) were the one hit wonders The Kalin Twins, Hal and Herbie with their recording of the song 'When' in 1958.

Twins have featured in chart positions since then, even reaching number one but always as part of a larger group.

Almost 40 years since the Kalin Twins hit the top, identical twins Charlie and Craig Reid, as The Proclaimers got to the top of the UK charts with 'I'm Gonna Be (500 miles) but this was a re-recording for charity (of the highest placed Proclaimer's version - number 11 in Great Britain / number 3 in America) featuring the comedians Peter Kay and Matt Lucas so it was not strictly a twins duo.
The Proclaimers as a duo have, however had a number of hits with their accented singing 'Letter from America', 'I'm on My Way' and the cover 'King of the Road' as well as strong album sales.

Twins Robin and Maurice Gibb have scaled the charts in many countries, reaching the top and gaining many awards as part of The Bee Gees along with elder brother Barry.

Another singing Barry had a singing twin and together they had a successful musical partnership. Paul and Barry Ryan had a few minor hits in Britain during the mid-sixties before Paul moved away from the limelight and concentrated on composing, mainly for twin brother Barry for whom he wrote, 'Eloise' which Barry sang to the top of the charts in seventeen countries in 1968 and continued the melodramatic theme with 'Kitch', 'The Hunt' and 'Love is Love'. Sadly twin Barry was left entirely solo when Paul Ryan died in 1992, at the age of 44.

In 1964, teenage all girl group The Shangri-Las helped popularize the melodramatic singles with 'Leader of the Pack' and 'Remember (Walking in the Sand)'. Twin sisters Marge and Mary Ann Ganser were members of the group and their most famous song was re-released and became a hit twice again in 1972 and 1976 but Mary Ann did not benefit from this, having died at the age of 22 in 1970, Marge died 26 years later, aged 48.

The American band Styx was popular from the mid-1970's through the mid 1980's mainly with their rock ballad sound exemplified in 'Lady' and 'Babe'. Twins John and Chuck Panoza were drummer and bass player with the band until John's death in 1996 aged 47. Chuck still performs on occasion with the band but is battling HIV/AIDS.

In 1970, twins Tom and David Farmer formed the band 'Blackfoot Sue' and had a top 5 single in the UK two years later with 'Standing in the Road' but never managed to maintain success.

Identical twins Billy and Bobby had a top 10 UK single in 1977 with 'Oh Lori' under their surname Alessi , but apart from a minor chart placing in their native America with 'Savin' the Day' a few years later, their other releases were largely forgotten and they moved into jingle writing.

As these examples show, there have been a few acts containing real life twins who shared more than their similar appearances in that they also enjoyed the popularity of their public appearances together. Other twin acts include Transylvanian imports Monica and Gabriela Irimia aka The Cheeky Girls, Irish hair raising twins John and Edward Grimes aka Jedward and Matt and Luke Goss the two brothers from Bros.

Scottish band Biffy Clyro came to prominence via their many live performances including support slots for a number of major artists. The power trio consists of guitarist Simon Neil and twin brothers Ben and James Johnston and they continue to be Festival favourites in addition to UK hit singles 'Mountains', 'That Golden Rule', 'The Captain' and strong album sales.

'Lifestyles of the Rich and Famous' was the breakthrough single for the US band 'Good Charlotte' which was taken from their equally quirky titled second album 'The Young and the Hopeless' and following the group's eponymous first album, interesting named releases followed with 'Chronicles of Life and Death', 'Good Morning Revival' and

'Cardiology' all of which sold well.

Identical twins Joel Madden on lead vocals and Benji Madden on guitar and backing vocals along with bassist Paul Thomas have been with the band since its inception in 1996, guitarist Billy Martin joining in 1998 prior to their success, but the drum stool has had four different members.

Guitarist Johnnie Marr has added his talent to a number of groups since leaving the band in which he gained his reputation, The Smiths and from 2008 until 2011 he was a member of The Cribs along with drummer Ross Jarman and his older twin brothers Gary and Ryan.   They have achieved top 10 albums in the UK and tour extensively.

Brothers in Arms

Leaving twins and moving on to actual brothers, one family produced 3 brothers, all of whom were born in India and achieved hits individually with no recognition that they were related.

Eden Kane had a UK number one in 1961, his younger brother reached the top of the charts in 1969 in a number of countries and the youngest of the three reached number 3 in the UK four years later. The family name was Sarstedt and the stage name Eden Kane was actually Richard whose biggest hit was 'Well I Ask You'.

Brother Peter scored a major success with his own song 'Where Do You Go to My Lovely' and a top 10 follow up 'Frozen Orange Juice' and eponymous first album.

Clive Sarstedt used his middle name Robin when he recorded the Hoagy Carmichael standard 'My Resistance is Low' in 1976.

Another three brothers started as a successful 'boy band' with their globally successful single 'MMMbop'. Isaac, Taylor and Zachary Hanson perform under the title of their   surname and Hanson has progressed from 'child' act to mature performers with hits on both sides of the pond.

Three brothers in Australia started a band in 1977 with singer Michael Hutchence as frontman and have continued in INXS since the flamboyant vocalist's death 20 years later, with three different singers as well as touring celebrity vocalist's Terence Trent D'Arby and Jimmy Barnes standing in. Tim, Andrew and Jon Farriss along with fellow co-founders Garry Gary Beers and Kirk Pengilly maintain the Aussie band's legacy.

Lesley Evans lives in Australia and breeds dogs, but life could have been so different for the mother of seven, who once performed in a sell-out concert at London's

Talk of the Town in 1969. Although she toyed with the idea of a musical career and even recorded a few numbers, Lesley (maiden name Gibb) did not follow the same path as her four younger brothers but her singular performance was to 'stand in' as a Bee Gee, for brother Robin Gibb when he became estranged from siblings Barry and twin Maurice.

The Bee Gees had begun as child performers in their native UK before moving to Australia in the early 1960's but the 'brothers Gibb' soon showed promise via song writing and harmony singing reaching number one down under just as they sailed back to the UK to try and break through, which they did. The boys enjoyed their first wave of stardom with the number one record of 'Massachussetts' and other celebrated songs 'To Love Somebody', 'I've Gotta Get a Message to You' and 'Words' being covered by other major artists. The confines of family group working resulted in Robin going solo with a debut hit single 'Saved by the Bell' with Barry and Maurice continuing with the Bee Gee name, including the live performance assisted by sister Lesley.

Following this initial split, the three brothers reunited under the Bee Gees banner and experienced their second wave of acceptance beginning with US number 1 record, 'How Can you Mend a Broken Heart' and other hits ' Run to Me' and 'My World' before their popularity waned in the mid 1970's.

The brothers next found fame with a more soulful sound in the dawning era of 'disco' as their compositions for the soundtrack to the film 'Saturday Night Fever' rocketed them to a level of popularity that no one could have conceived. 'Night Fever', 'You Should be Dancing', 'Too Much Heaven' and 'Tragedy' kept the Bee Gees at the top of musical acceptance for a couple of years before the inevitable fall from grace. By the early 1980's the brothers were no more than a parody of themselves and another few years in the wilderness ensued.

However, younger brother Andy Gibb had now come into his own and three number one US hits, 'I just want to be Your Everything', ' Love is Thicker than Water' and 'Shadow Dancing', kept the Gibb name in the charts. Unfortunately as the Bee Gee brand declined in popularity, so too did Andy Gibb, not helped by unreliability due to drug use, but as he was apparently getting his life back in order, the just turned 30 year old died as a result of myocarditis.

Although this was a devastating blow to the family, the remaining Gibb Brothers continued with their contribution to popular music and found acceptance, recognition and popularity as songwriters in yet another wave of acknowledgement, in this case not only by audiences but also by performers who found their own careers boosted by their covers of Gibb material.

Barbra Streisand, Diana Ross, Dionne Warwick, Celine Dion, Kenny Rogers and Dolly Parton all benefitted from Bee Gees recordings and the brothers Gibb were again on top. Even their back catalogue was plundered when 'Boyzone' recorded 'Words' creating yet another hit, 'Steps' version of 'Tragedy' and the covers continued with Destiny's Child's remake of 'Emotion'.

Whether in fashion or not, as songwriters the Gibb's material has been covered by a diverse range of artists including Dweezil Zappa, Elvis Presley, Faith No More, Status Quo, Flying Burrito Brothers, Janis Joplin, Rita Marley, Roberta Flack, The Beautiful South, Glen Campbell, Richie Havens, Gladys Knight and even Ozzy Osbourne. Sadly their legacy was to end in 2003 when the group's multi-instrumentalist, 53 year old Maurice Gibb died of a heart attack during surgery to clear an intestinal blockage.

The remaining two brothers performed together infrequently thereafter and although Robin produced a 'Requiem' with his son Robin John, a few collaborations and some charitable performances, his untimely death from colorectal cancer at the age of 62, in May 2012, also buried the Bee Gees in all but the rich legacy of material they left behind.

Patriarch and ex-bandleader / drummer Hugh Gibb died three years after his youngest son Andy but Gibb matriarch and ex-singer Barbara outlived not only her husband but her three youngest sons Andy, Maurice and Robin with her two oldest children Leslie and Barry to share the grief.

However there is a future for the Gibb sound as some of the children of all three Bee Gees Barry, Robin and Maurice have followed in their fathers' footsteps into music.

Another major harmony vocal group that began in the sixties also had three brothers as members, in this case, along with their cousin and family friend. Brian, Dennis and Carl Wilson were joined by their cousin Mike Love and friend Al Jardine and The Beach Boys were born. Surfing, cars and girls were the subject matter for the group's many releases from 'Fun Fun Fun' 'Sloop John B', 'California Girls', Do it Again' through to 'Kokomo' their hits were synonymous with American summers and the band's image progressed from clean cut all American boys in striped shirts through long hair bearded Kaftan wearing hippie types to Hawiian shirt adorned middle aged men.
In addition to the usual personal, legal and commercial pressures, the public were always rewarded with strong melodies and pleasant harmonies. The unique Beach Boys sound was maintained through all facets of their career including the mental breakdown of main contributor Brian

Wilson, the much publicised presence of meditative Mike Love along with The Beatles and Donovan et al in India, the downward spiral of Dennis's personality affected by drink and drugs and ultimately early death and also Carl's illness and passing.

Three brothers and a cousin was also the make-up of a more recent successful American band.
The Followhill brothers Nathan, Caleb and Jared were joined by cousin Mathew Followhill to form Kings of Leon and their first album release in 2003 garnered interest more so in the UK than at home. Singles 'The Bucket', 'On Call' and 'Sex on Fire' along with another 3 albums and many live appearances established Kings of Leon as a major act until the end of 2011 when the members announced that they would 'take a rest' for a while.

Two brothers and a cousin along with a friend was the membership of The Canadian band 'Nickleback'. They began in 1995 and six years later, the album 'Silver Side Up' and lead single 'How you Remind Me' propelled them to popularity.
Brothers Chad and Mike Kroeger joined their cousin Brandon and friend Ryan Peake to create this indie pop rock outfit.

Two American duos 'Seals and Croft' and 'England Dan and John Ford Coley' produced soft rock material popular in the 1970's. Jim Seals and (England) Dan Seals are brothers. Between them, more than 30 albums have been released and numerous singles and although not massive sellers, many broke the top 100 in the US. The latter's biggest hit was 'I'd Really Like to see You Tonight' and the former's best known song was 'Summer Breeze' which was popularized by another group of brothers.

In addition to recording 'Summer Breeze', The Isley Brothers had hits with other covers including 'Twist and Shout', 'This Old Heart of Mine' and 'Behind a Painted Smile'. However, self-penned success came with the popular 'That Lady' and 'Harvest for the World' as well as the much covered single that launched the career of a teenage 'Lulu', the song 'Shout'. Various permutations of 'Isleys' featured brothers Rudolph, O'Kelly jnr., Vernon, Marvin, Ronald, Ernie and Chris Jasper who was brother-in law to Rudolph.

The Christians came to prominence in the latter part of the eighties with a soulful pop sound. The Merseyside group's name was not used for religious significance but was the surname of brothers Garry, Roger and Russell and coincidently the middle name of equal partner member Henry Priestman. Their first two albums were Top 3 in the UK and singles 'Forgotten Town', 'Ideal World' and their remake of the Isley Brothers 'Harvest for the World' were very popular in the era. Although the brothers have parted, vocalist Roger Christian still performs under the name along with a backing band.

Along with falsetto vocalist Philip Bailey, brothers Maurice (vocals/percussion) and Verdine (bass) were the mainstays for many years, along with younger sibling Fred (drums) for a time, of genre crossing showband (complete with lasers and levitation) Earth, Wind and Fire.

There have been numerous pop and rock bands throughout the history of rock 'n' roll containing two brothers.

Pre-punk outfit The Stooges are known as the band that backed Iggy Pop and during all incarnations from formation in 1967 and beyond the millennium, brothers Ron and Scott Asheton played guitar and drums respectively.

Jason Freese plays keyboards in Green Day and his brother Josh is a session drummer who used to play with 'Nine Inch Nails'. Josh took over the sticks in the group 'Paramore' at the end of 2010 when the original drummer Zac Farro and guitarist brother Josh Farro quit the band they co-founded with singer Hayley Williams and bassist Jeremy Davis in 2004, when Zac was only 14 and Josh 17. The band's profile was given a boost in 2008 when their songs 'Decode' and 'I

Caught Myself' were featured in the soundtrack to the popular film 'Twilight'.

Actor Jared Leto has featured in many independent and mainstream films including 'Fight Club', 'American Psycho' and 'Lord of War' but he is also vocalist and songwriter in the band '30 Seconds to Mars' along with his drumming brother Shannon.

A band formed in California back in 1972 that has seen many changes is anchored by two Dutch brothers. Guitarist / keyboard player Eddie Van Halen and drummer Alex Van Halen changed the name of their band a couple of times before settling on their own surname. Van Halen also changed vocalists throughout their career and maintained success with each line-up. Since their formation the lead singer roster reads David Lee Roth, Sammy Hagar, David Lee Roth, Gary Cherone, Sammy Hagar, David Lee Roth. As well as the man at the microphone, in 2006 long term bass player Michael Anthony left to be replaced by Eddie's son Wolfgang Van Halen. Van Halen's record sales, especially in America are excessive for a heavy rock band, their tours extensive, shows extravagant and they were instrumental in introducing contract riders into formal agreements in the music industry.

Staying with heavy rock brothers who emigrated and found global success with a band they formed in the early seventies and is still performing, Scottish born Malcolm and Angus Young moved to Australia where, in 1973 they formed AC/DC.

Record sales for AC/DC eclipse even Van Halen and their album 'Back in Black' has sold approx. 50 million copies worldwide ranking it in the top 5 best sellers of all time.   School uniform wearing lead guitarist Angus and rhythm guitarist Malcolm were forced to recruit a new lead singer when vocalist Bon Scott died in 1980 and the band's popularity actually increased when Brian Johnson took over microphone duties.

Coincidently, Angus and Malcolm's oldest brother Alexander Young was bass player and singer with UK based 1960's outfit 'Grapefruit' who scraped into the charts in the UK and Germany. Confusingly he was referred to as Alexander George but it was his younger brother George Young who co-produced a number of successful albums for their younger siblings' band AC/DC.   George also co-wrote material for other artists such as 'Love is in the Air' a hit for Jean Paul Young (no relation) but prior to this he beat Malcolm and Angus into the charts with an international hit in 1966 as rhythm guitarist in The Easybeats with his co-written song 'Friday on my Mind'.

The first group to have consecutive number one singles with their first three releases 'How Do You Do It', 'I Like it' and 'You'll Never Walk Alone' was Gerry and the Pacemakers.   Gerry Marsden was lead vocalist and guitarist and following the three number 1 covers, he wrote some of the band's follow up hits including 'Ferry Cross the Mersey' and 'Don't Let the Sun Catch You Crying'.   His brother Fred was The Pacemaker's drummer.

Another Liverpool group had the UK number one single in 1968 through Christmas and New Year and it featured a McCartney but it was not Beatle Paul.   His brother Mike McCartney used the stage name McGear and as part of the humorous poetic trio Scaffold, climbed to the top of the charts with 'Lily the Pink'. McGear's composition 'Thank U Very Much' gave them a second hit but musical success after that dwindled and Mike eventually reverted back to his birth name of McCartney and concentrated on his major career as a photographer.

Irish trio The Bachelors had a string of hits in the mid-60's in the UK, Ireland, with a few charting in the USA. The strong harmony sound was created by brothers Con and Dec Cluskey along with friend John Stokes but they split acrimoniously in the eighties when they were reduced to the cabaret circuit with the brothers staying together.

The sound of another Irish group, The Cranberries is epitomised by Dolores O'Riordan's vocals but the music is driven by the guitars of Noel Hogan and his brother Michael on bass.

Two brothers were at the centre of one of the UK's most influential bands from the early sixties through the various cultural and musical changes of a generation with observational lyrics and a driving sound.

Ray and Dave Davies hit a winning formula with Ray's song writing and lead vocals supported by younger brother Dave's harmony singing and strong guitar playing and it served their band The Kinks well for many years.

Success began in 1964 with 'You Really Got Me' when Ray was 20 years old and Dave only 17. Other classics followed, 'All Day and All of the Night', 'Tired of Waiting', 'Waterloo Sunset', 'Sunny Afternoon', 'Days', 'Lola' and other, clever, humorous and typically English songs.

However, personality clashes between the brothers, drummer Mick Avory and bass player Pete Quaiffe were prominent throughout the history of the band leading to onstage fights, some requiring treatment in hospital, and verbal battles in the music press which resulted in them being banned from touring America for 4 years in the late 1960's and impacted on US sales and popularity.

Ray and Dave had reasonable success as solo artists but the strength of their combined talents kept them performing under The Kinks banner for as long as they could tolerate working together over the years with The Kinks effectively splitting in 1996.

Fighting brothers was the theme of the sarcastically named Tour of Brotherly Love in 2001 which featured three bands including brothers who were known to get involved in the occasional spat. Vocalist Chris Robinson and guitarist brother Rich helped fly the Black Crowes to the top of the US album charts and sold out live performances like the 2001 tour where they were joined by English band Spacehog including brothers Royston and Anthony Langdon. Also on the bill was Mancunian band Oasis featuring the 'moody' Gallagher brothers Liam and Noel. From the formation in 1991 until the break-up in 2009 Oasis were synonymous with controversy due mainly to the behaviour of the Gallaghers but also allegations of plagiarism and unoriginality. Despite these claims, Oasis have their own legacy with many newer band citing them as an influence, over 70 million records sold worldwide and 22 UK hit singles.

Another group that it is claimed sold 70 million record was 1970's teen sensations the Bay City Rollers. Brothers Alan and Derek Longmuir were in the most successful line-up of the group who apparently received very little in the way of royalties for the amount of popularity and sales they achieved in the UK, Canada and the USA.

In the 'new romantic' period of the 1980's Spandau Ballet were a popular band fronted by vocalist Tony Hadley with Martin Kemp on bass and brother Gary Kemp as guitarist, keyboard player and main songwriter. 'True', 'Gold' and ' Through the Barricades' ensured their popularity for a few years but they split in the late 1980's with the Kemp brothers moving into acting, although the original members reunited for a tour in 2009.

Contemporaries Duran Duran had, in addition to singer Simon Le Bon and keyboard player Nick Rhodes, three members John, Roger and Andy all with the surname Taylor, but they were not related.

In the early seventies, rhythm guitarist Tom Fogerty quit the successful Creedence Clearwater Revival fronted by the writing, singing and lead guitar playing of brother John. Tom felt increasingly marginalised as John became the main focus.

About ten years later a similar circumstance was played out when David Knopfler quit Dire Straits. The band broke into the music scene showcasing the fretboard talents of Mark Knopfler and providing rhythm guitar on the band's first two albums and hit single 'Sultans of Swing' was Mark's brother David.

The younger sibling left after three years in the shadow of his brother and embarked on a low key solo career.

Dire Straits breakthrough first album was produced by Melvyn 'Muff' Winwood who also produced the brothers Ron and Russell Mael's most successful recording – Sparks 'Kimono my House' and the popular single, 'This Town ain't Big Enough for Both of Us'.
The Mael Brothers had a weird image with energetic Russell cavorting out front with his often falsetto vocal while Ron on keyboards gave an appearance of an escaped mental patient with his deadpan expression, squinting eyes and Hitlersque moustache.

Muff Winwood had previously been bass player with the Spencer Davis Group when they had the smash hits 'Keep on Running', 'Somebody Help Me' and 'Gimme Some Loving'. Muff was 22 when Keep on Running hit the top of the UK charts in 1966 but the singer and keyboard player on the song was his younger brother Stevie who was only 17 at the time. Stevie went on to further acclaim as a writer, singer, guitarist and organist with Traffic, Blind Faith and Eric Clapton as well as his solo work on albums 'Arc of a Diver', 'Back in the High Life' and the chart topping single 'Higher Love'.

Still there are more bands featuring brothers playing in musical combinations, in different decades and across musical styles.

Nils Lofgren is known as a member of the E Street Band but prior to joining Bruce Springsteen the diminutive guitarist supported Neil Young on record and on tour. However, Nils was also a classically trained accordionist who fronted his own band 'Grin' and enrolled his brother Tom as rhythm guitarist when he toured.

Late 60's /early 70's rock / psychedelic / progressive outfit, the nearly made-its Edgar Broughton Band had Rob (Edgar) supported by brother Steve, among others.

Vinnie Paul Abbott and younger brother Darrell Lance Abbott aka 'Dimebag Darrell' were the founders of heavy metal band Pantera who released nine albums including 1994's 'Far Beyond Driven' which was the first extreme metal sound to reach the top of the US charts. In 2003, the brothers created a new band 'Damageplan' but the following year, guitarist Darrell was murdered.

Multi-instrumentalist Will Butler plays for the Montreal based band Arcade Fire, for which his brother Win is vocalist and songwriter. The band has received international acclaim and is the recipient of many awards including a Grammy for album of the year in 2011 for 'The Suburbs' and they contributed to the soundtrack for the movie, The Hunger Games.

UK boy band Brother Beyond initially had brothers David White and Francis, nicknamed Eg, but the latter left when the group got involved with Stock, Aitken and Waterman and ironically then had success.

Having so far only mentioned the 'Isleys' as a group who used their surname followed by the actual word brother to depict the family relationship, there are a few others of note.

Influential on many modern acts were The Everly Brothers. Don Everly was born in 1937 and Phil two years later and by 1957 the duo had their first number one with their debut single 'Bye Bye Love'.   This was followed by countless other melodic renditions including 'Wake up Little Susie', 'All I have to do is Dream', 'Walk Right Back', 'When Will I be Loved' and their biggest self-penned hit 'Cathy's Clown'. However relations between the two were not always as harmonious as their voices and the pair often argued leading to splits and inevitable reconciliations. Although the hits dried up in the mid 1960's, tours, albums, solo material, guest appearances and occasional reunions kept them in the public eye and among the many awards received by The Everly

Brothers, is the prestigious Grammy for Lifetime Achievement.

New Orleans singer Aaron Neville had his first US hit back in the mid-sixties but it was over two decades later before his tremulous vocals came to prominence both as a solo artist and specifically on his Grammy winning duets with Linda Ronstadt. However, he has also featured over the years as part of The Neville Brothers along with real life brothers Art, Charles and Cyril and more recently including his son Ivan. The Neville Brothers are an institution in the New Orleans area with their Cajun/jazz influenced R&B attracting reasonable commercial and critical success.

Brother bands featured in all musical genres.

The Gibson Brothers were Alex, Chris and Patrick Gibson who had a few top 50 hits in Europe in 1979/80 with their disco infused sound.

American act the Jonas Brothers began as a 'boy band' in 2005 when teenagers Joe and Kevin sang on younger brother Nick's solo material. A child actor and product of the Disney Chanel, Nick along with his brothers combine their music with television appearances and acting.

Country crossover act The Bellamy Brothers hit the pop charts in 1976 with the infectious 'Let your Love Flow' but David and Howard Bellamy seemed more at home with country tinged material such as another popular Bellamy track 'If I Said you had a Beautiful Body Would you Hold it Against Me'.

The mid-seventies also saw The Sutherland Brothers and Quiver charting with 'I Don't wanna Love You (But You Got Me Anyway)' and the bigger hit 'Arms of Mary'. Prior to the amalgamation with Quiver, brothers Gavin and Iain Sutherland had made a couple of albums and gained some recognition with 'The Pie' and Gavin Sutherland's 'Sailing' which was covered with great success by Rod Stewart.

Brothers Duane and Greg Allman gave their name to the Southern blues sound of The Allman Brothers band and Greg continued to perform with the other musicians from the group when founding guitarist Duane Allman was killed in an accident in 1971.

Families of brothers also came to prominence, one of the earliest being the Mills Brothers who began their unique harmony sound back in 1928 and continued with chart entries in the 50's an 60's. Initially the four brothers John Jnr, Herbert, Harry and Donald sang bass, tenor, baritone and lead tenor respectively but on John Jnr's death at the age of 26, their father John Snr took over the bass role. The Mills brothers are cited as an influence on later harmony groups from the pop world such as The Bee Gees.

In 1964, a trio of teenagers called themselves The Jackson Brothers but it was not until Jackie, Jermaine and Tito were joined a year or so later by younger brothers Michael and Marlon that they began to get noticed and The Jackson Five were created. Berry Gordy quickly signed the act to Motown and honed the brother's image as The Jackson 5 with early successes 'I Want You Back', 'ABC' and the ballad featuring a young Michael, 'I'll Be There'. Simultaneously, Michael, Jermaine and Jackie had parallel solo releases whilst part of the '5' and when the group changed record labels and moved to CBS they also altered the group's name to The Jacksons and membership to include youngest brother Randy in place of Jermaine who stayed with Motown, having married Hazel Gordy daughter of the owner Berry. Television appearances at this time also featured the three Jackson sisters Rebbie, La Toya and Janet, all of whom proved popular and launched solo careers although oldest sibling Rebbie kept a lower profile having married and with a family of her own. Although The Jacksons continued, output and popularity diminished as individuals concentrated on solo work and the family could only look on as Michael's career reached superstar proportions following the release of 'Thriller'.

However, family squabbles were played out in public as was the questionable behaviour of Michael and any possibility of a return of The Jacksons was ruled out in June 2009 when Michael Jackson died due to complications following administration of inappropriate medication by his personal doctor, who was subsequently charged with manslaughter.

The Jackson family legacy continues with individual releases and performances by remaining family members as well as the back catalogue of the various solo and combinations of the members of the first Afro-American family to have their own television variety show.

In 1958, four young Mormon brothers sang harmonies of the 'barbershop' style. Allan, Wayne, Merrill and Jay Osmond appeared as a regular act which became five as younger brother Donny was added. The variety Osmond Brothers evolved into the pop group The Osmonds despite the suspicion of the boys' father that the genre was not suitable for his religious outlook. 'One Bad Apple', 'Yo Yo', 'Go Away Little Girl' and 'Crazy Horses' maintained the group's success but Donny was also groomed as a solo performer and became the 'star' of the family with his crooning renditions of 'Puppy Love', 'The Twelfth of Never' and ' 'Go Away Little Girl'.

Also coming out of the shadows was youngest brother Jimmy who had a UK number one with 'Long Haired Lover from Liverpool' and teenage sister Marie who began her success with the country crossover 'Paper Roses'. The Osmonds had another hit 'Love me for a

Reason' and Donny and Marie continued the name as a duo. As committed members of the Church of the Latter Day Saints, The Osmonds juggled family life, fame, recording and touring with the duties of their religion and musical output dwindled.

However, the Osmond name lives on with occasional recordings and hits mainly in the country charts, tours by assorted members and a next generation of Osmonds following in their fathers' footsteps.

Little Sister

Having introduced a musical sister, there are more male and female sibling acts

Steve Earle has had a successful career as a songwriter and country recording artist. His sister Stacie is also a country singer and prior to her own solo career and duo role with husband Mark Stewart, both were members of Steve's band.

Inez and Charlie Fox were a brother and sister singing act whose biggest hit was their self-written and much covered song 'Mockingbird' but they had a reputation of providing an exciting live show during their most popular period in the mid-sixties.

Richard and Karen Carpenter were a brother and sister act who had major success in the 1970's with Grammy wins, album sales, television shows, live tours and number ones singles. Commonly referred to incorrectly as The Carpenters, the group the siblings fronted had no definite article and was in fact 'Carpenters'.

Musically their output was a mix of covers and songs co-written by pianist Richard, whose other main roles were production and the arrangements which often consisted of complex multi-layered sound.

Sister Karen was initially the drummer but relatively reluctantly soon found herself out front as her contralto lead vocals proved popular across the spectrum of music buying public. However, the wholesome image of the brand 'Carpenters' pigeonholed them into easy listening which did a disservice to the quality of their music. The 'squeaky clean' persona also belied the behind the scenes dominant nature of Richard who eventually became addicted to quaaludes and had to seek help, but even more disturbing was the self-doubt suffered by Karen which lead to her living with the eating disorder anorexia nervosa for a couple of years and although medical intervention tried to cure her problems, 32 year old Karen Carpenter passed away in 1983 from a cardiac arrest resulting from her weakened state caused by complications from the illness. Carpenters musical legacy can be appreciated by the sound of classic tracks 'Yesterday Once More', 'Close to You', 'We've Only Just Begun' and 'Goodbye to Love' but Karen's personal legacy is that being one of the first high profile deaths from an eating disorder, anorexia and bulimia received much greater publicity, understanding and positive attention following her demise.

Another musician writes songs, plays and sings backing for his younger sister's lead vocal but Jim and Andrea Corr are only half of The Corrs line-up with Sharon on violin / backing vocals and drummer Caroline who also plays piano and backing vocals. The Irish family have experienced incredible success since their debut album 'Forgiven Not Forgotten' in 1995 and the follow up 'Talk on Corners' released two years later. Some critics were of the opinion that the attractive appearance of band members assisted their popularity but there is no question that the family has musical talent and they tapped into the general music buying public's wish for melodic pop with a hint of tradition.

Gladys Knight and the Pips were a family singing act consisting of Gladys as lead vocalist with brother Merald 'Bubba' Knight and cousins Edward Patten and William Guest as support backing singers. Although they were signed to Tamla Motown in the 1960's and even had a moderate hit with their version of 'I Heard it Through the Grapevine', it was not until the early 1970's when they had left Motown and signed with Buddah Records that GK and the Pips really broke through. 'Midnight Train to Georgia', 'You're the Best Thing that Ever Happened to Me' and her version of

Kris Kristofferson's 'Help Me Make it Through the Night' gave Gladys Knight global success and she recorded for a time Pipless' including a Bond theme with 'License to Kill'.

Multi-instrumentalist Mike Oldfield has an older brother Terry and sister Sally, both of whom are musicians and assist Mike when he plays his Tubular Bells and other works live.

Sisters are doing it for Themselves

Moving on to bands that contain no brothers but in which sisters contribute, the first being triplets. Rachel, Petra and Tanya Haden continue the legacy of their musician father, Charlie Haden whose upright double bass playing can be heard on numerous recordings by Jazz greats, particularly Ornette Coleman, his own releases and collaborations with pop/rock musicians from Rickie Lee Jones, Ginger Baker and Beck. His three daughters released a country album as The Haden Triplets and all play in individual bands achieving recognition as does their brother Josh and Tanya's husband 'Tenacious D' performer and actor Jack Black.

Twin sisters Kim and Kelley Deal began as an acoustic duo, Kim was later in The Pixies but the sisters both played in The Breeders.

B*witched was a four piece all-girl singing group from Ireland who had strong record sales in the four year period from 1998-2002. Lindsay Armaou and Sinead O'Carroll along with twin sisters Edele and Keavy Lynch sang their way into the top 10 in the UK (number 1) and the US with their debut single C'est la vie and continued with two platinum selling albums and a string of hit singles. Armaou married Lee Brennan from boyband 911 and the Lynch twins' brother Shane was a member of Boyzone.

An Irish family consisting of father, mother, two sons and five daughters moved to Blackpool in England and played the club circuit in the area. The girls emerged from this act to become The Nolan Sisters and eventually shortened to the name to The Nolans.

The sisters biggest success was the catchy 'I'm in the Mood for Dancing' and this as well as other very 'poppy' tunes sold well in the UK, parts of Europe, down under and the group became a major favourite in Japan. With a pool of six sisters, they performed in various formats as some left for solo careers or family reason over their 30 year career.

The Staves are a modern harmony act made up of three English sisters Emily, Jessica and Camilla Staveley-Taylor who are tipped for success.

Back across the Atlantic there were a few Sister acts who graced the airwaves and dented the charts over the years.

One group of sisters had a number of hits, their biggest being a dance title and family reference. Kim, Debbie, Joni and Kathy make up Sister Sledge, the Philadelphia quartet who enjoyed popularity in the disco era with 'He's the Greatest Dancer' and 'We are Family'.

Contemporaries, Californian born sisters Ruth, Anita, June and Bonnie Pointer had toyed with country music and jazz but found greatest success with the ballad 'Slow Hand' and upbeat dance numbers 'I'm so Excited', 'Jump (for your Love), 'Automatic' and a cover of Bruce Springsteen's 'Fire'. Again the Pointer Sisters' line-up consisted of variants from duo, trio and quartet and on occasion solo performances.

Sisters Patty, Maxine and LaVerne were a singing trio from the 1930's through the war years entertaining troops as the Andrews Sisters. They reformed in 1956 and sang together for another 10 years with their harmony sound influencing more modern artists such as Bette Midler who covered the catchy 'Boogie Woogie Bugle Boy'.
This song was also covered by the Puppini Sisters a trio of non-related girl singers who model their vocal style on the Andrews Sisters but although the music is

quaintly old fashioned, their lyrics are more modern and suggestive.

Considered by some as Canadian, the band 'Heart' are actually American but first found success north of the border in the 1970's with their 'Dreamboat Annie' sound and the single 'Barracuda'. A lull in popularity readied the ever changing line-up for the most successful period as AOR balladeers with 'Alone', 'These Dreams', 'Who Will you Run to' and 'All I Wanna do is Make Love to You' and Heart fronted by sisters Ann and Nancy Wilson were established as major artists in the genre.

Also American despite their first hit being called 'Going down to Liverpool' were The Bangles who had a few catchy pop songs in the eighties. Singer Suzanna Hoffs was supported by sisters Debi and Vicki Peterson on popular songs 'Manic Monday' and 'Eternal Flame'.

Two Australian sisters found popularity as singers and entertainers. Following acting roles in Australian soaps, Dannii Minogue released her first records in 1990 and has had a number of hits, mainly in her country of birth and the UK with emphasis on the dance charts. In her later career she veered towards musical appearances and television. Older sister Kylie also began in Australian soaps and via the Stock, Aitken Waterman stable, found great popularity as a pop singer in the 1980's. As she matured, so did her projects recording with members of The Manic Street Preachers and Nick Cave. From 2000 onwards, Kylie Minogue's star status was global from 'Spinning Around' through movie appearances, extravagant tours, fashion and gay icon, personal life and tabloid exposure, Kylie has never been out of the media in the past decade. The positive aspect of this was her very public declaration of her fight against breast cancer with which she was diagnosed at the age of 36 and has been treated successfully. Doctors have referred to the 'Kylie effect' as many young women have checked for signs of the disease and reported for professional diagnosis as a result of the singer's profile and advice to do so.

Family Affair

There are a number of musical families, some becoming melodious dynasties as generations of talent continue to produce prolific offspring.

One such example is Nelson spawning from big band leader Ozzie Nelson and his singer wife Harriet. Their band had hits through the 1930's and 40's and then moved to radio and subsequently television with their early version of reality shows 'Here Come the Nelsons' and 'The Adventures of Ozzie and Harriet' (50 years before Ozzy and Sharon Osborne's show). These shows portrayed the couple raising their two sons,

David who went on to be a movie producer and Ricky who developed into a successful musician in his own right. As a result of the fictional setting of his televised life, Ricky Nelson was already financially set up by his early teens but the money was held in trust and not released to him.

What was released in 1957 was the 18 year olds first album which reached number one. His musical career had started on the back of his television and teenage appeal and within five years he featured 30 times in the US top 40 with his best known recordings being 'Travellin Man', 'Young World' and 'Hello Mary Lou'.

When the singer turned 21 he dropped the 'y' and became the more adult sounding Rick Nelson, achieving his last hit with 'Garden Party' in 1972. Despite his clean cut image, Nelson had been a drug user since the early sixties. He was involved in a number of relationships but was only married once to Kristen Harmon with whom he had four children. Twins Mathew and Gunnar Nelson continue the family's musical legacy fronting the rock band 'Nelson' and have had a few US hits including a number one single in 1990 with '(Can't Live Without Your) Love and Affection'.

Therefore, three generations of the Nelson family have reached the top of the charts in their country of birth.

Two generations reached number one in 1972 at the same time when The Staple Singers, Stax single 'I'll Take You There' hit the top spot. Sisters Mavis, Cleotha and Yvonne along with brother Pervis and their father Roebuck made up the gospel singing family that crossed over into mainstream after a lengthy career.

'Pops' Staples was almost 60 years old and his offspring in their thirties when their chart run including 'Respect Yourself' and 'If You're Ready (Come go with Me)' began.   The family patriarch died aged 86 but Mavis continued to keep the Staple name in prominence recording, performing and collaborating with other artists including Bob Dylan, who she claims once asked her father for her hand in marriage.

Mavis Staples won the Grammy for Best America album in 2011 at the age of 71.

In a different part of the world two families were responsible for spreading the influence of their musical traditions to a wider audience.

Ricardo Baliardo came to prominence in the mid 1960's popularising a style of flamenco guitar playing. Known by the stage name Manitas De Plata (Little Silverhands) he was actually a gypsy guitarist born in France and although illiterate, played throughout the world, sometimes solo and on occasion he recorded with flamenco singer Jose Reyes.

Reye's sons Nicolas, Canut, Patchai, Paul and Andre joined with De Plata's three boys Paco, Diego and Tonino to form the Gipsy Kings.

From humble beginnings busking, the GK's hit mainstream popularity with genre defying 'Bambeleo' and 'Volare' and their rhythmic strumming and powerful vocal style crossed many borders.

Back in America, a couple of family names became musical institutions due to their prolific recorded and live output.

The name Carter is well established in the genre of Country music with the Carter Family's first recording back in 1927.   A.P. Carter, his wife Sara and sister-in-law Maybelle were the initial members of the singing 'Family' which at one stage included A.P. and Sara's children Janette and Joe as well the daughters of Ezra and Maybelle Carter, Helen, Anita and June. The act evolved into 'Mother Maybelle and The Carter Sisters with the last four named continuing the legacy. Thereafter, all three sisters had individual careers and success as writers and performers.

June's first marriage produced daughter Carlene Carter a successful singer / songwriter (who was married to musician Nick Lowe for a time), her second marriage saw the birth of her second daughter Rosie

Nix-Adams who was also a country singer but died of carbon-monoxide poisoning at the age of 45.

June Carter's third marriage was to the established singer songwriter Johnny Cash whose reputation as a songwriter and singer of favourites 'I Walk The Line' and 'Get Rhythm' as well as June's co-written 'Ring of Fire' were about to be eclipsed by his prison songs 'Folsom Prison Blues' and 'San Quentin' and his version of 'A Boy Named Sue'.

Thus the Carter Family tree branched out to become Carter / Cash and the musical legacy encompassed a wider number of performers and evolved from traditional country music into a wider Americana genre. June and John had one son together and John Carter Cash is a performer and sought after producer. Johnny Cash had four daughters from his first marriage, the eldest of whom, Roseanne is also a Grammy award winning singer songwriter. Although both Johnny Cash and June Carter died in 2003, the Carter / Cash Family continues the musical journey that began back in the 1920's.

Jimmy Webb is a musician who achieved minor success as a singer but major plaudits for his song writing. Webb material has taken a diverse range of artists into the charts, such as actor Richard Harris and electro / disco queen Donna Summer with Jimmy's epic 'McArthur Park'. Jimmy Webb songs have been recorded by elite vocalists of the pop / rock era including Frank Sinatra, Elvis Presley, Art Garfunkel and Linda Ronstadt. Vocal Group 5th Dimension scored a hit with 'Up Up and Away', The Highwaymen' recorded his song 'Highwayman' and used it for their album title and various versions of Webb songs have been resurrected through the years, a recent example being 'Rumer's version of his eponymous tribute to fellow songwriter 'P F Sloan' in 2012.

However, the most prodigious purveyor of Jimmy Webb compositions was Glen Campbell who achieved major success with 'By the Time I Get to Pheonix', 'Wichita Lineman' and 'Galveston'.

Jimmy Webb's sons Christiaan and Justin started a band called the 'Webb Brothers' and were soon joined by brother James, their most successful album 'Maroon' reaching just outside the UK top 100. Jimmy and his sons, including brother Cornelius on bass and Jimmy's Baptist minister father recorded an album 'Cottonwood Farm' in 2009 and the three generations of Webb musicians toured the release with Cal Campbell, Glen's son on drums.

Glen Campbell's 50 year career has taken him from session guitarist, one time Beach Boy, actor, songwriter, television host and country singer. In addition to his Jimmy Webb written hits, Campbell popularized 'Gentle on my Mind', 'Southern Nights', 'Honey Come Back' and the karaoke favourite 'Rhinestone Cowboy'. He was an Academy Award and

Golden Globe nominee and has numerous pop and country music awards including a number of Grammy's, four of which were won in 1967. A popular live draw, Glen Campbell embarked on his farewell tour in 2011, having announced that he was suffering from Alzheimer's disease and his backing band for this final outing included three of his children,

The Cowsills are an American family of harmony singers who achieved success in the late 1960's with the million sellers, 'The Rain, The Park and Other Things', 'Indian Lake' and their version of 'Hair' from the musical of the same name. Brothers Bill, Bob and Barry were joined by siblings John, Susan and Paul as well as their mother Barbara to create tight harmony singing in their many live performances. A version of the act still performs but a number of the original members have since passed away.

The idea for the television musical spin-off The Partridge Family apparently came from the popularity of The Cowsills' formula and featured heart throb David Cassidy and his real life stepmother Shirley Jones. Although a manufactured act, a number of hits were attributed to The Partridge Family, the biggest being 'I Think I Love You'

Other acts with the word Family in the title who had no familial connections include English progressive rockers 'Family' whose first two albums had the domestic sounding titles 'Music in a Doll's House' and 'Family Entertainment'. However no related personnel were in this band which brought us the singles 'The Weaver's Answer', 'In My Own Time' and 'Burlesque'.

The Lighthouse Family, best known for the radio friendly song 'Lifted' and debut album 'Ocean Drive' from the mid-1990's were in fact two students who met while working in a bar. Keyboardist Paul Tucker had written a number of songs which found popularity when the easy listening vocals of Tunde Baiyewu were added.

Similarly, Family Dogg, one hit wonders with 'A Way of Life' were neither canine nor related but was an early vehicle for the talents of Steve Rowland (producer of Dave Dee, Dozy, Beaky, Mick and Tich's string of hit singles, aspiring songwriters Mike Hazelwood and Albert Hammond and singer Christine Holmes aka Kristine Sparkle).

On the other hand, the multi-racial outfit who sang about 'Family Affair', advised 'Im Gonna Take You Higher' and urged us to 'Dance to the Music' did have some familial connections. Sylvester Stewart (Sly Stone) had brother Freddie on guitar, sister Rose on keyboards and another sister Vaetta as one of the

backing vocalists in 'Sly and the Family Stone.
Other important members in the funk outfit were
Larry Graham, innovator of the slap bass style of
playing and trumpeter Cynthia Robinson. The final
two members, strange for the time were Caucasians,
drummer Gregg Errico and Saxophonist Jerry Martini.
The band's influence has been recognised by
musicians across styles from dance to hip-hop, soul to
pop and Sly and the Family Stone were inducted into
the Rock and Roll Hall of Fame.

The single most negative connotation of the word
family with a musical connection was the failed singer
songwriter Charles Manson whose 'Family' of
followers did his bidding to the extent of mass murder
leading to his incarceration for life. Manson had
tentative musical links to the Beach Boys but his
fascination with The Beatles manifested itself for the
outside world to see at the scenes of the murderous
crimes with lines from Beatles' songs written on walls
and kitchen appliances, some in blood.
He considered many songs from The Beatles (White
album) to be lyrically in tune with his thoughts on
racial tensions and pending war. The songs 'Helter
Skelter' and 'Piggies' supposedly had specific
significance and were used at his subsequent trial to
prove that Manson was obsessed and delusional.
Although some of Manson's recordings have been

released since his imprisonment without garnering any commercial interest, a few of his songs were covered by mainstream artists. The Beach Boys reworked his 'Cease to Exist' and recorded it as 'Never Learn Not to Love' and Guns N' Roses did a version of Manson's 'Look at Your Game, Girl'. Some of Charles Manson's lyrics have also been used by namesake, but no relation, Marilyn Manson.

Chapter 5

I've Got a Name

I've got a name, I've got a name, and I carry it
with me like my daddy did,

but I'm living the dream that he kept hid,
moving me down the highway,

rolling me down the highway,
moving ahead so life won't pass me by" — (vi)

by Jim Croce

When parents name their children there are not many
who consider whether the appellations would sound
good on the radio or stand out from the front of an
album cover but a catchy memorable nomenclature
can improve chances of getting noticed in the world of
entertainment. As far as pop / rock musicians go, the
sound of the name must relate to the image and
genre to avoid confusion and assist with marketing.
Registered surnames are required to identify
individuals but forenames and middle names are
more adaptable, whereas nicknames tend to be more
individualistic. Nevertheless, many opt to adopt stage
names, assumed names, aliases, nom de plumes, aka's
or formally change their official identifier by deed poll.

As rock and roll music emerged from the dancehalls and concert venues onto radio and then television programmes, entrepreneurial managers were keen for their acts to share in the opportunities. Many recording artists were 'given' new names that supposedly portrayed a 'cool' image as opposed to those that appeared on birth certificates. Thus the charts were filled with names such as Cliff Richard, Billy Fury and Adam Faith as opposed to their actual designations Harry Webb, Ronald Wycherley and Terence Nelhams.

A few took on more elaborate or 'glitzy' sounding names, perhaps with a view to standing out against the mundane, so Robin Peter Smith became Crispian St. Peters and Paul Gadd tried Paul Raven before settling on Gary Glitter and Bernard Jewry became Shane Fenton and evolved into Alvin Stardust. Michael Barratt is not as rocky as Shaking Stevens and of course the transformation of Vincent Furnier to Alice Cooper was more glam than glamorous but became a well-known epithet for the singer.

In the case of David Jones, a musician trying to break through in the mid-60's a slight change from Jones to Bowie ensured that Ziggy, the Thin White Duke and the many faceted Starman would not be confused with fellow English singer Davy Jones of Monkees fame.

Some artists 'official' names did not roll off the tongue as easily as their lyrics and they took on more appropriate personas. Dionysius P.A. O'Brien and his sister Mary Isobel Catherine Bernadette O'Brien came to prominence in the folk trio The Springfields with Mary assuming the name Dusty Springfield, with which she became known as one of the best female singers to come out of the UK and her brother, who became a songwriter responsible for many of The Seekers hits, taking on the name, Tom Springfield. A similar circumstance arose more than 10 years later when the individuals in the group The Ramones took on the band's moniker as their surnames.

Definitely Maybe

When it came to group names, the definite article seemed to be a requirement in the early sixties, thus we had The Zombies, The Animals, The Easybeats, The Kinks, The Searchers, The Fortunes, The Turtles, The Casuals, The Tremeloes, The Who and The Move. A slight deviation in spelling gave an individual identity and would hopefully be more identifiable like, The Beatles, The Hollies, The Byrds and The Monkees. Some bands had two words often because they were named after something such as The Rolling Stones, taken from a blues song, The Mindbenders copied from a movie of the same name and The Moody Blues which was expanded from the initials of a local brewery M&B's.

As the decade progressed, the music became more experimental and so too did the names of bands. 'Grateful Dead' was a phrase taken from a dictionary (as was Evanescence years later), 'Procol Harum' was supposedly a miss-spelling of a breed of cat, 'Jefferson Airplane' is a parody of a traditional blues singer's identity, 'Buffalo Springfield' was copied from the names on the side of a steamroller and 'Amen Corner' resulted from a record session in a Welsh Club.

The psychedelic era saw some bizarre band names appear and usually disappear with minimal impact or music legacy. 'Pacific Gas and Electric', 'Strawberry Alarm Clock', '13th Floor Elevators', Dantalian's Chariot' and 'The Peanut Butter Conspiracy' graced the airwaves for a short time. Slightly more commercially known were 'Captain Beefheart', 'Moby Grape', 'The Crazy World of Arthur Brown', 'The Incredible String Band', 'New Riders of the Purple Sage' and 'Country Joe and the Fish'.

Members from groups became known in their own right and some went solo or joined other musicians and produced collaborative sounds with competitive egos. The term 'supergroup' was bandied about as bands were formed and identified by the names of the participants without a communal 'the' to cement the venture.

So Crosby, Stills, Nash & Young aka CSNY operated as any combination of the four, Emerson Lake and Palmer sounded less like a firm of solicitors when shortened to ELP and they too had a similarly fluent relationship and various ex-members of the group 'Yes' would play together under their surnames banner, Anderson Bruford Wakeman Howe.

The Swedish pop sensations that used the initials from their forenames in a palindrome had no requirement to revert to surnames as they became globally recognised as ABBA.

X & Y

Using initials simplified the names of bands for disc jockeys and journalists and many groups became known by their shortened form such as ELO rather than Electric Light Orchestra or OMD without the need to pronounce Orchestral Manoeuvres in the Dark, Bachman Turner Overdrive became BTO, Creedence Clearwater Revival were known as CCR, Sensational Alex Harvey Band was SAHB, Barclay James Harvest regressed to BJH and the Average White Band could be truncated to AWB.

The seventies outfit who went by the initials CCS actually had a full title of Collective Consciousness Society.

Other bands had letters as the actual name of the group that were not abbreviations –   A-HA, ABC, XTC, INXS, TLC, REM, UFO, KLF, AC/DC, N SYNC and the combination of words and letters REO Speedwagon, ZZ Top, M People, Boney M and Tenacious D.

Nick of Time

Many amateur performers had hours of fun down at the pub trying to come up with the ultimate stage name or band identifier and inspiration came from the unlikeliest of places.

Those with ready- made nicknames were best placed to have a natural transition from obscurity to fame without the confusion of who was being referred to, thus few people mentioned Gordon Sumner as a member of The Police, but everyone knew who 'Sting' was. Similarly Paul Hewson and David Evans are not widely known as members of U2 but as Bono and The Edge they are instantly recognisable as is Slash (ex-Guns'N'Roses), Suggs (Madness) and Fish (ex-Marillion).
Others with a string of names or even just a string of letters took a shortened version and enjoyed fame with a single denomination. Cherilyn became Cher, Madonna lost the surnames as did Bjork, Jewel, Tiffany, Adele, Beyonce and Shakira.

Others known mononymously are Lulu, Beck, Shaggy, Yanni, Dido, Odetta, Fabian, Moby, Usher, Pink, Melanie, Donovan, Lobo, Jamelia, Dion, Liberace, Heinz, Falco, Enya, Nico, Prince, Fergie, Seal, Sade, Eminem, Anastacia and Twinkle.

'Coolio' and 'LL Cool J' are certainly cooler names than Artis Leon Ivey Jnr. and James Todd Smith, 'Kid Rock' and 'Iggy Pop' are much more rock 'n' roll than Robert James Ritchie and James Newell Osterberg Jnr. and from 'Ice T' to 'Jay Z' slips of the musical tongue a lot more credibly than Tracy Marrow to Shawn Corey Carter.

For No One

Some bands used abbreviated or adapted versions of members' names as in the case of Fleetwood Mac, the mainstay rhythm section of drummer Mick Fleetwood and bassist John McVie providing the title. Similarly Guns 'n' Roses came from an amalgamation of the bands 'LA Guns' and 'Hollywood Rose' as well as prominent members Tracii Guns and Axl Rose (whose own moniker is an anagram of oral sex).
Whereas, although the Bee Gees name fits easily to the family title 'Brothers Gibb', this was not the derivation of the name, which was in fact , based on the initials of two friends in Australia when the Gibb brothers were young, Bill Goode and Bill Gates (not Microsoft man).

A few band names were taken from films like the aforementioned Mindbenders, also Black Sabbath, My Bloody Valentine, Golden Earring, Fine Young Cannibals, Sleeper and Bad Company while Duran Duran was based on a character from the movie Barbarella.

The origins of some band names supposedly came from the living conditions they endured as they struggled to make ends meet whilst trying to make it in the competitive world of music, notably 'Dire Straits' and 'Crowded House'.

A more erudite approach to naming of musical groups produced 'The Fall' taken from a book by philosopher Albert Camus, 'Steppenwolf' from a Herman Hesse novel and 'Mott the Hoople' from a novel by Willard Manus. Experimental jazz / rock exponents 'Soft Machine' took their name from a William Burroughs novel, 'Primal Scream' from a book of the same name by Arthur Janov and 'Savage Garden' from a novel by Ann Rice.   'Marillion' created the bands' original sounding identifier from a J.R.R.Tolkein collection, by adapting the title, 'The Silmarillion'.

Boo Radley was a character from the Harper Lee novel and Oscar winning film 'To Kill a Mocking bird' which was used by the nineties alternative Britpop group The Boo Radleys and the name 'Supertramp' is taken from the 'Autobiography of a Supertramp' by W.H.Davies

The French children's book 'Belle et Sebastien' was the basis for the band name 'Belle and Sebastian' and another publication for children 'Mr Crowes Garden' inspired a band of the same name who then amended it, to become 'The Black Crowes'.

'Good Charlotte' was also taken from a children's story and used for a music group.

The progressive outfit fronted by Ian Anderson that gave us 'Thick as a Brick' and 'Aqualung', 'Jethro Tull' took their name from an 18th century agricultural inventor and seventies heavy rock outfit 'Uriah Heep' used the name of a character from Charles Dickens' novel David Copperfield.

An English post punk goth band released a number of albums in the eighties that made respectable chart positions including a UK number 4. They took their name from a style of architectural design from 1920's Germany and called themselves 'Bauhaus'.

A Chicago group went even further into the geographical past and acquired the idea for their name from the mythical river 'Styx'.

'Genesis' is the first book from the bible's old testament and was thought to be a suitable name for a band and 'Avenged Sevenfold' adapted their name from the phrase 'vengeance seven times over' that appears in Genesis.

'Nirvana' relates to the state of mind aspired to in Buddhism and was the name of a relatively obscure

UK band in the sixties into the seventies. The American 'grunge' band that used the same name were iconic for the genre but the apparent suicide of frontman Kurt Cobain was at odds with the tranquil image of spiritual nirvana.

The not so cultured titles based on the seedier side of life include the Malcolm McLaren anointed 'Sex Pistols' a veiled reference to his fashion shop venture with Vivienne Westwood, 'Sex'.
Also with sexual connotations, 'Velvet Underground' and 'Joy Divison' which were both taken from books about S&M and 'Alice in Chains is apparently a sado-masochistic parodied slant on Alice in Wonderland.
'Iron Maiden' was named after a torture device and the name 'Pet Shop Boys' refers to practices in the gay scene.
Despite AC / DC being a slang term for transvestites, the Australian based rockers saw the letters on an electrical appliance and took the name whereas an appliance of a more sexual nature was the basis of the band name 'Steely Dan' lifted from the William Burroughs novel 'Naked Lunch' in which it is the name given to a vibrating pleasure implement aka dildo.

There are a number of musical links in the naming of bands such as 'Deacon Blue' being taken from a song by the aforementioned Steely Dan. The 'Cocteau Twins' was an early 'Simple Minds' song and Jim Kerr's band took the words 'simple minds' from David

Bowie's song 'Jean Genie' while another Bowie number, 'Kooks' was the origin of the band of the same name.

'Deep Purple' was a 1930's song popularised in 1963 by brother and sister Nino Tempo & April Stevens and again thirteen years later by brother and sister Donny & Marie Osmond and the name was used by seventies heavy rockers the 'Deep Purple' of 'Black Night' and 'Smoke on the Water' fame.

Martin Fry's 'ABC' was taken from a Jackson 5 hit and the group 'Sisters of Mercy' used a Leonard Cohen song for their name.

Even more bands took song titles as their own names such as boogie blues band 'Canned Heat' from the 1920's number 'Canned Heat Blues' and 'Radiohead' from the 'Talking Heads' track Radio Head.

Queen's anthemic 'Radio Ga Ga' was the inspiration for Stefani Joanne Angelina Germanotta to take the name Lady Gaga and Swedish duo Roxette are named after a Dr. Feelgood track of the same name.

'Shakespears Sister' took their name from a track by The Smiths, 'Starsailor' was from a Tim Buckley song of the same name as was 'Stiff Little Fingers' taken from The Vibrators' song.

Green Gartside created a band in the second half of the seventies and gave it the name 'Scritti Politti' as an homage to Italian left-wing writer Antonio Gramsci. The band's style varied from punk through soul and even jazz and they had minor commercial but greater critical success.

One sign of recognition is when fellow artistes record material written by another and also if a composition inspires a name for another performer. Both of these occurred in the case of Scritti Politti when one of their songs 'The Sweetest Girl' was covered by popular fun group 'Madness' but also jazz legend Miles Davis did a version of 'Perfect Way'.

The lyrics to another of their songs, 'Getting, Having and Holding' was the source of the name 'Wet Wet Wet' as used by the Scottish eighties pop sensations.

'Pink Floyd' is named after two blues musicians and The Boomtown Rats was the name of a gang in Woody Guthrie's 'Bound for Glory', so musicians inspired musicians.

Here There and Everywhere

A number of bands named themselves by a geographical location which is understandable for the civic minded or patriotic citizens who are proud of their heritage but many just took the name of a distant or glamorous sounding location.

Edinburgh's seventies tartan boy band the 'Rollers' stuck a pin on a map and christened themselves with the prefix 'Bay City'. Other Scottish musicians used the equally distant location of 'Nazareth' as their group's name but this was not due to any religious significance, they took it from The Band song 'The Weight'.

Fellow Scot Johnny McElhone had some UK success in the groups 'Altered Images' and 'Hipsway' but when he founded his next band along with singer Sharleen Spiteri and her lead guitarist brother-in-law Ally McErlaine they achieved much greater popularity across Europe, Scandinavia and Australasia.
Taking their name from the film 'Paris, Texas', the American market has ironically proved elusive for 'Texas'.

American States and cities have been a popular choice for band names with 'Orleans', 'Chicago', 'Kansas', 'Alabama' and 'Boston' all featuring as group names and of course the band 'America' itself.
There is also 'New York Dolls', 'Manhattan Transfer', 'Georgia Satellites', 'Miami Sound Machine', 'Atlanta Rhythm Section', 'Black Oak Arkansas', 'Ohio Players', 'Manassas' and a sampling dance band from the UK taking the name 'Utah Saints'.

More UK bands used the equally glamorous sounding local location names, 'Hatfield and the North', 'Portishead' and 'Lindisfarne' but two groups of

Englishmen who were popular in the eighties took their names from much farther afield, 'Japan' and 'China Crisis'.

A Scottish outfit baptised themselves The Blue Nile.

An American band whose biggest hit was 'Take my Breath Away', the theme song from the jingoistic navy romance film 'Top Gun' had the non-American name 'Berlin' and an equally overseas nomenclature was used by the English membership of the 'American' AOR sounding 'Asia'.

Slightly closer to home was the Scandinavian rock band who gave us 'The Final Countdown' Swedish group who called themselves 'Europe'.

Returning home after our sojourn to these various location band names we can sit in the comfort of our kitchen with 'Milk and Honey', 'Cream', 'Meatloaf', Red Hot Chilli Peppers', 'Chicken Shack', 'Hootie and the Blowfish', 'Blue Oyster Cult', 'Salt 'n Pepa, 'Bread' and even 'Half Man Half Biscuit'. Then settle back with Neneh Cherry, 'Peaches & Herb', The Cranberries and Bananarama before relaxing with 'Hot Chocolate'.

Lucky Number

There are many examples of bands that have used a combination of numbers and words / letters for recognition but only those that are recognisable are listed, beginning at the higher end with 10,000 Maniacs (adapted from a horror film called Two Thousand Maniacs).

1910 Fruitgum Company, Blink 182, 112, One Hundred Ton and a Feather, Haircut 100, Sham 69, B52's, 50 Cent, Level 42, UB40, 30 Seconds to Mars, Matchbox 20 and Heaven 17 all achieved hit records and recognition.

The lower numbers are used more often and three bands with 'ten' in their titles have charted. Woodstock performers, 'Ten Years After', the combination of songwriting and musical talent that emerged from 'The Mindbenders' and 'Hotlegs' to become '10CC' as well as the Edward Tudor-Pole fronted punk outfit called 'Tenpole Tudor'.

'Nine Inch Nails', 'Nine below Zero', 'S Club 7', 'Shed 7', 'The Temperance 7' and 'Sixpence None the Richer' have taken the number / letter combination into our headphones.

More than five prominent acts used the number 5, 'Five Star', 'Ben Folds Five', 'MC5, 'Maroon 5', 'Dave Clark 5' and of course the 'Jackson 5' and in excess of four with the number 4, 'Gang of Four', '4 non-blondes', the 'Four Tops', the 'Four Pennies' and 'The Fourmost'.

'The Three Degrees' were a popular pop / soul singing trio, 'Funboy 3' were three singers who emerged from ska band The Specials and American group 'Three Dog Night' were 3 vocalists along with backing musicians. The name for the last named was suggested from an Aboriginal legendary custom where the indigenous tribes people would sleep with a wild dog at night to keep them warm and on colder nights would have two dogs for heat whereas freezing temperatures would be a three dog night.

Different styles of music are represented by 'The 2 Live Crew', 'H2O', 'Boys II Men', 'U2' and 'Soul II Soul'.

'The Only Ones' are not the only ones to use the number one, but there are fewer than would be expected. The only chart topper was a remake of Cliff Richard's 1959 hit 'Living Doll' which was credited to Cliff along with four comic actors who made up 'The Young Ones'. This made for charity record hit the top in the UK, Holland and Australia.
However, there are a couple of good band names with as yet no hits under their belts but 'One Car Pile-up' and 'One Hit Wonder' are two names to look out for.

One band had a practical use for numbers when sixties combo 'Unit 4' added two members to their line-up and became 'Unit 4 plus 2'.

Colours

Another 'theme' is the use of a colour in a band title from the basic word 'Blue' to 'Simply Red' and various shades in between. King Crimson, Maroon 5, Orange Juice, Tangerine Dream, Rose Royce, Pinkerton's Assorted Colours, Frijid Pink, Pink Floyd and Pink Fairies were variations on red which was used directly in Red Hot Chilli Peppers.

There is Black Sabbath, Black Uhuru, Black Oak Arkansas, Ladysmith Black Mambazo, Black Eyed Peas and The Black Keys also White Stripes, Great White, Whitesnake and Average White Band.   The tasty shades of Cream and Hot Chocolate and the exotic sounding Pearl Jam and Indigo Girls were aurally bright.

Then there is Moody Blues, Swinging Blue Jeans, Blue Oyster Cult, Deacon Blue, Blue Nile as well as the Lemonheads, the Lemon Pipers, Green Day and Green on Red.

The richly coloured Deep Purple and New Riders of the Purple Sage were matched by Goldfrapp and Quicksilver Messenger Service and who could forget all the colours of the 'Rainbow'.

Individually Barry White, Cilla Black, Sam Brown, Macy Gray, Al Green, Yellowman, Jason Orange and Ruby Turner brightened our airwaves.

Sound of Silence

The only onomatopoetic band name was George Michael & Andrew Ridgley's duo of glam known as 'Wham' but many names conjure up a style of music as the sound of the artiste(s) define the genre in which their music fits or at least narrows it down. 'Howlin' Wolf', 'Screaming Jay Hawkins', 'Motorhead', 'Anthrax', 'Iron Maiden', 'Saxon' and 'Metallica' are not names that would associate readily with folk music or romantic ballads or anything that required the amplifiers to be set to anything but LOUD.

Similarly, groups and individuals referred to as 'Rat Scabies', 'The Clash', 'The Stranglers, 'Siouxsie and the Banshees', 'The Damned', 'The Vibrators' and 'Wreckless Eric' could only have come out of the punk movement and listeners would expect expectorate.

Clarification on the derivation of some band names highlight the obvious, but there are also a few surprising entries.

A 'B52' was an American 1950's design stratofortress bomber aircraft and also a three layered shot cocktail drink. However, the 'Love Shack' and 'Rock Lobster' singing band called the B-52's took their name from none of the above, but instead from the beehive hairdo of the same name, which was in fact named after the aircraft' s nosecone shape.

Southern rockers Lynyrd Skynyrd supposedly took the name of an old teacher some of the members had known called Leonard Skinner and came up with the abomination that few fans can spell. One of the stories about the origin of the name of Scottish band Biffy Clyro is similar but the group members tell many alternatives to confuse and amuse.

The Shirley Manson fronted band 'Garbage' reportedly assumed the moniker following criticism of their combined sound and heavy made up musicians 'Kiss' liked the sound of the word as being both dangerous and sexy.

The Kaiser Chiefs are not a reference to indigenous Germans but the English group took the name from a South African football team called Kaizer Chiefs.

REO Speedwagon was named after a model of fire engine, UB40 from a welfare form, Depeche Mode from a fashion magazine and Eurythmics is an old fashioned form of music instruction.

It is often difficult to categorically state the origins of group names because members tease the media with alternative views on this but there is usually enough evidence to make an educated guess.

For example, Jimmy Page is said to have named his band following The Yardbirds, Led Zeppelin, after a comment by either The Who's drummer Keith Moon or bassist John Entwhistle. When discussing the possibility of joining a group along with Page, one of them commented that news of that happening would "go down like a lead balloon" and Jimmy Page adapted the analogy slightly to create an original name with a unique spelling.

There are also denials of popularly held perceptions, one being the refutation by singer Michael Stipe that REM were named after the scientific phrase used in dream / sleep research - rapid eye movement.

Someone Someone

Well known musicians often had to use alternative names for contractual reasons when they appeared on other artistes' recordings.
George Harrison had numerous aliases some of which were not too difficult to decipher such as Hari Georgeson, Jai Raj Harisein, George Harrysong, George H, and Carl Harrison. However, the guitarist also guested under other guises Son of Harry and the exotic sounding L'Angelo Misterioso (Mysterious Angel).

Ex-Beatle colleagues and friends Ringo (Richard Starkey) has played as Roy Dyke and Richie Snare while Macca (Paul McCartney) has at various times been, Apollo C Vermouth, Paul Ramon, Percy Thrillington and booked studios to work in under the name Billy Martin.   John Winston Lennon used various names Dr.Winston O'Boogie, John O'Cean, Dr.Dream, Kaptain Kundalini, Mel Torment, Dwarf McDougall and the variants Reverend Fred Gherkin, Reverend Thumbs Gherkin, Dr.Winston O'Ghurkin, and Winston Leg-Thigh.

Over the years the name of Eric Clapton has featured near or at the top of polls identifying the Englishman as the best rock guitarist ever. However, in the late sixties he was given an even greater honour following graffiti messages on walls claiming 'Clapton is God', but his 'official' nickname is 'Slowhand' although he did appear on another recording as Eddie Clayton.

Fellow axeman Jimmy Page has used the pseudonym S. Flavius Mercurius and compatriot vocalist Robert Plant is known to have used the name Charles Obscure.

It is understandable that musicians may wish on occasion to play incognito but some also use pseudonyms when writing.

The Bangles hit 'Manic Monday' was credited to Christopher Tracy as writer and Sheena Easton's

'Sugar Walls' notes the composer as Alexander Nevermind but they are in fact both aliases for the artist sometimes known as Prince.

Prince Rogers Nelson' who has had both critical and commercial success as a performer, singer/ guitarist, writer, producer and actor, created an enigmatic persona by his behaviour and his carefully stage managed public appearances, none more so than during the phase when he opted to be known by no name, substituting instead, a symbol that could not be pronounced, prompting the media to refer to him as either 'Symbol' or 'the artist formerly known as Prince'.

Other names used by the Paisley Park producer have been Joey Coco, Jamie Starr and Gemini.

New York rappers Wu-Tang Clan took their name from the Chinese martial arts film called Shaolin and Wu Tang. Each of the group members use various aliases, too numerous to mention but the titles they are 'known' by are GZA, RZA, Method Man, Masta Killa, Ghostface Killah, Inspectah Deck, Raekwon and U-God with deceased founder member having used the name Ol' Dirty Bastard.

Back in the sixties Nanker Phelge appeared on the credits of some early Rolling Stones recordings and signified that writing contributions came from all members of the group. The writing and / or producing partnership of Mick & Keith was usually accorded to Jagger & Richards but has also been listed as The Glimmer Twins and The Unknown.

Also, the initial and surname L. Ransford appeared on a number of records by The Hollies in the sixties but this did not allude to a single writer but was a collective pseudonym for the early writing talents of group members Allan Clarke, Tony Hicks and Graham Nash.

When Nash left the Hollies in 1968, he crossed the Atlantic and settled in the States where he teamed up with ex-Byrd David Crosby and ex-Buffalo Springfield members Stephen Stills and Neil Young.
Canadian Young's recorded output has been prolific along with heavy backing from Crazy Horse, Country arrangements with the Stray Gators, various collaborations from Emmylou Harris to Pearl Jam and some work using the alias Bernard Shakey.

Throughout all the changes in musical styles, they were matched by associated changes in styles of band names but some bands continued using the definite article and similar to the sixties preserve 'The Marmalade' we were treated in the seventies to 'The Jam'.

In the sixties we had 'The Mugwumps' and by the eighties we found 'The Cure'.

In the sixties we heard 'The Sandpipers' but by the nineties we played 'The Waterboys'.

In the sixties we went through 'The Doors' and by the millennium emerged to dance in 'The Streets' and while interesting names still surfaced, 'Tears for Fears', 'Art of Noise', 'Inspiral Carpets', 'Massive Attack', 'Blur', 'Arctic Monkeys', 'Thirty Seconds To Mars', 'Franz Ferdinand' and 'Super Furry Animals', the three letter precursor is still prevalent.

'The Shadow Puppets', 'The Strokes', 'The White Stripes', 'The Killers', 'The Libertines' but from the 1980's, we had perhaps the best use of the definite article with the Matt Johnson creation, 'The The'.

I Write The Songs

"I've been alive forever and I wrote the very first song

I put the words and the melodies together

I am music and I write the songs:

I write the songs that make the whole world sing

I write the songs of love and special things

I write the songs that make the young girls cry

I am music and I write the songs" - (vii)

These words are synonymous with the image of Barry Manilow sitting at the piano serenading an audience of middle aged women in awe at the man's talent but what many of them don't know or possibly don't care about, is the fact that their idol did not compose this particular song. It was in fact written by Bruce Johnson, one time half of the singing duo Bruce and Terry (along with Terry Melcher), one time Beach Boy and also composer of the group's opus 'Disney Girls'.

Unchained Melody

Some songwriters only compose and are happy with others performing their material like the Motown writers Holland / Dozier / Holland or the sixties MOR composers Bacharach / David from the USA and contemporaries Leiber & Stoller, or the UK's pop writing teams of Roger Cooke and Roger Greenaway and Tony MacAulay with various co-writers, or the musicals pairing of Tim Rice / Andrew Lloyd Webber.

The importance of songsmiths cannot be emphasised enough as without them many artists would not have been discovered. Some musicians are capable of composing as well as playing but many singers depend on others to provide tunes and lyrics.

Diane Warren is a songwriter who has written hits for Cher, Gloria Estefan and LeAnn Rimes to name but three, examples of her compositions are Starship's hit 'Nothin's Gonna Stop Us Now', Aerosmith's epic 'I Don't Wanna Miss a Thing' and the Grammy award winning 'Because You Loved me for Celine Dion. At one time, Warren had seven hits in the American charts, all performed by different artists.

Composers such as Jimmy Webb and Albert Hammond wrote many hits for others but also recorded some of their own material with lower key success as recording artists than they had as writers.

Word Up

In the case of a few lyricists who wrote memorable words, they themselves kept low profiles while their tunesmith co-writers became the well-known faces of the partnerships. 'Whiter Shade of Pale', 'Homburg', 'A Salty Dog', 'Conquistador' and many other Procol Harum numbers were sung by the dulcet tones of Gary Brooker but the enigmatic lyrics were created by behind the scenes 'non-group' member Keith Reid. Similarly, Cream lyricist Pete Brown, co-composer with vocalist / bassist Jack Bruce of 'White Room' and 'I Feel Free' among others and the pair along with Eric Clapton came up with 'Sunshine of Your Love', but Brown remained offstage.

While pianist Elton John's costumes and persona became more flamboyant, the scribe of the majority of his career's highlights from 'Border Song' and 'Your Song' through 'Rocket Man', 'Daniel', 'Don't Let the Sun Go Down on Me' as well as classic albums 'Madman Across the Water' and 'Goodbye Yellow Brick Road' the rarely seen but much respected lyricist Bernie Taupin enjoyed his incognito status.

Guy Chambers is a musician and producer who played with Julian Cope, The Waterboys and World Party for a time, before really breaking through as a writer / composer when he co-wrote the majority of hits for Robbie Williams including 'Rock DJ', 'Millenium', 'Let Me Entertain You' and 'Angels'. Chamber's song writing credits continued with co-composition duties alongside Kylie Minogue, Melanie C, Katie Melua, Beverley Knight, James Blunt and many others proving that popularity can be achieved behind a keyboard as well as in front of a microphone.

Another more recent pop writer is James Bourne who has co-written numerous hits for McFly, a few for The Jonas Brothers and contributed to material for Melanie C, Boyzone, Backstreet Boys and Pixie Lott among others thus proving that individuals have a composing style that can be replicated to produce different songs in a similar vein.

From Tin Pan Alley and the Brill Building, from writers such as Lennon / McCartney, Jagger / Richards, Ray Charles to Ray Davies, Van Morrison to Morrisey, Carole King to Queen, John Sebastian to Belle & Sebastian, Laura Nyro to Laura Marlin, the importance of songs and the creativeness of their creators cannot be underestimated.

I'd Like To Teach The World To Sing

While some fans prefer melodies, others harmonies, some appreciate musicianship and a few just enjoy the celebrity, many just know songs – tunes and words – songs are important to us as they are to the many writers who even named their albums in honour of the simple word that describes the not so simple formula of song.

There is 'Songs of Leonard Cohen' and from the same artist 'Songs from a Room', 'Songs of Love and Hate', 'Recent Songs' and 'Ten New Songs' while Neil Diamond released an album called '12 Songs', Fugazi had '13 Songs' and The Magnetic Fields produced '69 Love Songs Vol.1,2 & 3'.
Graham Nash gave us 'Songs for Beginners' and 'Songs for Survivors' while his ex-lover Joni Mitchell's debut album was 'Song to a Seagull'. Stevie Wonder welcomed us to 'Songs in the Key of Life' and Eric Clapton in the guise of Derek and the Dominoes treated us to 'Layla and other Assorted Love Songs'.

Musicians are the tradesmen and women, instruments are their tools and songs are the crucial raw materials which together build our audio world.

Different tastes and marketing can help determine whether a song becomes popular and there appears to be no rules when deciding what is a good or bad song, when catchy becomes irritating, when overplay becomes overkill or even when a song sounds unoriginal.

Song styles have formulae that people relate to and some musicians strive to emulate and may even purposely or inadvertently copy.

Musical genres become typecast and many garage, grunge and goth bands sound similar as do many singer songwriters, dance music makers, exponents of Trad. Jazz and even purveyors of punk are not unique.

Oasis have been criticised for sounding like The Beatles, but ELO sound Beatlesque, early Bee Gees tried to emulate the fab four before arriving at their own obvious identity, as did The Monkees and many 'Mersey' bands.
Tears for Fears 'Seeds of Love' is a great piece of work but so too was the similar sounding Beatles song 'I am the Walrus'.
Neil Young has a distinctive voice but did not sing the America hit 'Horse with no Name' although it sounds like him.
Paul Weller has been referred to as the 'Modfather' but sounds like the son of Who, Kinks, Small Faces and other sixties 'mod' groups.

Many non-Jamaican ska and reggae bands were good but not altogether original and were Iggy Pop or the MC5 punks before The Ramones or the Sex Pistols. Heavy metal is formulaic, country music is repetitive in its themes and arrangements, disco is disco and folk is for folk that like to keep within safe parameters of words and melodies.

We Sing We Dance We Steal Things

The band 'Coldplay' were compared to many acts
when they first appeared and as they matured and
produced material with a different sound, they were
then said to sound like other acts.

In an interview for a magazine in 2005, Coldplay's
Chris Martin said, (19)

"We're definitely good, but I don't think you can say
we're that original – I regard us as being incredibly
good plagiarists".

Fellow band member Jonny Buckland remarked
"We've never so directly stolen off anyone before.
We've never paid for our plagiarism".

This is the point, sounding like is different from
stealing material. The music industry is big enough to
cater for all but what does matter is not the originality
of the sound or image, but the originality of the songs
because ownership and copyright determine that this
is important, not the views of fans.

Songwriters may create the work but in the
professional environment it is normally the publishers
that hold copyright rights and although most
songwriters are proud of the integrity of their art,
publishers are more business oriented and look on
songs as commodities to be exploited for income.

In the litigious world in which we live there have been a few court cases and judgements in relation to claims of plagiarism, mainly regarding tunes rather than words.

The highest profile copyright infringement case concerned George Harrison's first post Beatle solo 1970 release 'My Sweet Lord'.
The song, which topped the charts in 12 countries including the US and the UK where it was the biggest selling single of 1971, was an overtly religious piece lauding the Hindu God Krishna but including chants of the Christian/Jewish praise 'Hallelujah'.
Musically, a wall of sound blended numerous acoustic guitars, drums, some keyboard and Harrison's trademark slide guitar.
The overall atmosphere of the record was far removed from the 'doo lang doo lang doo lang' female vocal by The Chiffons of the Lonnie Mack song 'He's So Fine', recorded seven years previous.
However, the melody is so similar that following a lengthy court battle, the judge ruled in favour of Bright Tunes Music – the copyright holder of He's So Fine and Harrison had to pay a large sum to the music company. He had in fact tried to reach an out of court settlement and offered to pay them royalties for the song but this was refused. In this case, the writer did not consciously copy but did agree in hindsight that there were similarities in melody. Even although the infringement was not intended, Bright Tunes were

awarded somewhere between $ 500,000 and $ 1.5million.

Harrison later recorded a self-penned song called 'This Song' in which he sarcastically comments on the episode.

An even greater amount, reported to be over $ 5million was paid out by American singer Michael Bolton in respect of a song called 'Love is a Wonderful Thing' which was written and recorded by the Isley Brothers and deemed by the courts that Bolton's song of the same name was lifted from the original.

The 1963 hit 'Surfin' USA' was found to be so similar to Chuck Berry's 1958 song 'Sweet Little Sixteen' that Berry was granted co-writing credits and a share of the royalties for the Beach Boys' song.

Similar co-writing status and royalties were agreed for Albert Hammond and Mike Hazlewood in relation to Radiohead's 'Creep' because the melody was so similar to the songwriters' best-selling ballad 'Air That I Breath', as recorded by the Hollies.

An out of court settlement was granted in 1995 after a ten year battle, to Huey Lewis by Ray Parker Jnr. for allegedly stealing the melody for 'Ghostbusters' from the Lewis song 'I want a New Drug'.

Even Les Paul was sued for plagiarism back in 1953 as was Oasis in 1994, Avril Lavigne in 2008, The Black Eyed Peas in 2010 and Nickleback the following year.

Therefore it is apparent that in modern music copying is akin to stealing, although proving is more subjective.

A Belgian court ordered all copies of Madonna's song 'Frozen' to be removed and not given airplay in the small European country because in the judges view, it was copied from Belgian artist Salvatore Acquaviva's composition 'Ma Vie Fout le Camp'.

Killing Joke started proceedings against Nirvana with regard to using a 'riff' from one of their songs but did not proceed when Kurt Cobain died.

In June 2012, Will Loomis from American band Loomis and the Lust began the process of suing Jessie J for using his song 'Bright Red Chords' as a basis for her song 'Domino'.

One of the most bizarre cases of alleged plagiarism was made by Fantasy Records against ex- Creedence Clearwater Revival frontman and songwriter John Fogerty.
When Fogerty left Fantasy, the company retained copyright for his back catalogue and claimed that one his new releases 'The Old Man Down The Road' sounded too much like his previous song 'Run Through The Jungle'.   This extraordinary case, Fogerty V Fantasy was based on the fact that the singer's new work sounded too much like himself. The verdict was found in favour of John Fogerty.

Another strange case was brought about in 1989 by publishers Acuff Rose who had the rights to Roy Orbison's 'Oh Pretty Woman'. The band '2 Live Crew' released a parody of the song claiming that it was not a copy and the humorous version would not impact on future sales of the sixties hit. Initially the courts favoured the publishers claim but an appeal to the Supreme Court overturned the verdict and found in favour of 2 Live Crew.

The Verve's classic song 'Bitter Sweet Symphony' does not generate royalties for Richard Ashcroft or any member of the band who recorded the song despite being a hit on both sides of the Atlantic and being used in commercials (against the wishes of Ashcroft). Although the vast majority of the song is original, the orchestral 4 bar introduction is based on the melody of Jagger / Richards early 1960's Rolling Stones hit 'The Last Time'.
Because of this, Allen Klein, who owned the copyright of The Last Time via his company ABKCO, successfully managed to get the Verve to surrender all rights to the song, despite the 'plagiarised / copied / sampled' part being a very small section at the beginning of the song.

ABKCO also took out a case against Lil Wayne and his management / label over the rappers' song 'Playing with Fire' due to its similarity to the Jagger/Richards composition from 1965 'Play with Fire'.

Richard Ashcroft's song 'Bitter Sweet Symphony' was taken from The Verve's 1997 album 'Urban Hymns' but an album called 'Bittersweet Symphony' was released eleven years later by a totally different artist called Jade Valere. Although the titles appear similar, the former is three words while the latter is only two. Valere's real name is Jade Villalone and she had previously been a vocalist for 'Sweetbox' who had released an album simply called 'Jade' which proves that a unique name is important not only for identification but to prevent confusion over similar titles.

A song written in 1934 for the Girl Guides that many primary school children have been singing since is 'Kookaburra Sits in the Old Gum Tree'. Although the writer Marion Sinclair died in 1990, the copyright owner Larrikin Music sued the Australian based group 'Men at Work' because the flute solo at the beginning of their global hit 'Down Under' sounded similar. Writers Colin Hay and Ron Strykert claimed that Larrikin Music did not own the rights but they countered that they became official owners in 1990. The courts found in favour of the copyright owners that the flute segment of the song was taken from the Kookaburra melody.

Lawyers Guns And Money

An unusual and unfortunate case occurred in 1967 that resulted in the group who performed, and more particularly the member who wrote a hit song, not getting royalties. The song in question was the first record (but not the first tune) to be played on the newly created BBC Radio 1. (The first tune was called Theme 1 written for the opening by George Martin and then part of the Johnny Dankworth tune 'Beefeaters' was played, which was DJ Tony Blackburn's Breakfast show theme).

These instrumentals were followed by The Move's third single, 'I Can Hear the Grass Grow' written by guitarist Roy Wood.

However, the group's manager at the time, Tony Secunda had created a publicity stunt in order to market the single which had included sending postcards to select addresses depicting then Prime Minister Harold Wilson in a compromising position. Mr Wilson sued The Move (not the manager) for libel, won the case which resulted in the group having to pay costs and donate all royalties to charity.

This was a financial blow to group members, a double financial blow to Wood which was all the more annoying by the fact that Secunda's idea was all his own, the band knew nothing of it at all, and while they paid, he did not, although he was subsequently fired.

The Move replaced their errant manager with Don Arden who went on to manage the group's successful offshoots 'Wizzard' and the 'Electric Light Orchestra'. However, ex-singer / impersonator Arden's methods were not altogether without criticism and he had a reputation as a 'hard man' who was not averse to using violence and threats against his rivals to achieve his aims.

He previously managed The Small Faces and was accused of cheating by buying up enough copies of their first single to ensure a chart placing. The Small Faces did become popular and sold records on their own merit but saw very little financial return due to Arden's heavy handed control.

Other acts Don Arden managed including The Nashville Teens and Lynsey DePaul also claimed financial irregularities and they received very little for their efforts. He later managed Black Sabbath but had a major rift with his daughter Sharon who went on to manage and marry lead vocalist Ozzy Osbourne. Sharon Osbourne successfully steered Ozzy's and subsequently her own and their children's careers via reality television shows.

In 2003, the members of 1970's 'light rock' band 'Blue' instigated a court case against 'boy band' members Simon Webbe, Duncan James , Lee Ryan and Antony Costa for using the same band name. However, the judge determined that it would not be difficult to tell the two bands apart and the case was thrown out.

In 2012 an American pop / punk group called 'One Direction' asked for a court order to make the British 'boy band' with the same name, change it to a different identity.

Modern established artists who 'sample' from existing songs generally come to an agreement regarding copyright and royalties with the original writers / publishers.
An example being Janet Jackson who sampled to great effect in 1997 when she 'used' Joni Mitchell's 'Big Yellow Taxi' for her single 'Got 'til it's Gone' and again in 2001 when the guitar introduction from America's 'Ventura Highway' was incorporated into Janet's 'Someone to Call My Lover'.

In March 2006 the decision was taken by the UK chart organisers to allow downloaded material to be included. The first number 1 of the new system was Gnarls Barkley's 'Crazy' which itself was sampled from a tune used in a 'spaghetti Western' movie.

Another massive global hit and Grammy winner was 'Gangsta's Paradise, by Coolio featuring L.V., the chorus of which was sampled from the Stevie Wonder song 'Pastime Paradise'.

However, in the early days of sampling, a number of rap artists borrowed illegally. Vanilla Ice released 'Ice Ice baby' using the sample riff from the David Bowie / Queen collaboration 'Under Pressure'. Ice Ice Baby hit the top of the charts and the rapper settled without going to court.

Another rapper, Biz Markie asked permission to use a sampled melody and three words from the Gilbert O'Sullivan song 'Alone Again Naturally' but was refused. Taking a chance, he went ahead anyway, but the judge called the act theft and even threatened him with a criminal charge.

It is usually melodies, riffs, hooks that are plagiarised, not so often words, but one musician did blatantly use another writer's words.   John Lennon was sued for lifting words from a Chuck Berry song to use in his own song 'Come Together'. Lennon used the lines "Here comes up flat top, He was groovin' up slowly", merely changing the first 'up' to 'ol' and 'was' to 'come'.   The matter was settled out of court.

Considering there are only seven notes on the diatonic scale, 12 notes on a six string guitar (with a number of pitch variations), only 88 keys on a regular piano keyboard, there are limited combinations on how they can be arranged to create melodies and it is inevitable that some commonality will exist on occasion. Whereas there are endless words available to be used as lyrics for songs, but in pop music there is an unwritten rule that rhyme schemes are expected and popular subject matter is around kissing, loving, dancing and thinking.

Therefore, the same words do tend to be used often and yet no one has been sued for reusing the phrases, 'I want to kiss you', 'I want to make love to you', 'I want to dance with you' or 'I can't stop thinking about you'.

This is maybe just as well because substituting osculate, copulate, gyrate and contemplate doesn't have the same ring.

There is an art to lyric writing as there is to melody creation and it is easy to subconsciously regurgitate something that you as a listener have heard but you as a writer, thought you had created.

It is allowable to record older uncopyrighted material and credit it as 'traditional – arranged by…" or acknowledge known writers of the original songs even if they are re-recorded and arranged in an entirely different format.

Deep Purple's epic 'Child in Time' was created as a group effort with original lyrics and musical parts. Ian Gillan's vocal performance, Richie Blackmore's guitar virtuosity, Ian Paice's drumming and use of cymbals to create atmosphere, Roger Glover's bass lines and the keyboard skills of Jon Lord are classic purple.

However, the melody played on the organ by Lord is identical to the instrumental piece 'Bombay Calling' by the San Francisco outfit 'It's a Beautiful Day'. This was recognised at the time and in response, the American band adapted the Purple track 'Hard Road'

(Wring that Neck) to make their own song 'Don and Dewey'.

One major band with a string of hit albums, members of the Rock and Roll Hall of Fame, icons of rock, had a unique instantly recognisable sound. Led Zeppelin were the real deal when it came to arrangements, instrumental ability and vocal histrionics but a trawl through the band's many recordings undercovers numerous cases of plagiarism.

Before Zeppelin, drummer John Bonham and singer Robert Plant were mates and played together in Band of Joy.

According to the Small Faces' vocalist Steve Marriot (20) "Percy Plant was a big fan. He used to be at all the Small Faces gigs. We did a gig with the Yardbirds which he was at and Jimmy Page asked me what that number was we did "You Need Loving"……"Anyway we used to play this number………..After we broke up they took it and revamped it".

The song in question in its new format was the Led Zeppelin favourite 'Whole Lotta Love' which although given the 'Zeppelin treatment', was perhaps copied vocally from Steve Marriot's singing style, perhaps copied phrasing wise from the Muddy Waters version but there can be no question that the basis of the song was written in 1962 by bluesman Willie Dixon. This was eventually recognised in 1987 when Dixon was paid substantial back royalties.

In a separate case, Dixon was again recognised as the original writer of 'Bring it on Home' which Zeppelin copied for their song of the same name.

Led Zeppelin have also had to pay out for copyright infringement for their not quite original 'Lemon Song', 'Boogie with Stu' and one of the most contentious claims with regard to 'Dazed and Confused' has yet to be resolved. This song, Jimmy Page played in the Yardbirds and re-recorded with his new band and credited it as a self-written number, however, the original version was written in 1967 by American Jake Holmes who the Yardbirds saw play it live, bought the album and adapted the track.

Similarly Led Zeppelin's treatment of the song differs from the previous two versions, but it is not entirely original work.

The song that is popularly considered as Led Zeppelin's 'piece de resistance' is 'Stairway to Heaven'. Again the lyrics, arrangement and performance is all Zep but the introductory melodic run is a direct copy of a tune called 'Taurus' by the band 'Spirit' who toured with Zeppelin in 1968.

There is no denying the musical talents of Led Zeppelin members especially John Paul Jones and Jimmy Page who played on numerous recordings by other artists as session men, but a little humility and recognition of sharing, copying and adapting would not diminish the appeal of Yardbirds or Led Zeppelin songs.

A final word on another of Jimmy Page's iconic images: that of bowing the electric guitar with a violin bow to produce a haunting sound. According to producer Shel Talmy, guitarist Eddie Phillips from the band 'Creation' was doing that in 1966, (21) "Jimmy Page stole the bowing bit of the guitar from Eddie. Eddie was phenomenal".

Page denied this and in a way does it matter, it was as much a prop as it was a style of playing and used for dramatic effect as part of the live stage show.
Props and acting are not subject to infringement.

In Meatloaf's dramatic Bat out of Hell performance the singer clutches a handkerchief as he sweats out the lyrics but so too did Louis Armstrong in many a performance.

Bruce Springsteen famously collapsing as part of his act, because he supposedly couldn't take anymore, only to be revived by E Street band members to give the audience another powerful performance is reminiscent of James Brown falling to his knees to be helped up by his band colleagues.

U2 stopped the traffic as they performed live on a roof in the 1980's as the Beatles had in 1969.

Joss Stone often performs in bare feet, similarly 60's songstress Sandie Shaw did the same.

Even the famous Michael Jackson moonwalk had been done by others many times, the first filmed version being in 1955 by Pearl Bailey's brother Bill. It is believed that Jackson copied the idea and style from Shalamar's Jeffrey Daniel.

Image is important but the strength of the song is even more so.
The image of Bill Haley with his trademark kiss curl was not particularly appealing but the power of 'Rock Around the Clock' in its day, meant a lot to that generation.
Elvis's pelvis movements were so shocking for the censors at the time that he had to be filmed from the waist up and the naivete of his films still did not prevent record sales because the songs were, in the most part, good.
However, PJ Proby had the looks and voice that could have succeeded like the 'King' but mention his name to the nostalgic few and they will comment on his 'trouser splitting' image rather than his deep baritone voice.

The Singer Sang His Song

Many female singers from the sixties lost their way when the decent songs ran out. Following Sandie's moody vocals on 'Always Something There to Remind Me' and 'Girl Don't Come', Ms Shaw was reduced to 'Monsouir Dupont' and the Europop 'Puppet on a String'. After Cilla Black's powerful renditions of 'Anyone who had a Heart' and 'You're My World', she disappeared (from a musical perspective) down the middle of the road due to mediocre songs. Unfortunately Dusty Springfield's attempt to be recognised as a serious contender with 'Dusty in Memphis' did not quite work, perhaps because her previous 'pop' image was too strong, although she retained popular credibility later in her career with her Pet Shop Boys' collaboration.
Lulu also reinvented herself following 'Shout' and 'To Sir with Love' when she then veered off course to Eurovision and pop trivia only to discover the power of a good song and record Bowie's 'Man who sold the World'. The little Scot with the big voice later discovered her own song writing ability and is still a popular act unlike her contemporaries Vicki Carr, Clodagh Rogers, Julie Rogers, Anita Harris and Jackie Trent who faded from earshot due to lack of decent songs.
More recent Scots singer songwriters Amy MacDonald, KT Tunstall and Sandy Thom have shown a bit more originality.

American female singers seemed to fare better with a harder edged image that kept them in the limelight a bit longer, backed by decent song selection.

Janis Joplin covered Kriss Kristofferson's 'Me and Bobby McGee' and gave it her own style and may have been a force to be reckoned with, but for her untimely death.

Grace Slick moved from Airplane to Starship and maintained chart presence, while Linda Ronstadt plundered the best songs from Roy Orbison and Buddy Holly as well as contemporaries Warren Zevon, Karla Bonoff, Lowell George and Andrew Gold and with the benefit of her vocal talent and the cream of LA's musicians, she merged performance with material to produce a quality sound.

Englishwoman Christine McVie was good song writer and competent singer but her American Fleetwood Mac colleague had stage presence and the rock star image in addition to an emotive voice and quality songs.

Joan Jett knew how to play the leather clad front woman while in the UK, fellow countrywoman Suzi Quatro was a poor copy. Even the popularity of the new wave Debbie Harry from Blondie overshadowed Britain's own Banshee Siouxie Sioux who had to resort to a Beatle's cover in Dear Prudence, for major appeal.

The power of the song is exemplified when the cabaret style career of Bette Midler can be taken to another level by her rendition of 'Wind Beneath my Wings'.

The recent brand of quality singers to come out of the UK such as Adele, Leona Lewis and Emeli Sande could be as big as Whitney Houston if they continue to write or record good quality songs.

What then of the male image in rock !

Prince certainly plays up to an image but his musicianship and song writing abilities from pop to funk, dance to trance ensure his continued success. The artist formerly known as the writer of Sinead O'Connor's biggest hit 'Nothing Compares to You' and The Bangles' 'Manic Monday' as well as 'Purple Rain', 'Raspberry Beret', Little Red Corvette', and 'Kiss' is still an innovator.

Elton John has written and recorded lots of excellent songs with the occasional questionable choice but his costumes, outrageous glasses and extravagant shows have meant that his image has always kept him in the limelight. However the strength of his songs have meant that his persona would not overshadow his contribution as a musician.

Pink Floyd and Roger Waters shows were even more over the top with jets, fireworks, explosions, walls being demolished, large inflatables not to mention the lazers and lights, but again, the musicians could play and the songs were quality.

Many newer bands and singers ignore or shun any image and are content to let the music do the talking. Mumford and Sons, Paolo Nutini, Bon Iver and Ed Sheerin to name only four.

As well as the quality of the material being an essential feature, arrangements can also elevate a good song into an identifiable classic sound.

Examples of unforgettable arrangements are the many Phil Spector 'wall of sound' records from the sixties, the saxophone introduction and solo on Gerry Rafferty's 'Baker Street' played by Raphael Ravenscroft, the iconic bass line in Lou Reed's 'Walk on the Wild Side' performed by Herbie Flowers, the fretless bass of Pino Palladino on the Paul Young version of 'Wherever I Lay my Hat', the 'Motown' sound produced by the 'Funk Brothers' and the many Stax records backed by the Memphis Horns.

There are also sounds that define a particular timeframe in the history of popular music and when that sound goes out of fashion it cannot be used again without 'dating' a recording. Hendrix use of the 'wah wah' on 'Voodoo Chile', Frampton's 'Talk Box' on 'Show Me the Way', Giorgio Moroder's electronic loops on the Donna Summer disco hits and the 'Cher effect' auto tune vocal on 'Believe' all signify the era in which they were recorded. Arrangements and effects can be arranged effectively but only after the song is composed.

While many sixties bands quickly fell into the hits package tours as did a number of seventies performers and then eighties acts, only those with access to new and decent songs whether self- written or available to record, managed to maintain a career beyond the 'nostalgia circuit'.

When it comes to performance, Elvis may have been the best in some people's eyes but try telling that to fans of George Michael, Cher may have appeared outrageous but no more so than Lady Gaga, did Ronnie Spector pre-empt Amy Winehouse without the tattoos ?

Then there is the ultimate showman Freddie Mercury but his death didn't prevent other members of Queen touring with ex-Free / Bad Company singer Paul Rogers taking the vocals or The Doors touring with Ian Asbury of The Cult standing in for the irreplaceable Jim Morrison not to mention re-formed Herman's Hermits without Peter Noone, versions of The Animals without Eric Burdon or the infamous mid-seventies conglomeration of musicians sent out by a miffed manager, masquerading as Fleetwood Mac, minus Fleetwood, McVie, Nicks, Buckingham, Green or any other associate, Oh Well !

As performances go, we don't always know who we are listening to but still enjoy the music because of the quality or aural persistence of the songs.

Eyes Without A Face

In 1970, in the UK, the BBC television pop show Top of the Pops was the medium for showcasing songs to the eager public bereft of any other televised pop show. On one unique episode, 3 of the acts that featured had lead vocals by the same person. Tony Burrows was a session singer whose vocals were heard on songs by The Ivy League, Flowerpot Men, First Class, the Pipkins and on this particular show he fronted Edison Lighthouse with the weeks chart topper, 'Love Grows (Where my Rosemary Goes), he graced the stage as part of Brotherhood of Man singing 'United We Stand' and he stood united as a member of White Plains, singing 'My Baby Loves Lovin'.

A number of 'faceless' groups emerged in the late sixties in what was described as the 'bubblegum' era. The fictitious act 'The Archies' were based on comic book characters but required real musicians to churn out the massive selling 'Sugar Sugar'. Written by Jeff Barry and Andy Kim (who later had the 'Rock Me Baby' dance hit) the vocalist was Barry Manilow's record producer Ron Dante, who coincidently also provided all the vocal parts for another created bubblegum 'group' – The Cufflinks hit 'Tracy'.

Jerry Kasenetz and Jeffrey Katz produced a number of bubblegum records using studio musicians and in some cases touring bands were formed. Kassenetz / Katz were responsible for the 1910 Fruitgum Company recordings (Simon Says), Ohio Express (Yummy Yummy Yummy) featuring Joey Levine on vocal as did their 'Singing Orchestral Circus' hit 'Quick Joey Small'. The bubblegum songs were simple and catchy but the bands simply did not catch on because they were only a front for the short lived popularity of sugary pop,

The Monkees were a manufactured act and although Davy Jones, Peter Tork, Mike Nesmith and Mickey Dolenz had acting, comedic and some musical talent, they depended on established writers Neil Diamond (I'm a Believer), John Stewart (Daydream Believer), Carole King (Pleasant Valley Sunday) and in-house team of Boyce and Hart to provide good songs.

Putting On The Style

Songwriters who can compose original work capable of being recorded in different styles, not genre specific, can count on positive returns.
Dolly Parton's country song 'I Will Always Love You' took on a different image and reached a wider audience when given the big ballad treatment with Whitney Houston's quavering vocal.
Similarly, writer Leonard Cohen's stark recording of 'Hallelujah' suited the song but so too did Jeff Buckley's emotive version and the song was again transformed when Alexandra Burke scored a major hit in Europe with a powerful vocal. There have been

numerous covers of this song with a number of them charting in different countries.

Willie Nelson is an American country music legend, author, actor and activist who writes and covers others material, including a version of 'Hallelujah'. His biggest genre defying musical hits were the Grammy award winning 'Always on My Mind' and a duet with Julio Iglesias 'To all the Girls I've Loved Before' neither of which he wrote. 'Always on my Mind' is another style crossover song with charting versions such as Nelson's countrified rendition, Elvis Presley's more dramatic vocal and the Pet Shop Boys' electronic option.

It is often surprising who actually did write popular songs.
In Willie Nelson's case, he penned the 1963 Roy Orbison hit 'Pretty Paper' and the 1962 recorded and still often played classic song by Patsy Cline, 'Crazy'. 'Skiffle' pioneer Lonnie Donegan actually wrote the 1967 Tom Jones hit 'I'll Never Fall in Love Again' and all round entertainer Kenny Lynch co-wrote the Small Faces 1966 single 'Sha La La La Lee'. Rob Davis the glam-rock guitarist from seventies band 'Mud' co-wrote 'Can't Get You Out of My Head', the 1981 smash for Kylie Minogue and ex-Manfred Mann vocalist Mike D'abo wrote the much covered 'Handbags and Gladrags' as well as co-writing the Foundations single 'Build Me up Buttercup.

Gallagher and Lyle were a Scottish duo who, as part of McGuinness Flint wrote and performed the folky 'When I'm Dead and Gone' and 'Malt and Barley Blues' as well as under their own name 'Heart on my Sleeve' and 'Breakaway' which was a major hit for Art Garfunkel.

There's was an easy listening style.

Terry Britten was a writer and guitarist working with Cliff Richard for a good part of his career before meeting Graham Lyle and forming a successful writing partnership. This pairing was responsible for two major hits that revitalised the career of Tina Turner, 'What's Love Got to do With it' and 'We Don't Need Another Hero'.

Again this proves that good writers can produce songs in more than one style and cross genres but it also proves that artists require well written material to allow them to express their own talent.

Another Scot teamed up with an established musician to write a couple of hits in what appeared to be an unlikely partnership. B.A. Robertson had sung a few novelty style songs such as 'Bang Bang', 'To be or Not to Be' and 'Kool in the Kaftan' and it was he who put the lyrics to Mike Rutherford's music for the more mature sounding Mike and the Mechanics' songs 'Silent Running' and 'The Living Years'.

The Rolling Stones, Spencer Davis Group, Yardbirds, Animals, the 1960's version of Fleetwood Mac and many other fledgling bands all played blues covers at the start of their careers but quickly saw the prestige and financial benefits of writing their own material. Many bands from that era would end their sets with Chuck Berry's 'Johnny B Goode' or 'Roll Over Beethoven' and it is ironic that his pioneering sound was copied by many sixties and seventies 'pop' stars while that generations fans identified Berry by his novelty song 'My Ding-a-Ling'.

In 1960, the album 'The Sound of Fury' was released containing 10 songs written by either the singer Billy Fury or credited to 'Wilberforce' as the composer. In fact Billy Fury wrote all the songs (half under the pseudonym) and this is the first known UK release of singer / songwriter material.

Even those musicians who write their own material can recognise the quality of a good song and on occasion cover songs that they appreciate.
For example, the composer of the iconic 'American Pie' had a major hit with Roy Orbison's 'Crying' while Madonna did her version of Don McLean's tribute to the 'day the music died'. The song's subject, Buddy Holly, had a short career due to his untimely death but his songs lived on in musicals, films and via the interpretations of Linda Ronstadt, The Rolling Stones and The Beatles.

Paul McCartney owns the rights to Buddy Holly's music, having lost out in the bidding for the rights to his own (Lennon/McCartney Northern Songs) to Michael Jackson before the singer's death, although 'The Beatles' retained artistic control. Jackson reportedly also owned Joni Mitchell's and Stevie Nicks' back catalogue but his financial situation was convoluted to say the least and he apparently made some deals with Sony and as the legal implications are private, the current situation is not common knowledge.

Fandango

The two most frequently played songs of the last 50 years were truly innovative and were praised for their originality at the time of their releases and coincidently they both contain the unusual word 'fandango'.

The 1975 epic 'Bohemian Rhapsody' that was written by Freddie Mercury and performed by Queen was operatic in style and managed to blend a piano ballad with multi layered harmony, progressing to hard rock, all in just under 6 minutes. Despite reservations by some critics and music executives that it didn't adhere to their view of what a hit single should be (ie. it was too long and had no chorus) the song's success and popularity proves that it is possible to 'think out the box' and still produce something that is pleasing to the ear.

Whereas Bohemian Rhapsody urged the listener to 'do the fandango' (viii), eight years earlier, many enjoyed the suggestion to 'skip the light fandango' (ix) This extract is from the lyrically progressive, for the era, 4 minute classic pop/rock song,

'Whiter Shade of Pale' by Procol Harum, with words by Keith Reid and the Johan Sebastian Bach inspired piano tune by Gary Brooker, who also sang the much praised work.

However, this song became the subject of a court case but not due to plagiarism. In this case, 38 years after the record's release, Mathew Fisher, a member of Procol Harum who played the distinctive organ on the record, claimed that he co-wrote the tune.

Following a protracted lawsuit lasting almost four years, including an eventual appeal to the House of Lords, the final verdict was given in favour of Fisher, despite waiting so long to stake his claim, and he was assured a share of future royalties and his name included as co-composer of the piece.

So maybe not much is original and that is why images, arrangements, styles, marketing, collaborations, sharing, sampling, mashing and even re-mastering are important to keep the music industry interesting and buoyant as we move from shellac, vinyl, reel to reel tape, 8-track, cassette, cd and nostalgically back to vinyl but progressively onto digital downloads.

My Way

However, there is always a market for new and original songs.

Songwriter and lyricist Bob Dylan recently remarked in a magazine about plagiarism, in his inimitable articulate form, (18)
"Wussies and pussies complain about that stuff".
Rocks most prolific songwriter has been accused on occasion of plagiarising sources that are unknown to the masses and he rejects all the criticism the same way he did when he was called Judas for moving from acoustic to electric guitar back in 1965. The veteran musician shared his wisdom,
"It's called song writing, it has to do with melody and rhythm and then after that anything goes. You make everything yours".

Chapter 6

Don't Let It Bring You Down

"Blind man running through the light of the night with an answer in his hand, come on down to the river of sight and you will really understand" - (x) Neil Young

Living with a disability is difficult enough in itself but to achieve something in spite of the disability adds to the character of the achiever. People who aspire to creativity should be admired by an appreciative audience and anyone whose artistic expression can entertain deserves the applause.

A number of musicians with adversity of some form of disability have proved themselves worthy of mention in that their talent shone through their particular physical limitation.

There are many musicians, amateur and professional with various forms of disability that are known in their local area but have not yet achieved recognition so although they are to be admired, they are not named in the following list of more famous acts. However with organisations such as US based CDM – Coalition for Disabled Musicians, Genie Cosmas' Stream Records and initiatives such as that by the organisers of the Glastonbury Festival in 2010 devoting a stage to disabled musicians, the barriers are slowly receding so that talent will determine acceptance.

Doctor My Eyes

Many of the blues musicians from the earlier part of the 20th century were not only ill- educated and poor, but also blind and used the word as a prefix to their names.
Blind Boy Fuller, Blind Lemon Jefferson, Blind Blake, Blind Willie McTell and Blind Willie Johnson were inspirational for many musicians who followed.
McTell for example, was the subject of a biographical song by Bob Dylan and his own composition 'Statesboro Blues' was revamped many years later by the Allman Brothers Band and Folk artist Ralph May was encouraged to change his stage name to Ralph McTell because his guitar picking style emulated the blues legend.
Others were blind but did not tend to use the definition in their name, such as Gary Davis who is cited by many more modern guitarists as a major influence. Davis became blind as a child and although was referred to as Blind Gary Davis on occasion, he was more generally known as the Reverend Gary

Davis. Acclaimed blues harmonica player Sonny Terry was not born blind but lost his sight when he was a teenager.

The Blind Boys of Alabama were formed in 1939 as a Gospel group and the multi Grammy award winners are still performing in 2012 albeit with a different line-up as the founding members died and were progressively replaced. The principles in the band are blind and as the band members changed the music also evolved to include contemporary material and collaborations with modern day artists. The Boys have toured with Tom Petty and Peter Gabriel and in 2010 played for the US President at the White House.

From the traditional blues through gospel, jazz and crossover into popular mainstream music, the name Ray Charles is often cited as the breakthrough artist of his generation, opening the doors for other R & B artists to follow. Early 1950's compositions such as 'Mess Around' and 'I Got a Woman' are still popular today and his catalogue continued with classics 'Georgia On My Mind', 'Hit The Road Jack' and 'I Can't Stop Loving You'.
When Ray was four years old, he witnessed the drowning of his brother and found it difficult to shake of the guilt because he watched the tragedy. A year later he began to lose his sight due to glaucoma and was blind by the age of seven, but despite this physical limitation the boy became a proficient

pianist. Over the years Ray Charles was subjected to racial discrimination personally and professionally and as a self- confessed drug addict was even jailed for possession. Although married only twice, Ray fathered 12 children to 9 different women.

The winner of a Grammy Lifetime Achievement Award, possessor of a star on the Hollywood Walk of Fame and one of the first inductees into the Rock and Roll Hall of Fame, Ray Charles died from liver disease in 2004 at the age of 73, the same year the Oscar winning biopic of his career was released.

Another blind keyboardist / singer / songwriter and multi-instrumentalist has enjoyed critical and commercial recognition even beyond that of Ray Charles. As the recipient of more Grammy awards than any other solo artist, an Academy Award for best song, album sales in excess of 100 million and many other achievements, this artist scored his first hit in 1963 at the age of 13.

Born Stevland Hardaway Judkins (changed to Morris), he took the stage name Little Stevie Wonder but soon dropped the 'Little' and as Stevie Wonder his innovative sound, distinctive harmonica, melodic tunes, expressive lyrics and emotional vocals have graced the airwaves with 'I Was Made To Love Her', 'My Cherie Amour', 'Superstition', 'Sir Duke', 'I Just Called To Say I Love You', 'For Once In My Life', 'Higher Ground', 'Living For The City', 'Isn't She Lovely' and many more. Wonder has duetted with many major artists including Michael Jackson and Paul McCartney, his harmonica playing is recognisable on The Eurythmics track 'There Must Be An Angel (Playing with My Heart)', he featured prominently on the USA For Africa song 'We Are The World' and wrote the music for the classic song 'Tears Of A Clown'.

Having been born 6 weeks premature, Stevie suffered retinopathy of prematurity (detached retinas) at the time of birth resulting in blindness. Despite this disability, Stevie Wonder became a major musician, composer and recording artist of the modern era.

There have been few notable blind guitar players since the blues men of the 1920's /30's but from the mid 1960's and still playing fifty years later, a Puerto Rican born singer has dazzled with his fretboard skills. Jose Feliciano records in both English and Spanish and his guitar playing is a cross between rock and flamenco. He has covered many standards in his unique style, playing material by the Beatles, Bee Gees and most notably The Doors, 'Light My Fire' as well as writing his own material such as the classic Christmas 'Feliz Navidad' and even courted controversy by rearranging in Latin American style, the Star Spangled Banner, prior to the Hendrix Woodstock version.
Having been born blind as a result of congenital

glaucoma, Jose Feliciano honed his guitar skills by constant practice and close listening to classical and jazz players.

In the genre of Country music, Ronnie Milsap has had the third most number 1 hits in the country music chart with 40 (only George Strait and Conway Twitty have had more). Milsap's initial recordings had more of an R&B feel but when he moved to Nashville he began his string of country music successes and also managed to crossover into the mainstream charts in the US.

Born with a congenital disorder, as a child he was almost totally blind and when as a youngster he developed a blood clot, both eyes had to be surgically removed.

As a pianist and vocalist, Ronnie Milshap continues to be a major concert draw in his native America well into his 60's

Another crossover artist afflicted by blindness is Andrea Bocelli, Italian vocalist from the classical / operatic genre who has recorded popular standards and worked with contemporary artists. As a child he learned to play a number of musical instruments while sighted but he was blinded at the age of 12 during a footballing accident.

Anyone who can bring pleasure to people through music deserves appreciation and unsighted people who can do so are an inspiration to aspiring musicians.

Perhaps the most tragic example of a blind musician who conquered adversity to create music was Canadian Jeff Healey.   Adopted as a baby, Jeff contracted retinoblastoma, a form of cancer and had both eyes surgically removed before he had reached the age of 2.   He learned to play guitar in the unique style of the instrument sitting flat on his lap and as a teenager played in clubs around his native Toronto. Healey's band and music featured in the film 'Roadhouse' and his first album 'See the Light' spawned a hit single 'Angel Eyes'.   He ventured into jazz and continued to tour and record the music he loved and over the years played with many of rock and blues best guitarists including Eric Clapton, Mark Knopfler, Buddy Guy and BB King.

Health problems dogged Healey and approaching the age of 40 he had operations to remove sarcomas from his legs followed soon after by operations on metastatic tissue in his lungs but at the age of 41, Jeff Healey died from cancer.

I Can Hear Music

Not being able to see the instrument but managing to become a proficient player is a remarkable feat but in the world of sound, not having the capacity to hear would be an obvious barrier to any musician.

However, it is well known that Ludwig Van Beethoven became progressively deaf as he composed his later works and was almost completely unable to hear by the time of his death.

In the 1950's, singer Johnny Ray had numerous hits despite being deaf in one ear and wearing a single hearing aid. His condition worsened and by 1960 he was almost totally deaf but continued to perform with the assistance of two hearing aids. Ray's act was to play to emotion, feigning crying and sometimes actually doing so but despite a scandalous personal life and alcohol problems, he was a teen idol for his time and an example to hard of hearing musicians.

The Who's writer and guitarist Pete Townsend damaged his hearing ostensibly by the rock and roll lifestyle of playing loud but standing close to band mate Keith Moon's exploding drums did not help.

Genesis drummer and singer Phil Collins also experienced damaged hearing after many years playing live music and Beach Boy Brian Wilson had impaired hearing in one ear rumoured to be as a result of his father hitting him on the side of the head.

Singer and writer of songs for other artists, Michael Bolton is deaf in one ear as was the Velvet Underground singer Nico.

Ryan Adams first appeared as a solo artist in 2000 marketed as an alternative country artist and has been prolific since then on his own and backed by The Cardinals averaging at least an album per year as well as producing duties for the likes of Willie Nelson, playing with the Grateful Dead's Phil Lesh and proving his skills as author of three books.

All this and he suffers from Meniere's disease which impacts on hearing and balance.

Scottish percussionist Evelyn Glennie has been recognised as the first full time solo percussionist and in addition to touring and playing with orchestras, she has also collaborated with rock / pop acts such as Steve Hackett, Elton John, Sting and Bjork.

She is passionate about music being taught in schools and has successfully campaigned to ensure appropriate funding.

Glennie has been profoundly deaf since the age of 12 but disagrees with the way the media reports her condition and in response she published a "Hearing Essay" (2A) in 1993 explaining the misconceptions about deafness and musicians.   This personal statement from someone who has learned to appreciate music from a perspective not limited to ears explains first hand better than any speculative writer or journalist could attempt.

Paul Stanley, guitarist with American Glam Rockers KISS, has a deformed ear. He was born with microtia which resulted in the fleshy outer part of his ear not forming properly. Long hair covers the abnormal appearance but he speaks in support of those with facial differences on behalf of an organisation called About Face.

I Want To Hold Your Hand

A few individuals had accidents either before becoming professional musicians or, in some cases after, which required adaptations to technique or development of a unique style of play.

The inspirational 'gypsy' guitarist Django Reinhardt was respected on the European jazz circuit in the 1930's along with violinist Stephane Grappelli but their partnership was interrupted by World War II. Reinhardt had learned the violin and banjo at an early age and as a teenager played for a living. He moved onto guitar but his potential was almost wrecked by an accident at the age of 18 when the caravan in which he lived caught fire.   Django was badly burned, almost lost a leg and from that time the third and fourth fingers had very limited movement due to paralysis, meaning all lead solos were accomplished by using his two undamaged fingers.   Having toured in Britain and America Reinhardt's talents found a larger audience but as a Romani free spirit, he did not adapt to modernisation and preferred beaches and woods to entertainment halls.

Nevertheless Django Reinhardt is arguably the first lead guitarist to impress audiences with his virtuosity and many have tried to emulate the sound of the 'two fingered' maestro'.

Two more guitarists had accidents resulting in damaged fingers with yet another player permanently damaging an entire arm which could have ended any chances of them making a living from music but luckily for them and the listeners, they overcame their injuries.

An innovative guitarist was a 'fan' of Reinhardt and actually got to meet him, developing a style influenced by his jazz playing hero.
Lester William Polsfuss not only played the instrument but even invented the solid body electric version played by many today and the instrument was named after him by manufacturer's Gibson, by his shortened name, Les Paul.
As an inventor and adapter of equipment, Les Paul was involved in the early use of reel to reel and multi-track recording and the use of effects.
As a player he found fame as guitarist to the layered singing voice of his wife Mary Ford and in addition to having hit records, the pair were initial radio and then television stars in the 1950's.
However, this success could have eluded the couple because in 1948, a car accident resulted in Les Paul seriously smashing his right arm to the extent that

amputation was muted but specialists advised him that his elbow could be set at a permanent angle, reducing movement but saving the limb. Les Paul elected to have the arm set at an almost 90 degree angle which would allow him to hold his guitar in an appropriate position for playing.

A recipient of many awards during his lifetime, Les Paul died in 2009 at the age of 94 and many younger musicians, including Steve Miller who was given his first guitar lesson from Les Paul, were quick to pay tribute to the man, his inventions and his playing ability despite the injury to his arm.

As singer and frontman of the infamous Grateful Dead, Jerry Garcia's influence spread far beyond his native San Francisco and he played sessions for other musicians including Bob Dylan and Jefferson Airplane in addition to many side project bands like New Riders of The Purple Sage and The Jerry Garcia Band. One memorable example is the pedal steel guitar on the Crosby, Stills, Nash & Young recording of 'Teach Your Children' which was played by Garcia.

During a 30 year career with The Grateful Dead, the band seemed to be constantly touring and were famous for playing long shows, which together with increased drug use, took its toll on Jerry Garcia and he died of a heart attack in 1995 aged 53.

There are many recordings to sample the work of this man who throughout his playing had a number of custom instruments but a childhood accident could have prevented this musical legacy.

At the age of 4, Jerry Garcia's hand was injured when he was struck accidently by an axe, resulting in the loss of two-thirds of his right middle finger by amputation. Although the result could have been more serious, the loss of one digit did not prevent Garcia becoming a respected musician.

Tony Iommi is known as the left handed guitarist from the bands Black Sabbath, Heaven and Hell and solo work. His playing is ranked among the best in rock despite having lost the tips of his middle and ring finger from his right hand in an industrial accident when he was 17. Iommi was a burgeoning guitarist at the time and was ready to throw in the towel following the injury but on discovering the capabilities of Django Reinhardt who had similar finger limitations, he vowed to carry on. Fitting thimbles to cover the ends of his injured fingers and using lighter gauge strings, the Tony Iommi sound was complete.

Behind The Mask

Covering an injury and continuing as a musician despite the results of an accident was also the tack taken by Ray Sawyer.

Sawyer had been playing mainly country music since the late 1950's with limited success to the extent that he decided to give it a rest for a while and try something different. In 1967, he was involved in a car accident resulting in the loss of his right eye. This accident did not prevent the singer reverting back to a musical career. Sawyer never lost his humour and complete with trademark eyepatch went on to share lead vocals in the all- round entertainment package that was 'Dr Hook and the Medicine Show'. His singing was on the bands' debut hit 'Cover of the Rolling Stone' and some of the other early material, 'Everybody's Making it Big but Me', 'Freakin at the Freakers Ball' and 'Sylvia's Mother', before he left the band in 1973.

The appearance of a single eye patch has been adopted by a couple of performers notably Frederick Heath in his alter ego Johnny Kidd, the writer of 'Shakin' all over', who backed by The Pirates was a pioneer of theatrical rock in the early sixties. Even Keith Richards sported an eye patch during a scene in the Rolling Stones Rock and Roll Circus, merely as part of his costume.

Another singer who wore an eye patch is London born Brit and MOBO award winner Gabrielle who has enjoyed popularity and steady sales since her debut chart topping single 'Dreams' back in 1983. Louisa Gabrielle Bobb is not inflicted with a sight problem, but does have ptosis which is a drooping eyelid, sometimes referred to as a lazy eye.

As a child, Radiohead frontman Thom Yorke had to wear a patch over his left eye for a time. When he was born, the eye would not open, requiring a number of operations to graft the muscles which, although successful, has resulted in a slight droop. Yorke overcame this physical hindrance and achieved great success as singer, songwriter and instrumentalist, although his relation with the press remains less than positive and he has a reputation for being distant with many other musicians.

Of the many images and personas adopted by David Bowie, he occasionally sported an eye patch during the seventies, around the 'Rebel Rebel' period. This was only part of his costume because the singer does not have a serious problem with his eyes, although he has suffered from limited depth perception since childhood.
Some people are under the false impression that Bowie's eyes are different colours but this is not the case. When the singer was at primary school, he was involved in a playground punch up in which his left eye was injured to the extent that it was feared he would lose the sight from that side. However, following a number of operations, he was left with a permanently dilated pupil giving the impression that the irises differ in colour.

Another myth that did the rounds was the rumour that Ian Paice, longest serving member of Deep Purple, who also drummed for Gary Moore's band and Whitesnake managed to thump those skins whilst only possessing one lung. This story is exaggerated as Paice only had a small section of his left lung removed when as a six year old he caught pneumonia and tuberculosis.

Away from rumours and back to actual incidents resulting in serious permanent disability, three musicians lost the use of their legs following different types of accidents but carried on with their musical aspirations as far as they were physically able to do taking cognisance of their restricted mobility.

Move On Up

 Musician, writer and composer Curtis Mayfield first showed his potential as a member of The Impressions in 1965 with his song 'People get ready'. This and other Mayfield compositions were adopted by 'black' protestors in the growing civil rights movement as unofficial anthems.
When he left the group, Curtis continued writing and produced his biggest hit 'Move on up' as well as the inspirational soundtrack to the ethnic film 'Superfly' which strengthened his reputation at the beginning of the 1970's. He continued writing and performing until

1990 when a lighting rig fell onto the stage, seriously injuring 48 year old Curtis Mayfield and paralysing the singer from the neck down. He managed to finish his final recording but his health deteriorated as a result of the accident. Mayfield had a leg amputated due to diabetes and passed away aged 57 in 1999 leaving a wealth of recordings, well deserved awards and a history of social activism.

Teddy Pendergrass was the baritone lead singer of Harold Melvin and the Blue Notes on such 'Philly' standards as 'If you don't Know me By Now' before launching a successful solo career in 1977. As well as being recognised as a major R&B singer, Pendergrass had crossover appeal and was informally labelled the 'black Elvis'.
However, an automobile accident in 1982 left him paralysed from the waist down and confined to a wheelchair. Following his accident, he established the Teddy Pendergrass Alliance to help victims of spinal cord damage and continued to work and perform, appearing at the Philadelphia show for 1985's Live Aid Concert.
Pendergrass had further recording success, retired from the music business in 2006 but died three years later.

Robert Wyatt was drummer and shared vocals with Kevin Ayers in the progressive 'underground' outfit known as Soft Machine from 1966-71 when he left to form Matching Mole with whom he made two albums but was prevented from making a third due to his accident.

In 1973 Wyatt was at a party when he fell from a fourth floor window and was paralysed from the waist down. Now confined to a wheelchair he could not drum in the conventional manner but continued to write, sing and perform on other instruments including hand percussion. Although his jazz infused progressive output did not sell particularly well, in hindsight they have been recognised as being innovative and influential.

Wyatt did find commercial success after his accident when he charted twice with covers of Elvis Costello's 'Shipbuilding' and the Neil Diamond penned 'I'm a Believer'. There was controversy when he was booked to appear on the UK TV show Top of The Pops in 1974 to promote his version of the latter song which had previously been a hit for the Monkees. The producer of the show said that his use of a wheelchair was 'not suitable for family viewing' but Wyatt argued the point and was allowed to perform. Recent portrayals of singers in wheelchairs in the popular music 'reality soap' Glee is accepted without hesitation by today's producers.

A few other musicians used wheelchairs on a temporary basis.

Leon Russell, veteran session player, writer, Rock and Roll Hall of Fame Inductee, collaborator over the years with many of the greats had brain surgery in January 2010. He used a cane and motorised wheelchair to assist mobility when he played with Elton John later in the year.

Singer Adam Faith was in a wheelchair for months following a near fatal car crash in 1973.

The band 'Pulp' came to prominence in 1995 with the release of the album ' Different Class' and the spin off singles 'Common People' and 'Disco 2000'. However, this was their fourth album and they had been playing as a group since 1983. Singer Jarvis Cocker performed onstage in 1985 from a wheelchair following an accident when he fell from a window, apparently trying to impress a girl with his spider-man impersonation.

Sheffield born Jarvis Cocker is not related to Sheffield born Joe Cocker, the gravel voiced singer.

Accidents are unfortunate events but some circumstances are hard to envisage and like the next example difficult to comprehend how it happened.

During the 'boy band' era in the early 1990's, East 17 was one of the most successful in the UK with 12 top 10 hits and a couple of albums but they did not progress as tastes changed and popularity declined. Despite attempts at reforming including a renamed E-17 and a single hit, they never troubled the charts again.

In 2006, singer Brian Harvey bizarrely ran himself over with his own car, suffering life threatening injuries and lapsing into a coma for a few weeks, although he eventually recovered.

Steve Ellis was the powerful vocalist who fronted the Love Affair in the late 1960's on such pop songs as 'Everlasting Love', Rainbow Valley' and 'A Day without Love'. He never managed to achieve commercial success on his foray into a heavier sound in the 1970's with his bands 'Ellis' and 'Widowmaker' and retired from the music business for a while.

Ellis worked on the docks for a time and continued to sing given the opportunity but just as he was ready to quit the manual labour and try for a return to professional singing he was involved in an accident. Steve's foot was very badly smashed in an incident which left him unable to walk for some time and the singer had a very long recuperation before he regained his mobility, albeit with a permanent limp, and finally got back to singing.

Motorcycle accidents are not uncommon in general terms nor are they for musicians.

Ex Generation X punk Billy Idol embraced the MTV approach to marketing and quickly became a popular attraction with 'pop' singles such as 'White Wedding', 'Eyes without a Face' and 'Rebel Yell' all performed with a sneering bad boy leather clad image.
It wasn't all for the camera as Idol did in fact ride a motorcycle but in 1990 he was knocked off his motorbike when a car hit him resulting in a serious leg injury, the limb being held together by a steel rod. Since then his career has been steady with film appearances, live dates and collaborations.

One of the Doobie Brothers double drummers, Michael Hossack was a keen Harley Davidson rider but came off his bike on the way to a gig in 2001, suffered multiple fractures and had to be airlifted to hospital for surgery followed by a very long recuperation before he could play again.

In 1972, Terry Melcher suffered serious injuries to both legs when he came off his motorcycle and could not walk for 6 months. This was yet another case of serious bad luck for the only son of singer / actress Doris Day. The famous actress was pregnant with Terry when she was only 17, but left his abusive father who had little to do with the boy who eventually took the name of his stepfather and Day's third husband Martin Melcher. Melcher senior also became his wife's manager and dealt with her business affairs but on his death in 1968, Terry discovered that his stepfather had mismanaged the finances and embezzled the family's fortune.

Terry Melcher's involvement in music had begun in the early 1960's when he teamed up with soon to be Beach Boy Bruce Johnston and the duo had a few minor hits in the US. Melcher went on to produce 'The Byrds' version of Dylan's 'Tambourine Man' and was involved in a few of the group's albums as well as working with the Beach Boys.

It was his connection with Beach Boys drummer Dennis Wilson that led to the darkest part of Melcher's story. The pair met aspiring musician Charles Manson and made some demos with the possibility of further collaboration, but this did not come to fruition as Melcher was 'put off' by Manson's domineering behaviour. The world was about to discover the extent of control that the hippie leader of the commune and followers known as the 'Family' had and to what extent his instructions would be followed.

The murder of (a minimum of seven) innocent victims by 'Family' members under the instruction of Charles Manson shocked the world due to the barbarism of the crimes, the fact that one of the victims was celebrity actress Sharon Tate who was eight and a half months pregnant and the symbolism of messages and reference to the Beatle's songs 'Piggies' and 'Helter Skelter', written in the victims' blood.

Manson and his followers were sentenced for the murders and other crimes and conjecture concerning the reasons for the massacre suggested that Terry Melcher was an intended victim, having previously resided at the property where the victims perished, with his then girlfriend, actress Candice Bergman. Melcher was called as a witness at the trial and became scared and reclusive, even hiring body guards. He suffered a nervous breakdown and rarely appeared in public, although following all these troubles, Terry Melcher released two low key solo albums and was a co-writer of the Beach Boys 1988 hit 'Kokomo'.

Melcher died in 2004 from melanoma, at the age of 62, and the final tracks he had produced for his mother were released in 2011, giving 87 year old Doris Day yet another hit album.

Wreck On The Highway

From motorbikes to buses and cars and yet more injuries.

The 'Queen of Latin Pop', Gloria Estefan received a fractured spine in 1990 when her tour bus was involved in an accident during a snowstorm. The singer was 'out of action' for almost a year and required intense rehabilitation to regain mobility after two titanium rods were permanently inserted into her back.

As lead vocalist with the English rock band 'Kaiser Chiefs' Ricky Wilson is known as an energetic performer often running and climbing onstage as well as crowd surfing.

In 2006, his agility prevented a more serious injury when he was struck by a car in a hit and run accident but managed to partially jump out of its path limiting potential fatal injuries to leg damage requiring the use of crutches for a time.

Peter Frampton was involved in a near fatal car crash whilst in the Bahamas in 1978, as a result of which he suffered concussion, multiple fractures and muscle damage.

Ten years earlier, he was a teenage heartthrob as guitarist and singer with The Herd, prior to progressing to a rockier sound in Humble Pie. However, his career high point came in 1976 with 'Frampton Comes Alive' and the follow up album 'I'm in You' the following year cemented his popularity, but then came the crash and mistaken career choices including starring alongside the Bee Gees in the much panned film version of Sgt. Pepper.

Coincidently, Frampton attended the same school as David Jones (later David Bowie) and were in rival school bands 'The Little Ravens' (Frampton's) and 'George and the Dragons (Bowie's).

The Head of the Art Department, Owen Frampton, was Peter's father and his teaching method encouraged artistic expressions and this may have influenced Bowie's style and personas in his later career.

In 1984, a car accident resulted in the amputation of 21 year old Rick Allen's left arm.
Allen had been drummer with 'heavy metal' band Def Leppard since his mid-teens and it was presumed his stint as sticks man had come to an end.
However, with encouragement from friends and an adapted custom made part electronic kit, Rick Allen and the band have continued their popularity and have amassed album sales in excess of 100 million worldwide and continue to draw the crowds at live gigs and festivals.

Ten years after Allen's accident his bandmate bassist Rick Savage, developed the facial paralysis condition 'Bells' Palsy'. Although he recovered, the symptoms occasionally return and are visible.

It's Getting Better

Medical intervention helped a few musicians to extend their careers.

John Martyn was an innovative and experimental guitarist who composed his own material, much of which featured unusual tunings and effects. Sometimes backed by other musicians but often playing solo and using loops, phasers and echo to create a backdrop over which he would sing in his mumbling fashion.

Initially, an act with his then wife Beverly, Martyn was a brash character who was often drunk onstage but still managed to perform some amazing fretwork. Musically respected for his output he did not court commercial success but did achieve mainstream popularity for a time.

60 year old John Martyn died in 2009 but a few years before, he had his right leg amputated below the knee as a result of a burst cyst, but ever the trooper, continued to record and play his music live to an appreciative audience.

In 2006, Aerosmith's flamboyant frontman and singer Steve Tyler had a ruptured blood vessel in his throat which required surgery and in 2009 whilst touring, he fell off the stage injuring his head, neck and breaking a shoulder, but having overcame a severe drug problem the showman was no stranger to adversity and he bounced back to continue solo work, Aerosmith work and surprisingly to appear as a judge on American Idol reality TV show.

Phil Anselmo, heavy metal vocalist, best known for his stint with Pantera from 1986-2003, suffered from degenerative disc disease and required surgery on his back to alleviate the symptoms. He also had surgery to his knee to correct damage caused when he jumped from a speaker cabinet during a Monsters of Rock gig in 1994.

Saul Hudson made his name as a guitarist but most people would not recognise that name. They would however, recognise the top hat and nose piercing and the nickname 'Slash' that the former Guns 'n Roses axeman goes by.
'Paradise City' and the riff driven 'Sweet Child O Mine' are the band's best known numbers but due to his session work, playing with 'Snakepit' and 'Velvet Revolver', Slash has been become a respected rock guitar player, often figuring in or topping polls of favourite guitarists. However the rock lifestyle caught up with Slash at the age of 35 when he was diagnosed with the heart condition cardiomyopathy and was fitted with a defribulator.

There have been scares recently on the effects of immobility on long haul flights and the possibility and dangers of Deep Vein Thrombosis (DVT). Thankfully the medical profession and the general public are better informed and can take more precautions and identify symptoms. However, not so long ago ignorance and scaremongering surrounded DVT.

The media at one time incorrectly reported the premature death of Jethro Tull front man Ian Anderson as a result of DVT.

The singer song writing flautist is still alive but although reports of his demise were exaggerated, Anderson had torn the anterior cruciate ligament in one of his legs when he slipped on stage in Peru. He continued on tour and by the time the band had reached Australia, DVT had set in and for a short time Ian Anderson thought he might not get to prove that 'Life's a Long Song'. Appropriate medical attention ensured that the vocalist, whose stage act often included standing on one leg (not in any way related to the condition), survived the ordeal.

Ian openly talks about the incident and speaks authoritatively regarding the reality of minimising the chances of DVT's occurring, cutting through the media hype.

Singer Gareth Gates had a number of hits throughout Europe, including topping many charts in the first half of the noughties before moving into musical theatre. Gates has been open about his obvious stutter and not only sought therapy to combat the speech impediment but has also become a qualified speech coach and instructor of a programme to assist other stammerers.

A Rush Of Blood To The Head

Many believe that music therapy can assist treatment and recuperation for certain medical and psychological conditions. Some professional musicians have benefitted from their involvement in music following seizures or Strokes that left them incapacitated and recuperation was assisted by striving to re-learn their craft.

As a member of the group 'Orange Juice', Scottish singer Edwin Collins had his first UK hit single with 'Rip It Up', in 1983 and is more recognised for 'A Girl Like You' released over 10 years later under his own name. As writer and producer Collins has worked with other artists but his career was halted in 2005 when he suffered a double brain haemorrhage. Neurological rehabilitation has been slow but Edwyn has shown remarkable strength in recovery and although he still has physical signs of weakness in his right side, Edwyn Collins is recording, playing and singing as good as ever.

Edwyn Collins recorded a cover version of a song called 'After All I Lived My Life' which was written by another Scottish singer who coincidently suffered a brain haemorrhage.
Frankie Miller's raw singing voice is instantly recognisable but despite regular output in the 1970's he only achieved minor hits with 'Be Good To Yourself' and 'Darlin' although his version of the

Dougie McLean song 'Caledonia' from the early 1990's is a firm favourite in his native Scotland. However, Miller's talents as a writer have been recognised and his songs have been covered by other major artists such as The Eagles, Rod Stewart, Bob Seger, Clint Black and Roy Orbison.

In 1994, Frankie Miller was in America to collaborate with Joe Walsh, when he had a brain haemorrhage leaving him in a coma for five months. Frankie's rehabilitation and progress has been extremely slow and limited but helped by music.

Poison's Brett Michaels suffered a severe sub arachnoid haemorrhage in April 2010 and the 47 year old was critical for a week. Whilst recovering, it was discovered that he also had a hole in his heart but the rocker is still rocking and continuing to appear on reality television programmes.

Paul Kantner has been the constant factor in the various incarnations of Jefferson Airplane and Jefferson Starship since the mid-1960's and still writes and plays guitar for Jefferson Starship as he has the right to the prefix Jefferson.
However, his career and life almost came to a halt in 1980 when the 39 year old musician suffered a cerebral haemorrhage.

He survived the incident and recovered without surgery and it was thought that a previous injury to his skull following a motorcycle accident resulting in the temporary insertion of a metal plate, actually saved him. Doctors believed that cranial pressure was relieved by holes in his skull following removal of the plate.

Two career musicians had their abilities and mobilities impacted following strokes.

Dave Davies was lead guitarist with The Kinks and his high harmony vocals were as distinctive as his guitar riffs creating the recognisable sound on his brother Ray's songs and lead vocals. Dave also had a solo career from his top 3 UK hit 'Death of a Clown' in 1967 through his album and live work beyond the millennium. Unfortunately, following interviews in the BBC, Davies was in a lift, ready to leave the building when he suffered a stroke which disabilitated his right side.
Like all stroke victims, rehabilitation was a slow process but his positive attitude and respect for his specialist therapists, helped him to get, what he termed 92% back to normal within 2 years. Davies maintains that singing and the regime of relearning the guitar along with yoga, meditation and spirituality assisted his recovery.
Dave Davies was 57 when he had the stroke in 2004.

Coincidently, George Grantham was 57 when he had a stroke in 2004.

Grantham was drummer with American country rock outfit Poco and the band was playing live when he seized up and was unable to move one of his arms. Instinctively he continued to play with his non paralysed limbs but immediately the musicians playing in front of him detected that the usual reliable drumbeats were missing and stopped to assist their colleague.

Again, the recuperative progress was very slow and it was a couple of years before he could carry out basic tasks. Occasionally Grantham has appeared at Poco reunion gigs and although unable to play his percussion, he has managed to sing for short periods.

Musicians are certainly not immune from cerebral haemorrhages but music can be used as an aid to recovery.

Dr Oliver Sacks in his book 'Musicophilia' relates a number of studies to back-up the claims that music can assist with many conditions. He quotes examples where communication with sufferers of Autism, Asperger's and Dementia was improved with the use of music and how rhythm can assist people with Parkinson symptoms and rehabilitation of stroke victims is improved by music therapy.

Many of the studies recognise the merits of classical music and in some cases traditional sounds but pop and rock music can also be beneficial.

Nordoff Robbins music charity is recognised in the UK as the leading educational programme that promotes music therapy and many modern musicians are affiliated to the cause.

In the USA, ex-Grateful Dead drummer Mickey Hart has written books about percussion, is an authority on world rhythms and is on the Board of Directors of the Institute for Music and Neurologic Function which continues the quest to recognise the healing powers of music.

Another of neurologist Oliver Sachs' publications is the 'The Man who Mistook his Wife for a Hat and other Clinical Tales' which is a collection of essays describing case studies of some of his patients.

Scottish band 'Travis' used an abbreviated version for their highly successful second album 'The Man Who' which built on the reputation from the first release 'Good Feeling'.

However, as their popularity soared, they released a third album but an accident all but halted the band's future. Drummer Neil Primrose dived into the shallow end of a swimming pool and broke his neck and it was only the quick actions of other group members that prevented him from drowning.

Travis was on the verge of folding but despite the seriousness of Primrose's spinal injuries, he recovered and the band continues with the original membership.

White Ladder

There are also examples of musicians whose conditions are genetic.

A songwriter born in 1912 was inspirational and influential to a number of folk / pop / rock artists such as Bob Dylan, Tom Paxton, Bruce Springsteen, Billy Bragg and his son Arlo Guthrie.
He is of course, Woody Guthrie writer of songs across styles from children's songs to protest songs. His most famous, 'This Land is Your Land', became an unofficial anthem for the anti-establishment movement and has been covered by numerous artists. Guthrie's material, some commissioned, others written in response to what he witnessed around him was topical and reflected reality as opposed to much of the lightweight lyrics in popular songs of the era. 'Grand Coulee Dam', 'Pastures of Plenty', 'Pretty Boy Floyd', 'Union Maid' and 'Deportee' are examples of Guthrie songs with observational lyrics emulated by singer / songwriters from the 60's onwards.
Having lived through the Great Depression and World War II, in 1952 Woody Guthrie was diagnosed with the hereditary disease that was responsible for the

death of his mother and possibly his maternal grandfather. Huntington's disease can cause early dementia and muscle deterioration and Guthrie's mental and physical state deteriorated for the remaining 15 years of life resulting in his final 11 years being spent in hospitals before dying at the age of 55. He left behind a wealth of material, much of it still available in recorded format as well as the written versions stored in The Woody Guthrie Archives, but for those who appreciate meaningful lyrics to go with the music, perhaps his main legacy is the example he set for the many troubadours who followed the original 'Dust Bowl Troubadour'.

Two of Woody Guthrie's daughters inherited Huntington's and both died at the age of 41, but Guthrie's own death in 1967 helped raise awareness of the disease.

Another 'legend' of the pre-pop music era was Hank Williams, a pioneer who popularised country music and had numerous hits many of which were recognised beyond the country genre.

Standards such as 'Take These Chains from My Heart' topped the charts and Williams was the writer of the classic 'You're Cheating Heart' and the much covered 'Jambalaya'. His musical legacy is all the more surprising considering he died in 1953 at only 29 years of age. Hank Williams was born with a disorder of the spinal column which although undiagnosed as such was a mild form of spina bifida which gave him pain throughout his short life and the numerous painkillers he took to alleviate this, along with excessive amounts of alcohol caused his early death.

He died whilst being driven between performances as a passenger in a car, just sat in the seat and passed away, but in addition to the substances in his bloodstream, bruises and haemorrhages were found, another mystery for the conspiracy theorists.

Another American musician was born with a mild form of spina bifida requiring hospitalisation as a baby but the condition did not prevent Johnny Cougar / John Cougar / John Cougar Mellancamp / John Mellancamp ramping up 40 million album sales and over 20 top 40 US hits as well as a Grammy, Rock and Roll Hall of Fame inductee, actor and political activist.

There are examples of musicians from across the genres that have been stricken by diseases of varying types and severity.

Founder member and leader of soul / funk / rock outfit Earth, Wind and Fire, Maurice White was diagnosed with Parkinson's disease in the late 1980's and stopped touring a few years later. As well as his major contribution to EWF, White collaborated with many other artists and produced records for Deniece Williams and The Emotions.

Tionne Watkins (T-Boz) from the most successful 'rap' trio TLC found that she was suffering from the anaemic disorder and became a spokesperson for the condition, 'Sickle Cell Disease Association of America'.

In the mid-1980's, ABC lead singer Martin Fry was treated for Hodgkin's Disease.

The band 'Free' are best known for the much played single 'Alright Now' which was co-written by singer Paul Rogers and bass player Andy Fraser. As a 15 year old, Fraser had played with bluesman John Mayal before joining Free and later he wrote the song 'Evry Kinda People' which became a hit for Robert Palmer.
He continues to play and record but his physical condition has deteriorated having been diagnosed with peripheral neuropathy and then Kaposi's Sarcoma. This immune deficiency is AIDS related and the father of daughters declared his homosexual activities later in life.

A different debilitating disease has impacted on the careers and lives of a few musicians from different backgrounds who performed covering different styles.

Multiple sclerosis is an inflammatory condition that can affect the sufferer in mild form where numbness and loss of sensitivity may occur, through various degrees of severity to immobility and lack of cognitive control.

Donna Fargo was a popular country singer in the early 1970's who had mainstream recognition with the song 'The Happiest Girl in the Whole USA'. She was diagnosed with MS in 1978 but the condition stabilised with treatment and she continued to perform at a slower pace and lower key. Also in 1978, Fargo was given her own Television show which was produced by the Osmond Brothers.

The oldest of the pop singing Osmond family, Alan was forced to retire from performing due to contracting MS. His son David is lead vocalist of the Osmonds 2nd generation and he also has MS.

Rock drummer Clive Burr played with Samson and then Iron Maiden's first three albums. He was diagnosed with primary regressive Multiple Sclerosis around 1997 and is dependent on a wheelchair for mobility.

Mellon Collie And The Infinite Sadness

Few people would speak publicly about mental problems for fear of stigma and for those in the public eye, retaining privacy in these matters could be understood, although difficult to maintain in the era of intrusive media. The following few pages lists numerous singers, musicians and recording artists who have suffered from depression, many contemplating or attempting suicide and a few names will surprise the reader.

Brian Wilson was the main writer of the Beach Boys material as well as a vocalist, bass player, keyboard player, arranger and producer. After a few years that saw the group's popularity outgrow its initial 'surfing' image and sound as a result of Brian's input, he was burned out, had a nervous breakdown around 1964 and quit touring.

This was the start of Wilson's mental troubles which became exacerbated due to his long hours spent in the studio perfecting the album Pet Sounds and the innovative tracks 'God Only Knows', 'Good Vibrations' and 'Heroes and Villains'. Legal issues, personal problems and stress resulted in the follow-up album 'Smile' being cancelled and Brian Wilson again had a breakdown.

Over the years his weight ballooned, drug intake was excessive, he stayed indoors and in bed most of the time and a controversial psychiatrist was hired to try and sort the musician out. Brian Wilson continued to write for the group and solo material but his output slowed compared to his early prolific period. He also played with the band sporadically but the low years had taken their toll and the one time 'genius' was visibly showing the effects of his disorderly mental state.

Brian Wilson's solo career took off again following the untimely death of his two younger 'Beach Boy' brothers and he toured with a talented group of younger musicians playing his concept albums in their entirety, as well as performing Gershwin's classics and although the performances are professional, Wilson still bears the signs of previous mental problems.

14 year old Judy Collins tried to commit suicide and although the event may have been a cry for help, the vocalist with the crystal clear inflection did continue to have bouts of depression and problems with alcoholism.

This image does not fit with the public persona of the 1960's protest singer, interpreter of aspiring songwriters' material responsible for introducing the early works of Leonard Cohen, Joni Mitchell and Randy Newman to a discerning public.

The daughter of a blind alcoholic father, Judy also had problems keeping away from the bottle as did her only son who eventually killed himself at the age of 33 due to the effects of alcohol dependence.

As the inspiration for Steven Stills 'Suite: Judy Blue Eyes', reproducer of the haunting *A cappella* 'Amazing Grace' and performer of the melancholy 'Send in the Clowns' Judy Collins has given aural pleasure to many whilst battling her own demons, but the singer has confessed to the darker side of her life in order to help others be aware of the pitfalls and steer clear, especially of suicidal thoughts and she has become an advocate of speaking openly about this normally taboo subject.

Depeche Mode Lead vocalist Dave Gahan made an attempt on his own life in 1995 by slashing his wrists but if it was a cry for help he was lucky because he was found in time and saved. The following year he overdosed but again survived although he damaged his heart which had previously suffered a slight attack. Gahan also had to have a tumour removed from his bladder and other medical problems caused gigs to be cancelled but the suicidal tendencies did not return.

In 1970, a depressed, struggling, young singer songwriter left a suicide note and tried to kill himself by drinking furniture polish. He was treated in hospital for the effects and depression and put on suicide watch.

This was the low point for a performer who went on to win 6 Grammy's from more than 20 nominations, in excess of 30 top 40 self-penned hits in the USA, inductee of both Songwriters and Rock and Roll Hall of Fame.

From his first hit 'Piano Man' through ' Always a Woman', 'Just the Way You Are', 'Uptown Girl', 'We Didn't Start the Fire' and many more, Billy Joel does not give the impression of someone battling depression.

However, more than 30 years after that incident he still required psychiatric help for alcohol related problems.

Joel has written songs whose lyrics tell of his troubles.

Another American singer songwriter and Grammy winner – in this case 9 – admitted to "growing up in the presence of melancholy". Sheryl Crow considers that her depressive mood swings are inherited as her father has similar symptoms. Ex music teacher and singer of jingles, backing vocalist to established artists before releasing her first album in 1993, Crow quickly became established with upbeat positive songs 'All I Wanna Do' with its strap line – is have some fun – and 'If it Makes You Happy' but she also touched on more serious issues.

Coincidently, Crow's song 'Safe and Sound' from her 2002 release C'mon C'mon was dedicated to her boyfriend at the time, actor Owen Wilson who also suffered from depression and attempted suicide in 2007. Following their split in 2002, Sheryl Crow had a three year relationship with the shamed road cyclist extraordinaire Lance Armstrong who had previously battled and beat testicular cancer and not long after the couple called off their engagement, Sheryl Crow was diagnosed with breast cancer.

Following treatment she was also given the all clear, however in 2012, aged 50, she revealed that she also had a brain tumour, but it was benign.

Sheryl Crow continues to be positive in life – adopting children – and musically with numerous collaborations and new recordings, in spite of the depressive moods that she has learned to live with.

From Sheryl Crow to Counting Crows who also released their debut album 'August and Everything After' in 1993.

The single 'Mr Jones' was a hit, helping the album sales and the band were popular almost immediately. Fame did not sit well with lead singer Adam Duritz who had a history of depression and he had a nervous breakdown. He touched on this theme on some of the material on the follow up 'Recovering the Satellites' and his introspective lyrics come from his 'dissociative disorder'.

Duritz admits to having been crazy and said 'it was scary when the world isn't real' and it was some time before his problem was diagnosed. Adam Duritz co-wrote 'Accidently in Love' with the rest of the band and it appeared in the 'non-real' world of the movie Shrek 2. However, on the band's fifth album, a double called 'Saturday Nights and Sunday Mornings' the mental illness theme returned as Duritz explained "the album is about a downward spiral, losing my mind and about trying to get it back".

John Denver and Olivia Newton-John were very popular musicians of the 1970's both with clean cut images and high record sales on the back of television and film appearances.

Yet despite John Denver's public persona, he battled depression throughout most of his career, more so when his personal life was affected by divorce and confirmed that he attempted suicide.

Denver also admitted in his Autobiography that he had used marijuana, LSD and cocaine and told of his 'unloved' upbringing by a stern military father and alluded to his domestic abuse. On the positive side his songs such as 'Leaving on a Jet Plane', 'Annie's Song', 'Sunshine on my Shoulders and 'Rocky Mountain High', television appearances, his paintings, environmental work and even political activism made Denver one of the era's best loved entertainers.

His other passion was aviation and he supported the work of NASA and was a qualified pilot.
Ironically, he was killed whilst 'flying solo' an experimental plane when it crashed into the sea and because of a previous drunk driving conviction, he did not have the appropriate medical certification authorising the flight.

Newton-John was a moderately successful singer for the first half of the 1970's with covers of songs such as John Denver's co-written '(Take me Home) Country Roads' and Bob Dylan's 'If Not for You' but her appearance in the record breaking movie 'Grease' and her iconic duets with John Travolta 'You're the One That I Want' and 'Summer Nights' catapulted the Australian songstress to stardom.

Her career and private life were fine for a time but in 1992 during the same week that her father died, Olivia Newton-John was diagnosed with breast cancer but like Sheryl Crow, she recovered.   In 1994 Olivia divorced but it wasn't until 2007 when she admitted in a magazine article that, (22)
"I've been through cancer and divorce but nothing compares to this – I took anti-depressants, I had to". Now re-married, depression behind her, the low time referred to was when her partner of nine years disappeared, initially feared dead but following claimed sightings it was suggested that he staged his disappearance for financial reasons.

Siobhan Fahey was a member of Bananarama, one of the most successful singles selling acts in the UK but left to form Shakespears Sister in 1988 in which she was the main writer of a more mature sound. However, Fahey suffered from depression and admitted herself for psychiatric help in 1993.

Another successful girl group member spoke out about depression and eating disorders following comments about her shape and sexuality. Despite being arguably the fittest 'sporty' and the most credible singer to emerge from the girl power 'Spice Girls', Melanie C (hisolm) was affected by the negative comments in the press.

Billy Corgan was the frontman of the 1990's popular version of The Smashing Pumpkins and as well as solo work, still fronts different line-ups bearing the name. Corgan has battled with depression and suicidal thoughts for years which he blames on mental and physical abuse by his stepmother when he was a child.

Despite being a member of one of the best-selling bands to come out of America, Joey Kramer, drummer with Aerosmith since 1970, suffers from depression. He has written about his highs and lows in a confessional autobiographical book, "Hit Hard : A story of Hitting Rock Bottom at the Top".

Kramer's image is not readily associated with the type of person who could suffer from depression but that is the very nature of the condition, it is often hidden, not talked about and festering in the unlikeliest of person, another example being the next talented musician.

Guitarist extraordinaire and astro-physics expert Brian May battled with depression and contemplated suicide following the break-up of his first marriage, the death of his father, the illness and passing of band mate / friend Freddie Mercury which also meant the end the band Queen.

These events all occurred in a short period of time and May sought therapy to help him through the dark times.

As well as the much publicised arguments and fights with Kink's band mate and younger brother Dave, Ray Davies had a similarly tempestuous and public relationship with girlfriend Pretender's front woman Chrissie Hynde in the 1980's.

It has been suggested that they were ready to be married but the Registrar refused to carry out the ceremony due to their behaviour, nevertheless the couple had a child together but split up soon after.

There are further stories of Hynde's behaviour with rumours that she got fired from Malcolm McLaren / Vivienne Westwood's shop SEX, for fighting with a customer and that she attacked fellow musician Carly Simon for telling Hynde to 'shut up' during a Joni Mitchell performance.

Nevertheless, Chrissie Hynde has the reputation of being tough enough to survive in the male dominated world of rock music.

Ray Davies on the other hand wears his heart on his sleeve and is open about his problems as he explains in his one man show 'Storyteller' and his 1995 book 'X Ray'. Three times married Davies apparently attempted suicide following the break-up of his first marriage, another marriage ended as a result of his affair with Hynde, in 2004 he was shot in the leg and he has also admitted to being bipolar.

A much younger performer, lead singer, guitarist and writer for McFly Tom Fletcher admitted in his autobiography that he was a sufferer of bipolar affective disorder.

South African born Robert Calvert was a lyricist and singer for seven years from 1972 with the space rock band Hawkwind and then embarked on a number of solo projects. Calvert was much involved with the band's live double album showcase 'Space Ritual' and co-wrote with Dave Brock the seminal single 'Silver Machine'.
He suffered mental problems, was diagnosed bi-polar and was actually sectioned at the time that vocals were required to be overdubbed for the single, so bass player 'Lemmy' Kilmister (pre-Motorhead) sang lead on Silver Machine.

Drummer Jack Irons was a co-founder and member of the Red Hot Chilli Peppers but left the band in 1988 suffering from depression following the death of friend and band mate Hillel Slovak.

Irons sought psychiatric help and around this time and was diagnosed as bi-polar. Whilst facing up to depression, Jack Irons has collaborated with a number of big name artists and been a member of the bands 'Eleven' and 'Pearl Jam' as well as releasing a solo album aptly called 'Attention Dimension'.

Following a career high back in the early 1990's, Irish singer Sinead O'Connor has had an erratic lifestyle with limited forays in a musical direction.
A planned comeback scheduled for 2012 had to be postponed when she admitted dealing with bipolar disorder and fighting mental illness.

Stuart Goddard was diagnosed as bi-polar when he was 21 and his life has been dogged by mental problems and he has attempted suicide.
Known to the musical world as Adam Ant, he broke through as a faction of the 'punk movement' moved into the 'New Romantic' phase with his theatrical numbers 'Stand and Deliver', 'Prince Charming', 'Goody two Shoes' and 'Ant Music'.
Success was not confined to his native UK, becoming a celebrity in the USA and dating a string of actresses, it was inevitable that Goddard would also veer towards acting in various film and TV appearances. His star waned somewhat in the fickle world of fashion and

although he has had a few reasonably successful comebacks, Adam Ant's mental condition has seen him hospitalised, sectioned under the Mental Health Act and the medication required to stabilise his condition also impacted on him physically. In his own words Adam / Stuart has stated (23)
"mental health needs a great deal of attention, it's the final taboo and it needs to be faced and dealt with".

Contemporary of Adam Ant, Gary Numan hit the charts with his electronic sound recognised in his biggest hits 'Are Friends Electric' (Tubeway Army) and 'Cars' as well as three top 20 UK albums. Again his career stagnated as fashions moved on but it recently reignited as newer musicians acknowledged Numan's work and his popularity improved.
Gary Numan's white faced, dark clad, emotionless and uncommunicative persona was not merely marketing but it stemmed from his self-consciousness and mild Asperger's syndrome and the fact that he was first prescribed anti-depressants in his mid-teens.

Whereas Numan has never been formally diagnosed with Asperger's, singer, guitarist and writer with Australian outfit The Vines, Craig Nichols condition was confirmed.
In 2004 following a serious of behavioural episodes, verbal abuse and outbursts of temper which culminated in assault and malicious damage, charges were brought against the musician.

Although the band's initial output was received positively, Nichols productivity took a back seat as he underwent treatment for his condition.

In 1968 an unknown teenage guitarist, Danny Kirwan, joined the established British blues band, an early incarnation of Fleetwood Mac, just in time to be featured on their first number one single, the instrumental 'Albatross'. The talented Kirwan stayed with 'Mac' until 1972 when his alcohol dependency and behavioural problems overshadowed his contribution to the band and he was fired.
Despite attempts at a solo career, Danny Kirwan faded from the music business and although there is no certainty as to what he did from then on, the sad rumours are that he was institutionalised and became a homeless statistic.

Of the two major musician 'mental' casualties of the 1960's, one was also from the early Fleetwood Mac. Peter Green fronted the band in its first wave of success writing, singing and playing distinctive guitar style on 'Albatross', 'Black Magic Woman', 'Man of the World', 'Oh Well', 'Green Manalishi' and many more. However, the attention, adulation and even money that his talent brought did not sit comfortably with the sensitive Green and he began to act irrationally. Following one particular incident when he was given unknown drugs, the talented Peter Green known to the public was 'lost' and the physical Peter Green began many years in the musical wilderness whilst undergoing treatment for schizophrenia. Green spent time in psychiatric hospitals and although he did return to music in the late 1990's his concentration and ability never reached the levels of his 1960's standards.

The re-invigorated Fleetwood Mac complete with new members, reached superstar status and the musicians as well as the appreciative public recognised the legacy of Peter Green and sympathised with his premature 'loss'.

There are many similarities in Peter Green's circumstances as with another innovative 1960's musician. Roger Keith Barrett, known as Syd Barrett was a co-founder of 'Pink Floyd' and was initially writer, lead singer, guitarist and a creative musician. Moderate success with singles 'Arnold Layne' and 'See Emily Play' as well as debut album 'Piper at the Gates of Dawn' and experimental live performances showed early promise but increased drug use and irrational behaviour mirrored the deterioration of Peter Green, Barrett showing similar problems.

Recruiting David Gilmour to stand in for and subsequently replace Syd Barrett, Pink Floyd's rise to Global stardom and record breaking album sales with 'Dark Side of The Moon', 'Wish You Were Here' and 'The Wall' was beyond Floyd's imagination but the success was tinged with sadness as Barrett's mental state denied him the opportunity to be involved. The band members ensured that Barrett received any due royalties and the song 'Shine on you Crazy Diamond' was inspired by their ex-band member who never recovered from his drug induced sojourn, eventually dying at the age of 60 from pancreatic cancer.

Although it could be argued that the irrational behavioural tendencies of those with mental instability would manifest themselves without the stimulation of drugs, the impact of an unquantified amount of unknown substances certainly took Peter Green and Syd Barrett beyond a state from which they could return to normality.

OCD (obsessive compulsive disorder) is a condition that sufferers' minds take control by repetitive actions, orderly control and as the name suggests they cannot relax until things are achieved in a certain way, they must be done, no option. Like all mental conditions there are different degrees of severity from the laughable colour co-ordinators, symmetrical and straight line order through to repeat speech, habit control freaks and some bizarre obsessions. A few musicians are known to have forms of OCD, some being mild phobias but others verging on irrationality.

Justin Timberlake claims to have OCD and ADD (attention deficient disorder). Like fellow superstars Britney Spears and Christina Aguilera, Timberlake was a former child performer on the Disney, Mickey Mouse Club. He went on to be a member of boy band N'sync before launching a solo career in 2002 and venturing successfully into acting and business in addition to his Grammy award winning music. His self-confessed OCD requires him to put objects in straight lines and ensure certain foods are always in his fridge.

Singer Katy Perry cites her phobia of animal hairs on her clothes and fingerprint smudges on sunglasses as examples of her OCD.

Ex-All Saints member Natalie Appleton is obsessed with cleaning and reportedly uses tissue when opening doors, flushing toilets etc. in public conveniences.

Tall, with awkward posture and demeanour could describe the appearance of 'punk' singer Joey Ramone of the eponymous band, but apparently his 'look' and behaviour stemmed from being an outcast due to his dysfunctional upbringing and OCD.

One major entertainer labelled with OCD was Michael Jackson but his history and biography highlights that the 'prince of pop' suffered, in addition to many abnormal personality traits, from BDD (body dismorphic disorder) which resulted in his having no fewer than 30 cosmetic surgery operations and constantly wearing make-up to disguise and cover his natural appearance.

Limp Bizkit frontman Fred Durst admits to having OCD but refuses to discuss it.

Actor and occasional musician Billy Bob Thornton struck up a close friendship with late rocker Warren Zevon when the pair discovered their habitual OCD compulsions.

Although not a recognised condition in children until relatively recently, many people were affected by undiagnosed dyslexia.
It is claimed that ex-Beatle, the late John Lennon was one such affected as is ex-Oasis Noel Gallagher and American singers 'Jewel' and 'Cher'.

Australian born Helen Reddy had international success beginning in the early 1970's with iconic songs 'Angie Baby' and her co-written, 'I am Woman'.
Her popularity continued with a number of 'easy listening' releases and some film work.
However, as a 17 year old, Reddy had one of her kidneys removed and in later life was diagnosed with Addisons disease which affects the adrenal glands and requires continual treatment.

Keen golfer, keeper of pet snakes and theatrical rocker Alice Cooper was diagnosed with chronic asthma as a child in Michigan USA and the family reportedly moved to Pheonix, Arizona to help his chances for improvement to his breathing.

'Amazing Grace' songstress Judy Collins was also asthmatic and chose natural remedies to moderate the condition.

Perfect Skin

There are different levels of disability and an often misunderstood condition is Albinism. There are also different degrees of Albinism which is a congenital disorder with limited or total absence of melanin production for skin pigmentation. Albinos are often recognisable by physical signs like white hair, pink eyes and are prone to poor eyesight and further skin damage by the sun.

In some cultures people with Albinism are ridiculed, shunned and even suspected of being witches, but in most civilised societies, there are no problems, save from those imposed by the condition.

There have been few noted musicians with Albinism but two sets of 'musical' brothers were born with the condition.

African American blues pianists Rufus (Speckled Red) Perryman and William (Piano Red) Perryman played low key gigs through the Depression and war years but Willie Perryman did have chart success in the early 1950's as 'Piano Red' and again in the early 60's calling himself 'Dr Feelgood' and the song of the same name was widely played. (not to be confused with the English pub rock band of the same name)

More successful Albino rock brothers have been Johnny and Edgar Winter.
Johnny Winter is a rock / blues guitarist with peer recognition of his talents and is subject to major bootlegging of his material. In addition to his live performances, Johnny Winter produced three Grammy award winning albums for blues legend, Muddy Waters.

Younger brother Edgar, treaded a more commercial route playing keyboards and saxophone, as well as providing vocals for The Edgar Winter Group and White Trash.   In the 1970's he had hits with 'Frankenstein' and 'Free Ride'.
He has also provided music for popular Television shows such as The Simpsons and Queer as Folk as well as a number of feature films, examples being Waynes World 2, What's Love Got To Do With It and My Cousin Vinny. Albinism did not hold back the brothers.

However, Mali born Salif Keita was treated differently. Ostracised by his community because they considered Albinism a curse, Keita sang with bands in Africa before moving to Paris in search of a wider audience, which he gained in the newly recognised genre of 'world music'. Having made numerous albums and played throughout the world, Salif Keita was always aware of the difficulties some born with Albinism have to suffer, often speaking out in support and in 2009 dedicating his album 'La Difference' to the struggle of the Albino community.

Winston Foster was similarly shunned in his native Jamaica due to his Albinism but overcame the stigma to become as 'Yellowman' a popular DJ and recording artist.

At the age of 26, he developed skin cancer and was given three years to live but following major surgery in 1986 to remove a tumour in his jaw, he survived but was left severely disfigured. Nevertheless, he resurrected his career and continued to play live throughout the world.

American hip hop artist 'Brother Ali' was born with Albinism and the condition lead to his blindness. His material is personally confessional and makes fun of the media who always begin articles on him by mentioning Albinism.

A different skin problem stalled and almost halted the career of American 'New Wave' band Blondie in 1983 when guitarist Chris Stein developed the skin disease pemphigus.

Lead singer Debbie Harry and Stein were an item at the time and she took several years off to care for him and although the pair romantically split in the late 1980's, they continue to perform, record and tour with Blondie.

Yet more musicians were inflicted with yet more skin conditions.

In 2010, Canadian artist, writer and musician Joni Mitchell declared that she had the rare and controversial condition 'Morgellons Syndrome' which gives sufferers the sensation that their skin is being bitten by parasites but according to some experts is a psychological problem leading to 'delusional infestation'.

A number of musicians suffer from the skin condition Psoriasis including Australian 'pin-up' Jason Donovan, laid back singer songwriter 'gravel voiced' Tom Waits, angelic voiced Art Garfunkel and child star turned country hit maker Le Ann Rimes who discusses her experience in the media in order to spread more awareness.

Shawn Lane died in 2003, aged 40. He suffered from psoriasis and also developed psoriatic arthritis and died from lung problems.

In 1978 Lane became guitarist for Black Oak Arkansas when he was only 14 years old and played with them for four years but moved away from 'rock music' and developed his own style of playing which he showcased on two studio albums, some instructional releases and collaborations.

Shawn Lane never achieved commercially what his recognised ability on the instrument promised but his guitar playing style was described as rapid fire notes with exceptional speed in the neo classical metal genre and another unique was unplugged before he had completed his act.

Another promising virtuoso guitarist from this specialist technical playing style was Jason Becker. By the time he was 20 years of age Becker had released two albums as half of the duo Cacophony, a solo album and was working on an album with David Lee Roth.

Becker, like Shawn Lane was technically proficient and played what was termed 'shred' guitar – sweep picked arpeggios. Unfortunately his virtuosity was cut short when he was diagnosed with Lou Gehrig's disease or amyotrophic lateral sclerosis and told that he could be dead by the age of 25.

His condition deteriorated rapidly and he could no longer play guitar, walk or even speak but his mental capacity is acute and he composes music translated from eye movements via computer.

Self-styled 'King of the 12 string guitar' back in the thirties and forties, Lead Belly suffered from the same disease in the latter years of his life.

English singer 'Seal' (full name Seal Henry Olusegun Olumide Adeola Samuel) has facial marks that have caused all sorts of conjecture as to how they came about, but they were actually caused by the skin condition discoid lupus erythematosus which he had as a child. His popularity was sealed with hits 'Crazy', 'Kiss from A Rose' and 'Love's Divine', steady album sales and live appearances. He was married to supermodel Heidi Klum for 7 years.

Other musicians who have been diagnosed with some form of lupus include the little lady with the big voice who is synonymous with the most popular songs from musical theatre, Elaine Paige and Grammy Award winning singer Toni Braxton.   Jazz songstress from the 1950's Theodora (Teddi) King died at the age of 48 from complications from the disease.

Sugar Sugar

Diabetes is one of the most common diseases in the world but with increasing knowledge, early detection and controlled medication, most who have it can continue to live normal lives. It leads to high blood sugar and requires stabilisation via prescribed drugs, appropriate diet and on some occasions, lifestyle. Musicians with diabetes often live lives with irregular sleep, intermittent meals, long periods of travel, potential to push mind and body to meet pressures of the industry and of course temptations of overindulgence.

A few diabetic musicians were diagnosed but died of other symptoms and the effect diabetes had on them is not fully known. Cass Elliot (Mamas and Papas) died of heart failure as did Gerry Garcia (Grateful Dead) and Bo Diddley, so too did James Brown (Godfather of Soul) although he was also fighting prostate cancer and jazz legend Miles Davis died of a stroke and pneumonia.

Country legend Johnny Cash had a colourful life for a musician known as 'the man in black'. Despite involvement with alcohol and drugs throughout his career, Cash's output was prodigious and his acting, writing and singing talents earned him the often overused term 'legend'.

Cash was type 2 diabetic but in 1997 was diagnosed with autonomic neuropathy associated with his diabetes and although he continued to record, he could no longer tour. Johnny Cash died 6 years later at the age of 71.

Syd Barrett, troubled founding member of Pink Floyd, dropped out of the music business and became reclusive and introverted. Having battled with mental illness for most of his life, it was reported by some that he succumbed to complications from his type 2 diabetes but he did in fact die aged 60 from pancreatic cancer.

Jazz singer Ella Fitzgerald had been entertaining since the mid 1930's and had played with the greats of the era such as Count Basie and Frank Sinatra. Fitzgerald was diagnosed with diabetes just before she turned 70, losing her legs to the disease and eventually her life in 1996.

Another unfortunate victim was Danny Joe Brown who had been lead singer with Southern rockers Molly Hatchett. He died from renal failure caused by diabetes at the age of 53.

Also 53 when she died in 1977 after lapsing into a diabetic coma was vocalist Mary Ford, ex-wife and singing partner of Les Paul. Mary' voice had graced 16 top 10 American hits in the fifties.

However, there are a number of high profile musicians across the genres who contain their symptoms by medication and moderating their lifestyles. In the case of overweight, ex drug addict and liver transplant recipient David Crosby, it is not before time.
Apart from stints in rehab and a penal penitentiary, the ex-Byrd and archetypal hippie harmony singer has lived the rock and roll lifestyle to the full.

Crosby has type 1 diabetes as has crooner Tony Bennett and at the other end of the musical spectrum, Brad Wilk drummer with Rage Against the Machine and Audioslave.

Crosby is in his 70's and Bennett is already an octogenarian so there is proof that the disease can be controlled even in the bizarre world of rock and popular music. Wilk is in his 40's, offers help to other sufferers, has donated to diabetic charities and even had a soft drink approved for sale that he 'invented' as a sugar free beverage called 'Olade' for consumption by fellow diabetics.

Brett Michaels, lead singer with glam metal band Poison whose biggest hit was the group's anthemic composition 'Every Rose Has its Thorn'.
Michaels, who is also a solo performer and mainstay of a number of US reality television shows was diagnosed with type 1 diabetes as a child and has lived with the condition and other health scares since the 1960's.

A number of other musicians have type 2 diabetes and continue to perform and live 'normal' lives by adhering to appropriate diets, they include Randy Jackson American idol judge who acts as spokesperson for the understanding of the condition, soul singer Patti Labelle, hard-rocker Tommy Lee erstwhile Motley Crue drummer, singer Meatloaf, Leslie West guitarist from Mountain and blues man BB King.

Mick Fleetwood suffered from hypoglycaemia whilst touring in the late 1970's which lead to him being diagnosed as a diabetic and the 'godfather of soul', James Brown was found to be diabetic while quite young and he lived until the age of 73.

I Want To See The Bright Lights Tonight

It is difficult for those in the limelight to retain privacy and many would agree that medical conditions are personal and should not be discussed in the media. However, in some cases, the artists are happy to share their experiences while in other situations it is impossible to disguise the symptoms.

Epilepsy is a neurological condition which causes seizures, in some cases spontaneously and in others caused by a trigger such as flashing lights. Again the lifestyle and environment that musicians find themselves in is not conducive to passivity and seizures whilst performing cannot go unnoticed by colleagues or audiences.

This was the case with Joy Division's Ian Curtis who took epileptic fits whilst on stage.

Prince admitted that he was born with epilepsy but the condition did not progress, Mike Skinner aka The Streets, had epilepsy as a child and teenager whereas Geoff Rickly singer from the band 'Thursday' and Lindsey Buckingham erstwhile Fleetwood Mac writer / singer / guitarist were both on tour and in their twenties when they experienced their first seizures.

Mike Nolan from UK / Eurovision singing quartet 'Bucks Fizz' began having seizures following a coach crash in which he was seriously injured and Adam Horovitz, actor, producer and one time 'Beastie Boy' wears a medical alert bracelet following a full on epileptic seizure.

Ex-Spandau Ballet bassist now an actor, Martin Kemp suffers from epilepsy following two brain tumours which required the insertion of a metal plate in his skull, but his condition is medically controlled.

Luckily, the above named epileptics continue to play with control of their condition and awareness.

However, American blues guitarist Jimmy Reed was not so fortunate as his epilepsy was not diagnosed for some time. Although mainstream success eluded him,

Reed was influential on artists such as The Rolling Stones, Van Morrison and The Yardbirds. He died in 1976, aged 50 from respiratory failure brought on by a major epileptic seizure in his sleep.

The website brainaneurysm.com reports that up to one in every 15 US citizens will develop a brain aneurysm in their lifetime and that more than 30,000 will suffer subarachnoid haemorrhage. More depressing statistics are mooted regarding the chance of survival and permanent brain damage. Brain aneurysms are often only detected when they rupture and in such cases, survival rates are increased if the patients are treated as quickly as possible.

However, in some cases, nothing can be done as was the situation with singer Laura Brannigan who suffered an aneurysm in her sleep and died as a result at the age of 47. The vocalist's father and grandfather had both died from brain haemorrhages but Laura, who suffered headaches prior to her death, assumed they were caused by stress and did not seek medical help.
Brannigan was at her peak in the 1980's with songs on various movie soundtracks such as 'Flashdance' and 'Ghostbusters' and even the best-selling video game 'Grand Theft Auto', in addition to hit singles 'Self Control', How Can I Live Without You' and the major seller 'Gloria'.

A brain aneurysm also killed original Styx guitarist John 'J C' Curulewski at the age of 37.

'World Party' writer, singer and frontman Karl Wallinger was a member of The Waterboys for three years during the 1980's, has played with Sinead O'Connor and Bob Geldof but his biggest commercial success was his composition 'She's The One' which was catapulted into the charts by Robbie Williams. Wallinger's potential was stalled for a while after suffering an aneurysm in 2001 and it was five years before he was fully recovered.

'Texas' guitarist Ally McErlaine collapsed from a brain aneurysm in 2009 and was in a coma for nine weeks. The 41 year old was in a serious condition and remained in hospital for more than six months but he progressively recovered to the extent that he has performed again.

REM drummer Bill Berry collapsed onstage from a burst aneurysm and although he recovered, he has since retired from the music business.

Jazz trumpeter and producer extraordinaire Quincy Jones, who has worked with the greats across musical genres – Miles Davis, Frank Sinatra and Michael Jackson to name but three had a near fatal cerebral aneurysm in 1974, but recovered after major operations.

Pat Martino was a guitarist in the early 1960's who toyed with pop music but was soon captured by the sound of jazz and became a top player in that genre but in 1976 he suffered a brain aneurysm and required surgery. Following the operation Pat was inflicted by severe memory loss including the ability to play his instrument. Slow recovery lasted years and he re-learned the skills of guitar techniques aided by listening and watching previous recordings of himself playing, eventually regaining the high calibre of musicianship that he had originally reached.

There are also examples where head injuries or illnesses impacted on musicians.

In 2006, Keith Richards, writer and guitarist with The Rolling Stones bizarrely fell out of a tree whilst on holiday in Fiji and injured his head requiring cranial surgery to reduce pressure in his brain.

'Foreigner' vocalist Lou Gramm, the voice behind 'I Want to Know what Love is', 'Cold as Ice', 'Urgent', 'Waiting for a Girl Like You' and many more was diagnosed with craniopharyngima in 1997.
This was a benign brain tumour which was operated on successfully and although it impacted on the quality of his singing voice, Gramm was able to resume his career.

Not so lucky was the influential gypsy guitarist Django
Reinhardt, inspiration for many of rock's axemen. He
suffered a fatal brain haemorrhage at the age of 43 as
he walked home from a gig in 1953.

Having mentioned that Sheryl Crow and Olivia Newton
John have successfully been treated against the
symptoms of cancer, so too has Aussie songstress
Kylie Minogue, sixties sultry singer Marianne Faithfull
and a trio of American singer songwriters Carly Simon,
Anastacia and Melissa Etheridge.

There are another couple of examples of people from
the music industry fighting back the big C.

The 'Barenaked Ladies' are an alternative rock band
who have achieved great success in their native
Canada with reasonable recognition in the US but are
perhaps best known in the UK as writers and
performers of the theme tune to the television
comedy 'Big Bang Theory. Keyboardist/ guitarist Kevin
Hearn had to undergo bone marrow transplant from
his brother in order to conquer the symptoms of
chronic myelogenous leukaemia.

Mike Peters, best known as lead singer from Welsh band The Alarm successfully beat lymph cancer in the mid-1990's but was faced with chronic lymphocytic leukaemia ten years later. Peters helped set up the 'Love Hope Strength' foundation to help fight cancer and fundraising includes fellow musicians staging concerts in unique locations.

A number of musicians were affected by the disease Polio when they were children.

English singer songwriter Ian Dury was well into his 30's when he broke through into mainstream success in the UK as leader of The Blockheads in the late 1970's. 'Hit Me with Your Rhythm Stick', 'What A Waste', 'Reasons To Be Cheerful Part 3' and 'Sex and Drugs and Rock And Roll' were his most famous compositions.

Often appearing onstage sporting a cane, Dury had contracted polio at the age of 7 which affected his mobility for the rest of his life. He apparently caught the disease from a visit to a public swimming pool. Dury's lyrics were often controversial, a case in point being 'Spasticus Autisticus' in which he wrote from the perspective of someone with a disability about the 'establishments' patronising attitude.

Other musicians who were affected by polio include saxophonist David Sanbourn who reportedly took up the instrument to strengthen his chest and improve breathing, 'Cockney Rebel' singer Steve Harley (Come

Up and See Me, Make Me Smile), Scottish singer / songwriter Donovan, American singer Judy Collins and multi-talented Canadian Joni Mitchell.

To overcome any of these ailments and find success deserves praise but one musician has achieved critical and commercial acclaim across a range of musical styles from country, rock, grunge, rockabilly, electronic and on occasion with hard hitting controversial lyrics, despite being affected by polio, epilepsy, diabetes and suffering a brain aneurysm.

He is Canadian singer / songwriter / guitarist / harmonica player / pianist, one time member of Buffalo Springfield, part-time frontman of 'Crazy Horse', the final quarter of super-group Crosby, Stills and Nash – Neil Young.

Six year old Young caught polio in the same Canadian outbreak that affected Joni Mitchell as a child and he was also diagnosed as being diabetic around this time. At the early stages of his breakthrough in the mid 1960's, Young was subject to epileptic seizures, a condition also experienced by his daughter Amber Jean, while his two sons are both inflicted with cerebral Palsy.

In 2005, Neil Young had an operation to relieve an aneurysm but collapsed in the street a couple of days later with bleeding from a femoral artery.

Ever the trooper, the Canadian troubadour recovered and was back on the road and in the studio soon after.

Despite these medical hindrances, Neil Young remains one of the most prolific and popular musicians of his era.

Young's occasional singing partner David Crosby put his body (and mind) through considerable chemical abuse throughout his life and as a diabetic this took its toll on the singer's internal organs to the extent that in 1995 he underwent a life-saving liver transplant.

In 2003, Jack Bruce the ex-Cream singer / bassist received a replacement liver via transplant, as did The Grateful Dead's bass player Phil Lesh in 1998 and Allman Brother Greg in 2010.

R&B, soul and jazz vocalist Natalie Cole, daughter of singer Nat King, received a kidney transplant in 2009 on the same day and in the same hospital that her adopted sister Carole died.

In 2004, Fairport Convention alumnus, Dave Swarbrick had a double lung transplant which gave the veteran fiddler a new lease of life and he continued to play and tour.

Hip replacements are generally considered to be carried out on older patients but two performers had the procedure performed on them

At the relatively young age of 57, Nils Lofgren required to have both hips replaced. Keen on sport as a youngster, the talented musician would on occasion incorporate his gymnastic ability into his performances by jumping onto a trampoline and somersaulting on stage after a guitar solo which obviously took its toll on his hip joints.

Electro-pop lead singer Andy Bell from 'Erasure' has avascular necrosis and also had both hips replaced at a much younger age than Lofgren. Bell is also HIV-positive.

However, as these many examples of accident, injury and illness show, ability can shine through from the shadows of disability

In conclusion, the headlines from an article in a UK newspaper puts an interesting slant on the topic by suggesting that actually being a musician could cause medical problems (ia)

"Was rock guitarist's brain tumour caused by his playing? Doctors speculate about link between professional musicians and condition"

The newspaper reports on the case of a British musician and guitar teacher who developed a tennis ball sized tumour behind his eye. A successful operation removed the tumour and the guitarist recovered and is able to play again but some of the comments in the article give food for thought;

"Guitarist told by doctor his life-threatening brain tumour was prevalent in professional musicians" and a comment from hospital staff,

"We don't half have a lot of musicians in here with what you've got".

To play or not to play, that is the risk but don't tell the kids or they will have an excuse to refuse to go to piano lessons!

Chapter 7

The Art of Dying

"There comes a time when all of us must leave here, there's nothing Sister Mary can do to keep me here with you, nothing in this crazy life of trying can equal or surpass the art of dying" - (xi) George Harrison

Many musicians have died young as a result of accidents, illnesses or natural causes but the deaths of many others were the results of excesses as part of the rock and roll lifestyle. Abuse of alcohol, prescription and illegal substances may have added to the consciousness and enigmas of aspiring talent but they often blurred the reality of these individuals and confusion surrounds the actual circumstances of a number of musicians' deaths.

The phrase 'death by misadventure' has been attributed to some who passed away in situations not altogether clear due to overindulgence or inexplicable reasons and misreporting and cover-ups have created a catalogue of conspiracy theories.

Too Close to Heaven

A coroner's inquest determined that the death in July 2011 of Amy Jade Winehouse was misadventure. Winehouse had first broke into the UK music scene in 2004 when her jazz influenced debut album 'Frank' was both critically and commercially acclaimed. Two years later her follow up was completed and 'Back to Black' went on to be the best-selling album of 2007 in the UK and was top 10 in USA resulting in the young singer becoming the first British female to win five Grammy awards. The quick rise to superstardom was however not all positive as Amy Winehouse had a troubled personal life which resulted in as quick a fall from grace. A severe drug problem, which was eventually treated, was replaced by serious alcohol dependency which was identified as the symptoms that lead to her early death.

In her short life, Winehouse had one marriage which was played out in the press as a drug fuelled violent affair and her substance intake affected her live performances on some occasions forgetting lyrics, slurring words and being booed by unappreciative audiences. She was, however, a major donator to charities and considered to be "a true jazz singer who sang the 'right way'" according to veteran crooner Tony Bennett with whom Amy Winehouse made her final recording, 'Body and Soul' which won her a posthumous Grammy.

Following her tragic death, Amy Winehouse records again charted with Back to Black becoming the best-selling album (to date) of the 21st Century but her demise at a relatively young age added yet another musician to the mythical '27 club' as well as exemplifying how not to deal with fame.

The session drummer Joe Porcaro was co-founder of the Los Angeles Music Academy and has played with the major artists of the era including Pink Floyd, Frank Sinatra and Madonna. He is also the father of drummer Jeff, keyboard player Steve and bassist Mike, all of whom made their names as respected session players and writers as well as being members of the very successful band Toto of 'Hold The Line', 'Africa' and 'Rosanna' fame. Although Toto continue with altered line ups, Mike retired from the band due to him developing amyotrophic lateral sclerosis and being unable to play.

Brother Jeff's departure was more dramatic having died in 1992, aged 38 in disputed circumstances, not so much misadventure more mistaken definition.

Jeff Porcaro first played in Sonny and Cher's backing band when he was only 17 and his session work was endless on classic albums by a list of major artists including Steely Dan, Barbra Streisand, Bee Gees,

Miles Davis, Elton John, Bruce Springsteen, Paul Simon, Michael Jackson, Pink Floyd and numerous others.

His unfortunate demise has been linked to a heart attack resulting from hardened arteries caused by cocaine but this is disputed by his family and the official Toto story is that he accidently inhaled poisonous pesticides during a family barbecue and the reaction caused his death.

This chapter identifies the causes given for musicians' deaths and in some cases alternative versions where opinions differ as to the reason why the music stopped.

Having mentioned the short but eventful life of Rolling Stones founder Brian Jones, controversy also surrounded his death. Officially, the coroner's verdict on Jones passing uses the very words 'death by misadventure'. The 27 year olds body was found at the bottom of his swimming pool on 3 July 1969 and the perception was that Jones had drowned, possibly under the influence of drugs and / or alcohol, as his liver and heart were enlarged through overindulgence.

Conspiracy theories abound, not least because his girlfriend at the time claimed that he had a pulse when he was removed from the water. A number of people had been at his house that evening and rumours persisted that some of the musician's possessions went missing from his home. Claims that Jones had been murdered were given substance when a builder, Frank Thorogood confessed to the crime on his deathbed.

This information was later disputed although the case was reopened as further evidence came to light, but allegations of a Police cover up were not substantiated and the Thorogood story not proven, therefore the case was again closed.

Whether or not Brian Jones drowned accidently or there was something more sinister surrounding his passing remains to be seen, but it is ironic that the scene of the death of a man who lived the sex, drugs and rock'n'roll lifestyle to the full was the same location where the children's favourite Winnie The Pooh was composed by AA Milne, a previous owner of the property.

Sea of Madness

Another musician from a 1960's institution who lived the life celebrated in the band's songs had an accidental drowning.

As the only Beach Boy who could actually surf, Dennis

Wilson's autobiography is a lesson in bad living through good times. The middle of the Beach Boys three Wilson brothers, Dennis was the drummer and occasional singer and although he was considered to contribute the least to the group's sound, he was the most outgoing, was more of a playboy than his brothers, had a lead part in the cult movie 'Two Lane Blacktop' opposite James Taylor and his first solo album 'Pacific Ocean Blue' was well received both critically and commercially.

As the Beach Boys evolved from the trademark harmony sound in the 1960's, by the mid 1970's, Dennis Wilson's deterioration through drink and drugs was evident.
He also had a number of relationships, including a couple of years with Fleetwood Mac's Christine McVie and was betrothed five times to four different women.
Dennis married Karen Lamm twice (who was ex-wife of Chicago keyboard player Robert) and at the time of his death in 1983 at the age of 39, he was married to Beach Boy cousin Mike Love's illegitimate daughter Shawn Marie, who was 20 years Wilson's junior. Coincidently, Shawn also died at the age of 39.

Another controversial aspect of Dennis Wilson's career was his short but disastrous connection with Charles Manson and his 'Family'.

Wilson was found at the bottom of a marina in which he was diving with his alcohol consumption and the cold temperature of the water being possible factors in the accident.

Singer / songwriter/ guitarist Tim Buckley died of an accidental heroin overdose at the age of 28 before his son Jeff, whom he had apparently met only once, reached the age of 10.   Buckley junior released his first album 'Grace' in 1994 to positive reviews and eventual major sales, especially in Australia.
The album included his critically acclaimed version of Leonard Cohen's 'Hallelujah' and with good feedback for his live performances, Jeff Buckley's musical future looked bright, but this was not to be.

Tragically in May 1997, the 30 year olds body was found in Wolf River Harbour / Mississippi River, a victim of accidental drowning. He was still wearing his clothes and boots and there were no suspicious circumstances or trace of alcohol or drugs.

Rockabilly singer Johnny Burnette was also drowned aged 30.
He had been a member of the 'Rock and Roll Trio' along with his brother Dorsey Burnette and friend Paul Burlison in the 1950's but had a few solo hit singles in the early 1960's, most notably 'You're Sixteen'.

In 1964, he was fishing on a lake when his boat was hit by another vessel and the musician fell into the water and did not recover.

Original drummer with Steely Dan, Jimmy Hodder was 42 when he drowned in a swimming pool in 1990.

The final accidental drowning of a musician is poignant in that the 45 year old guitarist managed to push his 12 year old son to safety prior to being swept to his own death by a wave.

Randy Craig Wolfe had been a teenage guitarist who played with an early Jimi Hendrix incarnation called The Blue Flame and it was Hendrix who referred to him as 'Randy California' a name that stuck throughout his career. California fronted the 'Californian' band 'Spirit' who had respectable sales of singles and albums in the USA, highest placings in the 20's and although considered influential, success outside America was elusive.

Father and son were surfing in Hawiian waters when Randy California reacted to rescue his son Quinn from a riptide but was himself drowned.

Whiskey In The Jar

Spirit had previously toured with English group Led Zeppelin in their formative years in the late sixties.

Led Zeppelin were one of the few bands who genuinely earned 'superstar' status despite never having had a hit single. Album sales, live performances and an autobiographical fantasy movie maintained the band's popularity from the late 1960's until they ceased playing in September 1980.
The reason for the sudden termination was the 'accidental' death of drummer John Bonham. Bonzo had always been a heavy drinker and during a session of rehearsals he incorporated a session of drinking and later went to sleep it off. The following day he was found dead with the official verdict being that he vomited during sleep and was asphyxiated.
Bonham was 32 years old and described by many as the best drummer in rock, often soloing for lengthy periods during concerts and his legacy in addition to the Zeppelin back catalogue and some session work is the influence and impact he had on many other percussionists who are quick to acknowledge him in tribute.

Another drummer also died from choking on his vomit following a drinking session.

Stuart Cable had been the original sticks man with Welsh band Stereophonics from their formation in

1996 until he left to concentrate on television work in the early noughties.

In 2010, 40 year Cable was found dead in his home.

In 1964, Ronald Scott began playing in his first band as the drummer with the occasional vocal slot and ten years later was the lead vocalist with AC / DC.

Bon Scott was born in Scotland but like band mates Malcolm and Angus Young, he had emigrated to Australia as a child. Scott was lead singer in AC / DC up until their international breakthrough album 'Highway to Hell' in 1979 and a bright future was predicted for the rock band.

Tragically, on a visit to London, 33 year old Bon Scott had too much to drink and was left to 'sleep it off' in a car but apparently vomited and choked, a similar demise to Bonham and Cable.

The band considered quitting following Scott's death but recruited Brian Johnson as replacement and completed the album they had started with Bon Scott, 'Back in Black' which became one of the best-selling albums ever.

The same cause of death was intimated by the doctor who attended to pronounce the end of guitar legend Jimi Hendrix at the age of 27 but this case is one of the most controversial in relation to the decease of a rock star.

The American who is considered to be the most innovative and natural electric guitarist of the rock era was in London on the night of 17 September 1970 and had attended a party.   A few hours later he was dead, supposedly having choked on his own vomit, having consumed wine.

However, Monika Dannemann, the girlfriend he was with and who discovered him unconscious, always maintained that he was alive when he was in the ambulance on the way to hospital.   Her recollection of times, alcohol and drugs reportedly consumed and who was present during events, differed from official reports. There was even a difference in her story and that of the ambulance crew as to whether she was present in the vehicle.

Dannemann remained adamant that her version was correct but she also had an on-going dispute with Kathy Etchingham, a previous girlfriend of Hendrix and in 1996 Momika Danneman found guilty of contempt of court and committed suicide, taking her version of events to her grave.

There were further rumours suggesting that Hendrix was murdered by a manager because he wanted to end his contract but this story was thought to have been created by a former roadie trying to cash in.

There is a popular saying regarding the formative years of the cultural revolution that shook the boundaries of acceptance and assaulted the ears of youth with 'pop' music,
"If you remember the sixties, you weren't there".
Many were there in body but the amount of alcohol consumed and experimentation with hallucinogenics and other chemicals dulled their senses and eroded the lives of a few.
It is only with hindsight that the excesses can be attributed to the shortened lives of some musicians.

The name David Byron is not widely known even by musical aficionados and his death at the age of 38 in 1985 went largely unreported. He had been battling alcoholism for many years and sometimes collapsed onstage due to inebriation but eventually alcohol problems caused his demise.
Byron had a short solo career, stints in bands called 'Spice' and 'Rough Diamond' and was lead singer on 10 albums by Uriah Heep.
Although Heep's heavy rock genre was not mainstream and had a select following, Byron's voice was heard by many, without them knowing who it was, in the late sixties and into the seventies. David Byron was one of the main vocalists who appeared on numerous budget albums of session musicians doing covers of hits that were sold in supermarkets in place of the higher priced original artists products available in record stores.

Jim Morrison was ostensibly a poet and when he teamed with John Densmore, Ray Manzarek and Robbie Kreiger in the mid-sixties, they formed 'The Doors' and he readily became vocalist and frontman. They had a run of hit singles and albums, producing classic tracks 'Light my Fire', 'Break on Through', 'Riders on the Storm', 'Roadhouse Blues' and 'Love Her Madly' as well as the slightly weirder 'People are Strange' and 'The End'.

Morrison's behaviour became progressively more disturbing as his intake of drugs and alcohol increased and his onstage performances were unpredictable, the most notorious being when he was arrested for indecent exposure and taunting the Police.

Following the Doors last performance as a quartet in March 1971, Morrison left to stay with his girlfriend Pamela Courson in Paris. On 3 July she found 27 year old Jim Morrison dead in the bath, apparently from a drug overdose, but the authorities did not carry out an autopsy and the cause has been disputed.

There was no authentic witnesses to clarify the circumstances as Courson was also under the influence of drugs and coincidently overdosed and died three years later when she too was 27 years old.

Death comes to all and can happen at any age and can occur for many reasons but the more abusive the lifestyle and the bigger risks taken can reduce the odds of long life considerably.

Streets of Philadelphia

Considering the promiscuous lifestyle and frequent drug use of so many, it is surprising that so few musicians have been infected and / affected by Aids. The highest profile demise and first major rock star to die as a result of Aids was born in Zanzibar and raised in India before moving to London, UK when he was 17. Named Farrokh Balsara, the art student had begun to call himself Freddie and in 1970 met future band members Brian May and Roger Taylor who evolved into 'Queen' along with the addition of John Deacon and Bulsara changed his surname to Mercury.

The rise and success of the band and the showmanship of Mercury onstage was without bounds. Freddie frequently topped polls as best frontman and best vocalist, his composition 'Bohemian Rhapsody' regularly appears in the top 5 best ever songs, Queens Greatest Hits is the best-selling album in UK history, total worldwide album sales by Queen has topped 300 million and the spectacular live performances were legendary.

However, away from the glare of publicity, Mercury was a private individual and more shy than his flamboyant public persona suggested, but on occasions he also lived a dangerous decadent lifestyle, eventually testing HIV positive in 1987 but denying the fact until the day before his death at the age of 45, four years later.

Freddie Mercury's cause of death was bronchial pneumonia resulting from AIDS.

Another singer had died from complications from AIDS, eight years prior to Mercury's death but 39 year old German born, Klaus Nomi was not widely acknowledged outside of the New York art scene although he did appear on US TV show Saturday Night Live as backing vocalist in David Bowie's band.

There have been a few other victims of the disease, one unfortunate casualty being Tom Fogerty ex-guitarist from Creedence Clearwater Revival. Tom played with the band in which his younger brother John sang and composed the bulk of material, during CCR's most popular period 1968-71 with 'Proud Mary', 'Bad Moon Rising', 'Down on the Corner' and 'Travelin' Band'.

At the age of 48, Tom Fogerty was having treatment for back problems and was given blood transfusions, through which he contracted HIV and died in 1990 from a tuberculosis infection resulting from AIDS.

Ray Gillen was an American vocalist who fronted the band 'Badlands' but for a time found himself lead singer for Black Sabbath to complete tour dates when the group's frontman at the time, Glen Hughes damaged his throat and could not continue. Unfortunately, management difficulties prevented

Gillen recording with Sabbath and he reformed Badlands, but had to opt out of playing and recording due to ill health and he died from AIDS at the age of 34.

Songwriter Peter Allen co-wrote a number of hit songs for other artists such as 'I Honestly Love You' – Olivia Newton-John, 'Don't Cry Out Loud' – Melissa Manchester, 'I'd Rather Leave While I'm in Love' – Rita Coolidge and Oscar winner 'Arthur's Theme (Best That You Can Do)' – Christopher Cross. He was also a major cabaret star in his native Australia and was married to Liza Minnelli for seven years before coming out as homosexual.
In 1992, he died from AIDS related throat cancer, aged 48.

Jermaine Stewart was a dancer and had provided backing vocals for the groups Shalamar and Culture Club. He also had reasonable sales of his three recorded albums and notched up international hits with 'You don't have to Take Your Clothes Off' and 'Say It Again'.
39 year old Stewart died of AIDS related liver cancer in 1997.

Another victim of Aids was disco singer and drag artist 'Sylvester' who was 41 when he died of complications from AIDS in 1988. His biggest hits were 'You Make Me Feel (Mighty Real)' and 'Do Ya Wanna Funk'.

Fela Kuti was a Nigerian born human rights campaigner and political activist but he is also considered, along with drummer Tony Allen, to be a pioneer of 'Afrobeat'.

Controversial for his political stance and refusal to play songs after he had recorded them, Kuti remained popular in parts of Africa but not considered commercial outside that Continent.

In 1997, the 58 year old died from Kaposi's sarcoma brought on by AIDS.

There were a few more Aids victims who did not reach their fifties.

American guitarist Robbin Crosby played with the glam metal band 'Ratt' whose album sales reached platinum status on a number of occasions. He married a Playboy bunny and was open about his drug addiction and the negative effect it had on his career and eventually life.

HIV positive since 1994, Crosby passed away eight years later at the age of 42 of AIDS related complications and heroin overdose.

The name Dan Hartman is remembered for his major dance hit from late 1970's disco era, 'Instant Replay' but he also wrote the Lulu/Take That smash, 'Relight My Fire' and 'Free Ride' a hit for the Edgar Winter Group, of which he was a member.

Hartman died from AIDS complications at the age of 43 in 1994.

Ricky Wilson was only 32 when he succumbed to AIDS/HIV and died in 1985.
Wilson's unique open tunings were a feature of the 'New Wave' band the B52's in which he was a member along with his sister Cindy and three friends.

The final name on the list of AIDS related musician deaths is the youngest to date, at only 31 years of age.
Ex-drug dealer turned Gangsta rapper Eric Lynn Wright aka Easy E co-founded Ruthless Records which was responsible for the rise of rap music by the likes of Dr Dre, Ice Cube and Snoop Dog.
Easy E attended hospital in February 1995 with suspected asthma but was diagnosed with AIDS and died one month later

How Come

Another debilitating disease caused suffering and eventual death to three musicians from different backgrounds.
The classical cellist Jacqueline Du Pre, was one of the most popular musicians from the classical genre from her professional debut at the age of 16 in 1961 and the decade that followed. However, she began to lose sensitivity in her fingers which soon spread to other parts of her body and was diagnosed with MS in 1973 causing an early retirement from professional performances.
The condition worsened and Jacqueline Du Pre died at the age of 42.

Ex-English teacher Clifford T Ward had a top 10 single in the UK in 1973 with his self-penned song 'Gaye' and on the back of this, a top 40 album.   Thereafter, his releases showed low to moderate sales but he maintained a faithful following.

Diagnosed with MS in 1984, Ward continued to write and record as much as his health allowed and as his condition worsened, it was said that he crawled across the studio floor in order to complete his final works. 57 year old Clifford T Ward passed away in 2001.

The final multiple sclerosis sufferer who was a successful modern musician was diagnosed with the condition in the mid 1970's and progressively deteriorated over 21 years until his death in 1997, aged 51.

Ronnie Lane, 'Plonk' to his friends, had found fame and recognition as co-writer of most of the single hits by the Small Faces. Lane played bass and sang backing vocals in the band and continued these roles in the Faces with and without Rod Stewart, prior to embarking on a solo outing under the banner 'Slim Chance' and achieving UK singles success with 'How Come' and 'The Poacher'.

However, despite having had co-written many hits for the Small Faces, controversial management decisions and contracts prevented royalties from reaching Lane at his time of need and as medical bills increased, musician friends including Jimmy Page, Rod Stewart and Ronnie Wood helped with financial assistance

Lane's friend and co-writer in the Small Faces had a tragic death, but not as a result of medical problems.

Heat Of The Moment

As cocky cockney singer, guitarist and co-writer with Lane of classic pop songs 'Lazy Sunday' and 'Itchycoo Park' for the band he fronted, The Small Faces, Steve Marriot epitomised the 'good-for- a- laugh' Englishman. Humour shone through his singing style, lyrics and stage presence but he could also rock and had a powerful, raw, bluesy voice.

On leaving the band that would morph into Rod Stewart and The Faces, Marriot had further 'single' success with 'Natural Born Boogie' along with Peter Frampton in Humble Pie and continued to tour with his 'tongue in cheek' named trio 'Packet of Three' but unfortunate experiences with managers resulted in limited payback for his talents and like Ronnie Lane, Marriot never achieved his potential commercially after his initial success.

(Eventually the surviving members of The Small Faces Ian McLaggan and Kenney Jones did get some financial recompense but this was sadly too late for Marriott and Lane).

An entirely different image of an Englishman was one time Bonzo Dog Doo Dah Band member Vivian Stanshall, who was working class but developed his idiosyncratic taste in clothes and language which gave a perception of eccentricity.

He shared a zany persona typified by his friend and practical joker Keith Moon and the pair were known as pranksters. Stanshall's recognisable vocal style was used for commercials, narrations including his fantasy 'Sir Henry at Rawlinson End' and as the master of ceremonies introducing the instruments on Mike Oldfield's 'Tubular Bells'.

Perhaps his 'off the wall' humour was too far out for major commercial success but he also contributed to mainstream rock, a fine example being his co-composing skills on Steve Winwood's 'Arc of a Diver' album.

However, Stanshall maintained reasonable popularity and his style of humour can be detected by the names given to his two solo albums, 'Men Opening Umbrellas Ahead' and 'Teddy Boys Don't Knit'.

These two differing but interesting talents not only provided us with interesting music and lyrics but while we enjoyed their showmanship in life, behind the humorous and positive façades, both became alcohol dependent and suffered tragically similar deaths.

Steve Marriot perished from smoke inhalation in a house fire in 1991 at the age of 44 and Vivian

Stanshall died four years later at the age of 51 when his flat caught fire.

Other tragic early deaths robbed the potential of 27 year old Les Harvey, 31 year old John Rostill and Keith Relf who was 33, all of whom were electrocuted by faulty musical equipment.

Les Harvey, brother of 'Sensational Alex Harvey' was guitarist in Scottish rockers Stone the Crows, fronted by the bellowing voice of Maggie Bell. The band was playing a live gig in Wales when tragically the guitarist touched an unearthed microphone and died onstage.

In 1963, John Rostill took over the bass playing role in successful instrumental and occasional Cliff Richard backing band The Shadows. Rostill was also a songwriter and his compositions were recorded by Olivia Newton John and Elvis Presley among others. He was found dead in his home studio by his wife and fellow Shadow Bruce Welch, having accidently touched badly wired equipment.

The Yardbirds achieved moderate singles success in the mid-1960's but are mostly remembered as the ensemble that produced guitarists Jeff beck, Jimmy Page and Eric Clapton.
On leaving the group, vocalist and harmonica player Keith Relf did not have such an illustrious career as the band's axe men, but he formed Renaissance with

whom he stayed for four years and Armageddon and continued to perform until the accident in his home when an improperly earthed guitar caused his death.

A different circumstance but similar result caused the demise of a popular French singer and composer. Claude Francois had record sales of over 70 million and along with Jacques Revaux wrote a song called 'Comme d'habitude' to which Paul Anka re-wrote English lyrics and it became the much covered and Frank Sinatra signature, 'My Way'.
Francois was also electrocuted, but not by faulty electronic musical equipment.
In 1978, 39 year old Claude Francois was at home in his bath when he touched a light fitment with his wet hands and death by electrocution was the outcome.

The deaths of these musicians from drowning, fires, electrocution and debilitating physical diseases were indeed tragic as were the final two deaths from a psychosomatic disorder in which the mental condition of the sufferers impacted on the physical with fatal implications.

Two young women in the musical limelight were effectively dying from eating disorders for a number of years but when the end came, a cardiac arrest was the actual cause of death for one and pneumonia in the case of the other.

No More Tears (Enough is Enough)

Lena Zavaroni had been a child star following her appearance on a UK talent show on the back of which she had a top 10 single and album in her homeland and appeared on many US television shows as well as singing with Frank Sinatra and a show at the White House. However, the diminutive Scot had battled with anorexia nervosa since the age of 13 and as her popularity diminished she became more depressed. Following a failed marriage, 34 year old Lena underwent an operation in an attempt to correct the psychological problem that was causing her distress but contracted pneumonia and passed away within days of the operation. Her reduced weight and lack of strength as a result of anorexia meant that she was unable to fight the infection.

Karen Carpenter died from heart failure at the age of 32, having also battled with anorexia nervosa for many years. The drumming sister of keyboard / arranger Richard, Karen's smooth contralto vocals had kept the musical siblings at the top of their game throughout the seventies but Karen was not a natural front woman and was never comfortable with the attention lavished on her.
Although Karen Carpenter's death in 1983 highlighted the problems with the eating disorder, the publicity

was too late to prevent Zavaroni's condition deteriorating to the ultimate similar sad end. However, apart from the Carpenters' legacy being in their recordings which are still popular years later, many teenagers have also benefitted from the knowledge gained about eating disorders since the singers' untimely deaths brought the illness to the wider publics' attention.

Travelling on various modes of transport is a requirement for many professionals but the basis of most musicians' success is the rapport they can share with live audiences which requires frequent journeys from city to city. Statistically therefore there is a high probability that some musicians would meet their end during travel and a number have perished as a result of aircraft, car and motorcycle accidents.

Flying On The Ground Is Wrong

"I was driving across the burning desert when I spotted six jet planes leaving six white vapour trails across the bleak terrain.   It was the hexagram of the heavens it was the strings of my guitar" (xii)   - Joni Mitchell

Statistics are often cited claiming that air travel is the safest form of transport and although not disputing this proposition, the number of deaths of musicians in plane crashes appears proportionately high. However, in many cases, bad weather or pilot error has been the cause.

The first high profile recording artist who ceased to record following a plane journey was an American musician, writer, band leader and innovative arranger whose aircraft took off from an airfield in England heading for Paris, France but the storyline cannot be completed.

The year was 1944, long before rock'n'roll but Glenn Miller was a musical hero throughout the second world war to an appreciative audience of 'swing' dance music for his enduring arrangements of 'Moonlight Serenade', 'Little Brown Jug' and 'Chattanooga Choo Choo' among many others. Major Miller set off in a small plane with a pilot and one other passenger and apparently went missing in fog. No plane was found, no bodies recovered and the trombonist and fellow flyers were presumed dead. However, speculation abounds with various conspiracy theories supposedly throwing light on the case many years later, but all the 'exclusives' appear to be conjecture. Examples of alternative theories are that Miller was sent on a secret mission to offer the few remaining

Nazi officers the opportunity to surrender peacefully as by that time the war was all but over, but Glenn was captured and tortured.

Another story is that he was shot by a jealous husband returning from being a POW to find his wife alone with the musician, yet another that he died in the arms of a French prostitute having suffered a heart attack.

Glen Miller was 40 when he disappeared / died and a popular musician whose fans prefer to accept the official story that his small aircraft most probably crashed into the English Channel during poor visibility.

'That'll be the Day' was a hit for The Crickets in May 1957 featuring bespectacled Charles Hardin Holley on lead vocals and guitar. Holley was misspelled as Holly on promotional material and was used for the remainder of releases by Buddy Holly until January 1959 when the short but inspirational life of the songwriter was prematurely terminated in a plane crash.

The emotive vocals on 'It's Raining in my Heart', 'Peggy Sue', 'I Guess it doesn't Matter Anymore' and 'True Love Ways' lived on for many years but a short flight in bad weather left 22 year old Buddy Holly dead.

The 21 year old pilot was killed as he lost control of the aircraft during a snowstorm and a wing hit the ground sending the plane crashing into a frozen field.

The other two passengers were also killed outright and they were fellow musicians who were accompanying Buddy Holly on tour.

Seventeen year old Richie Valens popularised the traditional Mexican folk song with his rocked-up version of 'La Bamba' but tragically could not capitalise on his hit as he perished in the accident.

The final victim was 28 year old J P Richardson who was known to music fans of the day as the 'Big Bopper' and in addition to his hit version of 'Chantilly Lace' he was a DJ and songwriter (composer of the song 'Running Bear').

Richardson was not scheduled to be on the plane but because he was suffering from a cold, Waylon Jennings gave up his seat to allow the Big Bopper to fly. Jennings would later become a country star of note but at the time, he was part of Buddy Holly's backing band. This goodwill decision saved his own life but following the fateful crash, the matter prayed on his mind and Waylon Jennings felt guilt for some time, considering his reported final banter with Buddy Holly. Holly is reputed to have joked to Jennings,(24)

"I hope your ol' bus freezes up"

to which he replied,

"Well, I hope your ol' plane crashes".

That was the infamous 'day the music died', as singer / songwriter Don MacLean would quote in his semi-biographical 'American Pie'.

However, further to the tragic deaths, Buddy Holly's wife of only six months was pregnant and miscarried the child following the trauma of hearing about the deaths on the news.

The Crickets continued to play and record after Holly's death and for a time, singer David Box took on Buddy's role.
In a tragic coincidence, he too died in a plane crash travelling between gigs.
21 year old Box was killed in an accident in 1964.

Patsy Cline was a country singer who became one of the first acts from that genre to have crossover hits in the 'pop' charts, not just once but on a few occasions with 'Walkin' After Midnight', 'I Fall to Pieces' and her signature version of Willie Nelson's 'Crazy'.
Having survived two serious car crashes, Cline was aware of her own mortality and apparently told friends that she would go when it was her time.
This message was ominous when the singer boarded a plane on 5 March 1963 in foggy weather against the advice of airport management and took off to her doom as the aircraft crashed shortly after in high winds and poor visibility with a pilot at the controls who was unable to use his instruments.
Patsy Cline was married with two children and was only 30 years old.

The following year, 40 year old singer Jim Reeves died when the plane he was piloting crashed in similar circumstances.

Coincidently, Reeves had been trained by the same instructor who had taught the pilot of Patsy Cline's fateful flight.

Having been recognised by country music fans in the late 1950's, the smooth baritone voice of Texas born Jim Reeves graced the popular music charts at the start of the following decade. Songs like 'He'll Have to Go', 'I Love You Because', 'Welcome to My World' and 'I Won't Forget You' gave him fame in countries as diverse as Norway and Sri Lanka and Reeves was a particular favourite in South Africa where he recorded in the Afrikaans language, toured and made a feature film.

His was another tragic death of a recording artist during a 'bad weather' flight but his popularity continued with strong record sales following his death, including the posthumous number one single 'Distant Drums'.

The next aircraft disaster involving musicians robbed the entertainment world, not only of the talented vocalist by the name of Otis Redding, but also four aspiring musicians, the teenage members of his backing band the Bar Kays.

Redding initially had recognition by a mainly black audience as a ballad and soul singer but by the mid 1960's had broken the ethnic barriers by appearing at the Whisky a Go Go and featuring at Monterey Pop to a universally appreciative public.

'Try a Little Tenderness' had given him widespread acclaim and 'Sittin' in the Dock of the Bay' was about to increase the singer's popularity. The single, Dock of the Bay and album of the same name, were hits but unfortunately posthumously as three days after recording the song, Redding was killed in a plane crash.

Again, the aircraft was flying in inclement weather against the advice of the authorities. Along with Otis Redding and his manager, guitarist Jimmy King (18), organist Ronnie Caldwell (19), saxophonist Phalon Jones (18) and drummer Carl Cunningham (18) all died in the accident.

Surviving members kept The Bar Kays name alive by recruiting new members and continued to act as backing band for many Stax artists.

You Don't Mess Around with Jim' and 'Life and Times' were the well-received first two album releases from singer / songwriter Jim Croce.

Unfortunately Croce's life and times were cut short and his third album 'I Got a Name' was a posthumous hit.

30 year old Jim Croce and sidekick guitarist Maury Meuhleisen who was only 24 had been playing together for a few years and had met with recent success at live gigs and chart positions with 'Bad Bad

Leroy Brown' and 'Time in a Bottle' but another aeroplane crash killed six people including the two musicians. The weather conditions were not too bad at the time but it was dark and the pilot did not gain enough altitude during take-off and the aircraft hit a tree.

Although different models of plane, the type Beechcraft was the same in the deaths of Buddy Holly / Richie Valance / Big Bopper, Jim Reeves, Otis Redding and the Bar Kays, and Jim Croce.

Jazz rock outfit 'Chase' lead by trumpeter Bill Chase showed promise in the early 1970's and were nominated for best newcomer at the Grammy's in 1971 (losing to Carly Simon). However, prior to recording their fourth album, 39 year old Bill along with keyboard player Wally Yohn, guitarist John Emma and drummer Walter Clark lost their lives in August 1974 when the plane they were travelling in crashed. The bodies of the pilot and another passenger were also found in the wreckage of the Piper Comanche which was the same type of aircraft in which Patsy Cline had perished.

Southern rocker band Lynyrd Skynyrd was known for live performances, visibly recognisable for playing underneath a Confederate flag, aurally recognisable for a three guitar sound and identifiable as the band that played one of the most requested tracks on music television, 'Free Bird'.

The band is also respected for the tongue in cheek retort to Canadian Neil Young's 'Alabama' and 'Southern Man' observations, with their 'Sweet Home Alabama'.

However, for rock music fans, the name Lynyrd Skynyrd also reminds them of yet another tragic aircraft disaster.

On 20 October 1977, a plane chartered by the band remarkably ran out of fuel and crash landed on an airstrip killing the pilot and co-pilot, the band's assistant road manager, lead singer Ronnie Van Zandt, guitarist Steve Gaines and his backing vocalist sister Cassie.   All other members of the band and road crew were injured, some seriously.

This tragic event ended the upward spiral of Lynyrd Skynyrd although some of the original members did attempt to play together in various line-ups including the most successful with replacement lead vocalist Johnny Van Zandt, Ronnie's brother.

However, bad luck continued to follow some of the original members.

Guitarists Allen Collins and Gary Rossington had both been involved in serious car accidents the year before the plane crash and 10 years later Collins was drunk driving and crashed his car killing his girlfriend and leaving himself paralysed from the chest down. Although he could no longer play, on occasions he was wheeled onto the stage during concerts to tell his sad story and advise the audience against drunk-driving, but he died from pneumonia in 1990.

Bass player Leon Wilkinson had never fully regained the use of his left arm following the air crash when doctors had considered amputation, but managed to continue bass playing by holding the instrument more vertically.
Wilkinson passed away in 2001, aged 49, from emphysema and liver disease and original keyboard player Alan Powell was 56 when he died from heart problems in 2009. Lynyrd Skynyrd, a tragic legacy from a true rock music era.

The next air incident causing the death of a musician was in 1982 when a 25 year old guitarist by the name of Randal (Randy) Rhoads, along with a hairdresser and the plane's pilot were killed in an accident.
At the time of his death, Rhoads was a member of Ozzy Osborne's band and played on 'Blizzard of Oz' and 'Diary of a Madman' but had expressed a desire to leave rock and study classical guitar. His guitar technique has been lauded by many and for a hard rocker, his style was called neo-classical metal.

Whilst the band were touring, their driver, who was also a licensed pilot took a short flight in an aircraft for fun with some of the entourage. He then took a second flight and for a joke 'buzzed the tour bus a couple of times but on the third fly over, misjudged the distance and clipped the top of the vehicle which spiralled the plane into wreckage, killing the three outright.

A child star in the 1950's, a pop star in the 1960's, an attempt to be taken as a more serious musician in the 1970's and induction into the Rock and Roll Hall of Fame in 1987.

However, the inductee Rick Nelson did not live to appreciate this honour.

On the last day of 1985, a plane with nine on board crash landed, hitting trees and although badly burned, the pilot and co-pilot survived the impact.

The seven others were killed, Rick(y) Nelson and his girlfriend, road manager / soundman Donald Clark Russell, Drummer Rick Intveld, guitarist Bobby Neal, bass player Patrick Woodward and keyboard player Andy Chapin.

Reba McIntyre is a successful country singer with a lengthy career and she had already released 15 albums by 1991 when a major tragic event impacted on her career.

A plane carrying her touring band, many members of which had played with McIntyre for years and were friends with the singer and her husband, crashed in a mountainous region near the California / Mexico border.

All on board perished in the crash including eight musicians and the two pilots.

McIntyre's next album release was dedicated to the deceased and it was called 'For My Broken Heart'.

All round entertainer, environmentalist, songwriter and milky bar kid lookalike John Denver was also a qualified pilot. Flying was one of the 'Leaving on a Jet Plane' composer's passions and he was qualified to fly various aircraft and experienced in different conditions.

However, in October 1997, the singer had just purchased a prototype Rutan LongEZ style experimental aircraft and was not yet used to the plane's controls which could have been the reason that it plunged into the Pacific Ocean with only Denver on-board. The pilot's head was so badly disfigured that only fingerprints identified the corpse as Henry John Deutschendorf aka John Denver. Although qualified, at the time of the incident, Denver's flying licence was not legitimate because appropriate insurances were not granted due to a previous drink driving conviction.

John Denver's squeaky clean image was not entirely accurate and an acrimonious divorce, drink and drug allegations tainted the positive persona. However, a couple of Grammy's, and Emmy award, various song writing and country awards as well as many pleasant, melodic songs remain to remind listeners of the musician's place in the pop / rock world.

In August 1999, ex-member of the Ozark Mountain Daredevils, Steve Canaday who was a tour manager and photographer was flying in a vintage aircraft with a friend when it hit the top of a house and crashed. Canaday was alive when the plane hit the ground but despite efforts to save him, the musician died shortly after.

By the age of 22, a young girl by the name Aaliyah had released three high selling albums, appeared in movies, modelled and her career was on the ascendance.
However, having just filmed a video shoot for her next single, the singer, record company personnel and crew were leaving the Bahamas on the last day of August 2001 in a small aircraft when it crashed shortly after take-off, killing all 9 on board.

The pilot was found to have cocaine in his bloodstream, did not have the appropriate certification for the flight, the plane was overloaded and had one passenger over the limit. All of these factors contributed to the accident.

Aaliyah achieved greater posthumous success and has been cited as an important link from traditional R&B to the more modern hip hop genre.

Three months later, a plane crashed just short of Zurich Airport killing three vocalists from the 'Eurodance' genre of pop.

Maria Serrano Serrano and Nathalie Van het Ende from the vocal group 'Passion Fruit' died along with former 'La Bouche' vocalist Melanie Thornton while Passion Fruit's third singer Debby St Maarten was seriously injured.

In addition to the deaths of musicians in fixed wing aircraft, a few have been killed in a mode of transport often used for delivering and extracting performers from certain external venues, examples of which can be seen in the movie 'Woodstock'.

An ex-musician had changed career but retained popularity until a helicopter crash ended it all.

American Jane Dornacker had written and sang with The Tubes, been a stand-up comedienne and was a traffic reporter for New York radio when the live broadcast she was giving from the air turned into a

'live' account of the death crash.
39 year old Dornacker died when the aircraft plunged into the Hudson River in October 1986.

Helicopter deaths also include Australian singer from the band 'Skyhooks' who became a popular television personality down under until the accident in 2001. Graeme Strachan, nicknamed 'Shirley' was 49 when the 'copter he was riding in crashed into a mountain.

In the same year, veteran tour promoter and entrepreneur behind San Francisco's Fillmore venue that showcased The Grateful Dead, Jefferson Airplane and Santana among many, Bill Graham was killed. The 60 year old catalyst for the burgeoning psychedelic scene in 1967 was still using his managerial skills when he and two colleagues died in a helicopter crash.

The final name on this tragic list of air accidents was a guitarist often quoted as one of the best modern blues players alongside Eric Clapton, Robert Cray, Buddy Guy and the deceased's brother Jimmie Vaughan.
35 year old Stevie Ray Vaughan was killed instantly when the helicopter taking him from an amphitheatre crashed into a hill during fog.

Drive

"Well the last thing I remember Doc, I started to swerve, and then I saw the Jag slide into the curve. I know I'll never forget that horrible sight, I guess I found out for myself that everyone was right. Won't come back from Dead Man's Curve" (xiii) - Jan and Dean

In contrast to the relatively lengthy list of well-known musicians' deaths as a result of air accidents, road accident fatalities of famous musicians are fewer but when lesser known acts are added, the number is quite significant.

One of the earliest rock'n'roll tragedies on the road occurred in 1960 in rural England and involved young American performers visiting the UK to build on their early popularity. Songwriter Sharon Sheeley, leather clad rocker Gene Vincent and singer/ pioneering guitarist Eddie Cochran were travelling in a taxi when it veered off the road with a punctured tyre and hit a lamp post.
The first two were badly injured in the accident but 21 year old Eddie Cochrane was killed. Sheeley was Cochrane's girlfriend and had co-written his hit 'Somethin Else' along with Eddie's brother (the song

was revamped and became a hit for the Sex Pistols). Cochran wrote with his manager Jerry Capehart, the much covered 'C'mon Everybody' and 'Summertime Blues' before the accident ended the potential of yet another young rising star.

Ironically, his last major seller was the posthumous release 'Three Steps to Heaven'.

A young Police Cadet removed Cochran's guitar from the scene of the crash and took it back to the Police station and reportedly played on it. Perhaps this gave Dave Dee the incentive to quit the Force and become a singer.

During the short tour, a young music fan, Mark Feld had carried Cochran's guitar case after a gig.

This teenager changed his name a few years later and made his musical journey through psychedelic tinged Tyrannosaurus Rex to become the Glam rock innovator and frontman of T Rex, Marc Bolan. Following a very successful few years in the early 1970's, especially in the UK with 'Get it On', 'Telegram Sam', 'We Love to Boogie', Jeepster', 'Hot Love' and many other infectious electric pop songs, as well as strong album sales, television and even a movie, Marc had retreated slightly from the limelight and settled with partner, singer Gloria Jones.

In September 1977, Jones was driving the pair home when the car went out of control and hit a tree, killing passenger Marc Bolan days short of his thirtieth birthday.

Johnny Kidd and the Pirates were a UK group from the late fifties into the sixties who dressed the part complete with eye patches and theatrical stage act. Musically their best known numbers were 'Shakin all Over' and 'Please don't Touch'.
Kidd was 30 years old when the car he was in as a passenger crashed killing the singer.

Cozy Powell was a drummer who, as a session player featured on most releases on Mickie Most's RAK label including records by Donovan, Suzi Quatro and Hot Chocolate as well as having hits such as 'Dance with the Devil' and 'The Man in Black' under his own name. Powell also toured as drummer with Jeff Beck, Rainbow, Whitesnake, Black Sabbath, Emerson Lake & *Powell,* and was working with Peter Green at the time of his death.
A keen petrolhead who had for a short time raced in the saloon car circuit in the UK, it is ironic that Powell died in a car crash in circumstances that were against all safety aspects of motoring.
On 5 April 1998, Cozy Powell was driving on a Motorway in poor weather conditions, he was well over the speed limit with alcohol content in his

bloodstream over the legal limit, the car had a slow puncture, Powell was not wearing a seatbelt and he was using a mobile 'phone at the time of the accident.

Another drummer had died in a Motorway crash almost 30 years previously along with the girlfriend of another of the band members. Martin Lamble was only 19 and had played on Fairport Convention's first three albums but his short career and life ended when the band's van crashed causing the deaths and injuries to the other occupants.

Also 19 at the time of his death was Californian born Adan Sanchez, a singer of Mexican descent whose father had been kidnapped and killed in Mexico when the boy was 8 years old. Having made a name for himself as a vocalist among the Mexican/ Americans, in 2004, Sanchez was touring in the area where his father perished when the car he was travelling in crashed, killing the young singer.

American heavy metal band Metallica was touring Europe to support the release of their third album but an incident in Sweden in 1986 almost halted the rise of the group.
The band's tour bus skidded and rolled over and

although most band members escaped unscathed, bassist Cliff Burton was trapped under the coach and died at the scene, aged 24. After considering their future, the remaining band members decided to carry on and Metallica became one of the biggest selling and popular bands in the genre.

Nicholas Dingley was a drummer known in the rock world as 'Razzle' who joined Finnish band 'Hanoi Rocks' in 1982.
However, before he tasted real success, Razzle was killed when as a passenger in the car being driven by Motley Crue singer Vince Neil, who was drunk, was involved in a collision with another vehicle. Neil survived as did the two seriously injured occupants of the other car but 24 year old Razzle died on the way to hospital.

There have been more deaths at the ominous number 27 years than any other age and those dying in car accidents include a few 27 year olds, many famous, some not so well known. However the age of 27 has taken on almost mystical perceptions in relation to musician's who play their final note or sing their final song as the curtain falls and their show ends.

Back in 1976, a Spanish singer by the name of Cecilia was killed along with one of her band members when the car they were travelling in returning from a performance, was in an accident on the way to Madrid.

Evangelina Sobredo Galanes had taken the stage name Cecelia from the Paul Simon song because the shortened version of her own name 'Eva' was already used by another vocalist. She was 27 years old when she died, one of a few musicians who became car crash victims at that age.

Rodrigo Bueno was the most popular singer of cuarteto music peculiar to Cordoba, Argentina and had become a local celebrity when the car he was driving hit a crash barrier, killing him and his passenger. This was in June 2000 and Bueno was 27 years of age.

Twenty years previously, 27 year old reggie artist Jacob Miller was killed in a car crash in his native Jamaica and another twenty years before that, R&B singer Jesse Belvin died along with his wife in a head on collision in Arkansas, he was also 27.
Another 27 year old was killed when he was thrown out of the rear doors of a van in Arkansas after the vehicle left the road. D.Boone (Dennes) had been co-founder, singer and guitarist with Californian punk outfit 'Minutemen'.

The final 27 year old musician killed in a car accident was American Chris Bell whose solo work and contributions to the band 'Big Star' in the seventies showed great promise, but two days after Christmas in 1978, his car hit a light pole, killing the singer, songwriter guitarist.

Austrian musicians are a rare entity in the world of pop / rock but Johan Holzel had a few hits, the best known internationally when he recorded under the name Falco, was 'Rock me Amadeus' in 1985.
Falco was driving in the Caribbean in February 1998, when a speeding bus hit his car and the singer was killed at the age of 40.

Other car deaths include one-time Byrd Clarence White who was struck by a drunk driver and died aged 29, Tommy Caldwell aged 30 from The Marshall Tucker Band, 37 year old 'Cat's in the Cradle' singer Harry Chapin, ex-Grateful Dead member Keith Godchaux aged 32, and 50 year old Dave Prater half of soul duo Sam and Dave.

R&B / rap trio TLC had four multi-platinum albums in their relatively short career which was ended when one of the members, Lisa 'Left Eye' Lopes was killed when driving in Honduras. Eerily, the 30 year old was being filmed at the time as part of a documentary and the footage caught the moment when her car veered off the road, throwing her out of the vehicle, to her death.

Before leaving the tragic circumstances of car crash victims, there is the case of the famous musician who did not die in a vehicle accident, but the conspiracy theorists pointed to evidence that he did.

The setting, late sixties UK, The Beatles had stopped touring, their manager Brian Epstein had died, there was disagreement between Paul and the others who should take over management.

Shock, horror, Beatle Paul killed in car accident cover up so that fans would not get distraught. There are messages contained in songs and if records are played backwards and / or slowed down, real fans will hear the news.

For those who don't follow, just look at the cover for Abbey Road where Paul is walking across the road leading with his right foot while the other three are left foot forward. Paul's feet are bare and he is wearing a grey mourning suit, RIP. John resplendent in white is obviously taking the role of religious officiator while dapper Ringo in black will act as undertaker and George walking behind the ghost of Paul is kitted out in denim gear, all set to be the gravedigger.

Some people started looking further into the possibility and invented further clues about Paul holding a cigarette, a bloodstain on the road, a police van in the background, a Beetle parked with wheels on the pavement and even the registration number of the Beetle which was LMW281F supposedly signified 'Linda McCartney Weeps' and 27 year old Paul would have been '28 if' he had lived.

The death conspiracy that became a series of exaggerated stories had to be silenced by a statement from the very much alive McCartney, but at least he did indeed get his Wings.

Motor Biking

"He rode into the night, accelerated his motorbike, I cried to him in fright, don't do it, don't do it" (xiv) - 'Terry' by Twinkle

The image of Peter Fonda and Dennis Hopper riding to the Easy Rider soundtrack, Prince in Purple Rain, Meatloaf's Bat out of Hell video, The Mods of Quadrophenia and Kris Kristofferson in A Star is Born; musicians and two wheels appear synonymous.
It is perhaps not surprising therefore that many who are attracted by the rock'n'roll lifestyle are also drawn to the freedom and excitement of motorbikes.
It is however surprising that there have been few musician fatalities as a result of motorcycle accidents.

It is also ominously strange that two were from the same band and occurred in almost the same location.

Duane Allman was a gifted guitarist, recognised for his bottleneck slide technique which featured on the first few releases by Southern rockers The Allman Brothers Band which he started along with brother Greg.
Duane's ability was picked up by Eric Clapton and the

pair collaborated on 'Layla and Other Assorted Love Songs' with Allman's guitar prominent on the much vaunted single 'Layla'. However, Duane Allman's potential ended on 29 October 1971 when he skidded his motorbike to avoid colliding with a truck and was thrown from the heavy Harley that then landed on him, trapping the musician and crushing him, leading to his death a few hours later in hospital.

Allman's accident occurred in Macon Georgia and just over one year later, Allman Brothers' Band bass player Berry Oakley was involved in a collision with a bus, just three blocks from where Duane's accident had occurred.
Oakley was also thrown from his motorcycle and struck his head causing the injuries that lead to his death a few hours later.

These connected motorcycle accidents were the highest profile in rock but a few other fatalities feature.

In 1966, Richard Farina had just published a book, 'Been Down so Long, Seems Like Up to Me' and released two albums of folk / protest songs with his wife Mimi, sister of Joan Baez. He left a party to celebrate his wife's 21st birthday to go for a ride as a passenger on a motorbike but the driver lost control on a bend and although he survived the crash, Richard Farina did not and died at the scene.

Greg Arama ex-bassist with American hard rockers Amboy Dukes was killed in a motorcycle accident in 1979 aged 29 as was American musician 34 year old Jimmy Spheeris and Buckaroos guitarist Don Rich, who was 32.

Pete De Freitas had joined Echo and the Bunnymen as drummer in 1980 just prior to the band's mainstream success in the UK and a modicum of recognition in the USA.
In 1989, returning from London to Liverpool, he was killed in a motorcycle accident at the age of 27.

Yet another musician on the '27' list died in 1973 and it is ironic that the musical career of Roger Lee Durham, as a singer and percussionist in the R&B/doo-wop group Bloodstone was interrupted by his stint as an airman in Vietnam, only to survive the war and die when he fell, not from a motorcycle, but in his case, from a horse.

The final death from two wheels was a freak accident on the island of Ibiza when legendary German born chanteuse Christa Paffgen fell from a bicycle after having a slight heart attack and struck her head on the ground and died later that day from a cerebral haemorrhage.

Known to the world of pop and rock by the singular name 'Nico', she had been a model, actress, released solo introverted material as well as cover versions and performed and recorded with The Velvet Underground.

Emerging from Andy Warhol's Factory, Nico was an enigmatic character and her image has been romanticised by nostalgia. In reality she had been a heroin addict for years but was fighting the addiction when the accident ended her life at the age of 49.

Wasted Time

"Why me, I need an answer, why me, I don't want this cancer, it's like I'm up against a wall, There's nothing that makes sense at all, why me?" (xv) - 'Why Me' vocal by Stephen Scott

The lives of many people are touched by cancer in one way or another and obviously musicians are no exception.

Having mentioned a few individuals from the popular music environment who have contracted the 'big C' but thankfully managed to overcome the symptoms, unfortunately there is a much longer list of those unfortunate enough to succumb to some form of the disease.

Despite having deep faith and deep pockets which allowed both a positive attitude and the best treatment available, George Harrison could not prevent the ravages of cancer spreading and ultimately ending his life at the age of 58.

Like many young men growing up in the 1960's Harrison was a smoker and the tobacco habit may have contributed to his eventual contracting of lung cancer in his fifties. A deeply spiritual person, George was a vegetarian for most of his adult life, kept himself fit and had interests in Formula 1 motor racing, movies (co-founder of Handmade Films) and he enjoyed his garden but there are also many references to drug taking with fellow musicians.

However, cancer is not discriminatory in who it can affect and in the case of the ex-Beatle it was first discovered in his throat but although treated in 1997 by early 2001 it had progressed to his lungs. In November of that year, the iconic musician was dead with the disease reportedly having also spread to his brain.

Although some cancers can be treated successfully and at the very least life expectancy may be prolonged for a time, George's chances were reduced as he had been weakened in an incident two years before his death.

An intruder had broken into the Harrison's home, Friar Park and attacked the man who had written 'Give me Love, give me Peace on Earth', inflicting a number of stab wounds, injuring a lung and causing a head wound. The violent intrusion could have been fatal had not Olivia Harrison rescued her husband by hitting the attacker with a poker and a lamp. However, in addition to the psychological trauma caused by this invasion, it certainly reduced the strength required to cope with the onslaught of cancer.

George Harrison joined the many individuals from the world of popular music whose contribution was cut short by cancer and proportionately it is still the biggest killer disease and as can be seen in the case of George Harrison can spread if not caught in time.

Another musician also died ostensibly from lung cancer although the disease had also spread to his brain. The Jamaican responsible for circulating and popularising Reggie music throughout the world in the 1970's is acknowledged to be Bob Marley. Along with his band The Wailers, Marley's ganga fuelled performances and recordings of 'No Woman No Cry', 'Buffalo Soldiers', 'I Shot the Sheriff', 'Redemption Song', 'Could You be Loved', 'Jamming' and numerous other rhythmic tracks introduced many westerners to Rastafarian images and sounds.

Having injured his toe playing football, Marley developed melanoma but did not seek treatment for the condition and as the disease spread he became weaker and it was too late for any treatment to be effective.

Bob Marley died in 1981 at the age of 36.

Most people nowadays are acutely aware that early identification of symptoms can increase chances of effective treatment but until recently ignorance regarding smoking habits, diet and exercise lead many to lead lifestyles that were detrimental to their health.

The mellow voice of crooner Nat King Cole soothed the ears of listeners with classic romance in such songs as 'Mona Lisa', 'Let There be Love' and 'When I Fall in Love'.

His baritone vocals were his trademark through the 1950's and into the 60's until his death in 1965 from lung cancer but Cole had begun his career years before as a jazz pianist and he worked his way from the clubs to become the first African American to have his own television show in the USA during the 1950's but throughout his career Cole had to fight against racism.

Unfortunately, his cancer was discovered too late to enable the singer to put up a similar fight against the disease. In fact, ironically and as a result of limited knowledge on the subject, Nat King Cole exacerbated the cancerous cells in his system whilst trying to cultivate his vocal style. A smoker of menthol cigarettes, which were thought to assist the texture of his voice, Cole smoked approximately 60 per day and chain smoked leading up to a performance.

Nat King Cole was 45 when lung cancer silenced the 'Unforgettable' singer.

Disco Queen Donna Summer epitomised the electronic dance sound of the late seventies with her co-written 'Love to Love you Baby', 'I Feel Love', 'Hot Stuff', her duet with Barbra Streisand 'No More Tears (enough is enough) and her danceable rendition of MacArthur Park'. Although output and sales diminished following this era, Summer continued to be an inspiration for other artists maintained a following and was still performing and recording up until her illness. Donna Summer was diagnosed with lung cancer and maintained that her condition was a result of inhaling particles following the 9/11 terrorist attack. She died from the symptoms in 2012 at the age of 63.

One of the inspirational figures from the rise of rhythm and blues music in the UK also became a victim of lung cancer.
Paris born Alexis Korner had co-founded 'Blues Incorporated' in 1961 (along with Cyril Davies) which was the training ground and springboard to success for members of The Rolling Stones and Cream to name but two. Korner had a stint in broadcasting and then joined forces with Danish musician Peter Thorup and the pair formed the successful ensemble Collective Consciousness Society which was recognised in the shortened version CCS as producers of hits 'Tap Turns on the Water', 'Whole Lotta Love' and 'Walkin'.
Korner passed away in 1984 at the age of 55.

Lee Brilleaux, frontman and singer of archetypal pub rockers 'Dr. Feelgood' had a sense of humour, a dapper appearance and was opinionated. In addition, the band were tight, the songs catchy and it is surprising that they never rose above the level of fame they achieved. Brilleaux was actually born in South Africa and the 'Back in the Night' singer and harmonica player gigged frequently but his untimely death from non-Hodgkin's lymphoma at the age of 41 ended his potential.

This same form of cancer was responsible for the death of guitarist Sterling Morrison who, along with John Cale and Lou Reed was a founding member of the influential 'Velvet Underground'.
Morrison had left the band in the early 1970's and returned to academia, earning a Ph.D before changing course again and becoming a tugboat captain whilst occasionally playing with ex members from the 'Velvets'.

One singer who was relatively unknown outside her local area of Washington DC, until she died and her music was posthumously recognised was Eva Cassidy. A singer who sang songs because she liked them and did not fit neatly into any genre had only released one studio album in 1992 but had a backlog of unfinished tracks recorded by 1996, when she tragically passed away from cancer.

Cassidy was only 33 and could have remained in obscurity had her version of 'Over the Rainbow' not been championed by BBC Radio DJ Terry Wogan who played it frequently gathering positive feedback and

generating interest in Eva's story and a ready-made
market for more material. Posthumous releases gave
Eva Cassidy the success she had not experienced in
her short life and her music featured in the charts
across the world from Australia to Scandinavia and
even her native USA eventually caught on.

Having had a melanoma removed from her back, it
was thought that Eva was clear of the disease but
tragically it had spread to her lungs and throughout
her body including bones and did not respond to
aggressive treatment.

Another American singer died in his thirties of
untreatable cancer.

Steve Goodman was a singer / songwriter from
Chicago who was a compatriot of John Prine and had
brief success in the 1970's in the US.

Goodman contracted leukemia and ever the
humourist, referred to himself as 'cool hand leuk'
knowing his condition was terminal and he passed
away in 1984, aged 36.

Steve Goodman left a legacy of over a dozen albums
but is most identifiable with the song he wrote about
a train, which has become a standard in many folk
singers repertoires. 'City of New Orleans' has been
covered by many artists including Willie Nelson, John
Denver, Johnny Cash and Arlo Guthrie and has also
been recorded in many other languages.

Singer/ guitarist Charlie Foxx who performed with his sister Inez on lead vocals, passed away in 1998 at the age of 58 as a result of leukemia.

Leukemia also ended the life of a singer songwriter with a strange name, known as a one hit wonder, but who also wrote songs that became country hits for other artists, notably The Oak Ridge Boys and Alabama.

Randy Vanwarmer was 48 when he succumbed to the disease and the ballad 'Just When I Needed You Most' was his best known work. With a keen interest in things beyond the earth's atmosphere, Vanwarmer had arranged for parts of his remains to be sent into space.

Over in the UK during the seventies, David Bowie progressed from 'ground control to Major Tom' through 'Starman' and 'Ziggy Stardust' phases, and his 'Spider from Mars' guitarist was never far from his side or his sound.
Mick Ronson released half a dozen solo albums, was a member of Bob Dylan's Rolling Thunder Review, recorded with artists as diverse as David Cassidy and John Mellancamp but was best known for his collaborations with Mott the Hoople's Ian Hunter and Bowie. Respected and acknowledged as an electric guitarist, Ronson was classically trained in a number of instruments but his abilities were unable to be

showcased beyond 1993 when Mick Ronson died from liver cancer at the age of 45.

Cypriot born Andonis Michaelides came to prominence as a musician in the era of art / new wave bands with his unique sounding fretless bass. A member of the enigmatic ethereal sounding 'Japan' he was recognised by his stage name Mick Karn. Japan had some commercial success as well as a cult following in, of all places, Japan.
Karn passed away from cancer in early 2011 at the age of 52.

Born on the Isle of Man in December 1949, by the summer of 1969 he was at number 2 in the UK charts (number 1 in New Zealand and South Africa) with his first solo single.
Not yet 20 years old, Robin Gibb had already experienced success in Australia and had hit albums and singles, including chart toppers with his brothers Barry and Maurice in the Bee Gees. Regrouping in 1970, the siblings went on to become one of the most successful writing teams and recording artists in the history of music.
Robin's faltering, emotional vocal style graced numerous songs across genres and over the decades until May 2012 when the teetotaling vegan succumbed to colorectal cancer at the age of 62.

Another singer from a harmonious sibling band, Carl Wilson was the youngest of the three Wilson brothers in the American musical institution that was The Beach Boys.

Carl's contribution cannot be underestimated especially as his brothers' reliability was uncertain and he toured with the band even while undergoing chemotherapy for cancer. Classic Beach Boy songs 'God Only Knows', 'Good Vibrations', 'I Can Hear Music', 'Darlin' and 'Wild Honey' all feature Carl on lead vocal but in 1998, Wilson's dulcet tones ceased when lung cancer halted his breath at the age of 51.

Another Carl, in this case Wayne had first experienced success as one of the lead singers along with Roy Wood in The Move and then as the vocalist behind the UK TV theme to 'New Faces' and a few acting and voiceover roles.

In 2000 when The Hollies original vocalist Allan Clarke retired from the music business, Wayne fronted this version of the Hollies but his stint only lasted four years as Carl Wayne contracted cancer of the oesophagus and passed away aged 61.

Drummer Randy Castillo got his break playing along with Lita Ford and then occupied the drumstool in Ozzy Osbourne's band for 10 years before beginning a brief stint with Motley Crue. Having survived a ruptured duodenal ulcer, Castillo was diagnosed with squamous cell carcinoma and died at the age of 51.

Session drummer Ian Wallace played with many of rock's elite including Bob Dylan, Peter Frampton and most of West Coast American musicians such as members of The Eagles, Fleetwood Mac, Traveling Wilburys, CSN and Jackson Browne. He had also briefly been in the Bonzo Dog Band but came to prominence in the progressive outfit King Crimson. Wallace died from oesophageal cancer at the age of 60 in 2006.

Another drummer had died aged 60 the previous year, in this case from stomach cancer. Also a singer who had a couple of solo hits, a songwriter (co-composer of 'Love Will Keep Us Alive' performed by The Eagles as an example) and collaborator with rock's 'A listers' George Harrison, Eric Clapton and Carlos Santana to name only three.
Jim Capaldi was also a member of the highly influential band 'Traffic' and co-wrote their hit single 'Paper Sun' among many other compositions. Having married a Brazilian and moved to that country, Jim Capaldi became involved in environmental issues and charities as well as working with local musicians until his demise.

Another 1960's act was The Tremeloes whose rhythm guitarist Alan Blakeley died from cancer aged 54 in 1996.

Two years later, Roger Christian from the eponymous group passed away at 48 from a brain tumour.

Although all deaths resulting from a wasting disease are tragic, younger victims tend to receive more sympathy but in the case of one particular singer who passed away at the age of 31, there was also admiration for her brave approach to the illness. Minnie Riperton had been in a couple of groups, sang backing vocals on a couple of hits and released a solo album by 1970 when she semi-retired to have a family. Persuaded back into the studio, her next album release 'Perfect Angel', in 1974 contained a single that would catapult the remarkable ranged vocalist as high as her singing voice.

'Lovin You' was a major seller in more than 20 countries and introduced Riperton to new audiences who marvelled at her vocal prowess. With an ability to sing more than five octaves, she could even enunciate in the highest 'whistle register' but irrespective of this talent, sales of her next three albums failed to match Perfect Angel.

In 1976, Riperton was diagnosed with breast cancer and despite having a mastectomy the disease spread to her lymph glands and she was given the news it was terminal.

Minnie Riperton continued recording and singing live despite this prognosis and became the national spokeswoman for the American Cancer Society. However, her condition deteriorated and she was hospitalised on 10 July 1979 where she died 2 days later. Having crammed so much into 31 years, Minnie Riperton had much more to offer but it was not to be.

Breast cancer also ended the life of Linda McCartney, who was initially a rock photographer until husband Paul encouraged her to play keyboards and sing backing in his post-Beatle band 'Wings'. Linda was known in her own right as an activist against cruelty to animals and one of the most famous vegetarians, she launched her own range of non-meat foods and numerous cook books.

Linda McCartney was diagnosed with cancer in 1995 but it spread rapidly and she died within three years, aged 56.

Sixties singing icon Mary Isobel Catherine Bernadette O'Brien contracted breast cancer in 1994 and bowed out five years later at the age of 59.

Known to the public as the panda eyed peroxide bee-hived with hand gesturing emotional voiced Dusty Springfield, she began her musical career along with her brother in the folk trio The Springfields. Early hits included 'Silver Threads and Golden Needles' and 'Island of Dreams' but by the middle of the decade she was a solo star with 'I Only Wanna Be With You', 'Son of a Preacher Man', 'You Don't Have to Say You Love Me', 'I Just Don't Know What to do With Myself' and many more.

Her musical pedigree was strengthened with the critically acclaimed 1969 release 'Dusty in Memphis' and she found another audience in the 1980's resulting from her successful collaborations with the Pet Shop Boys.

However, away from the public glare, Dusty's private life was not so positive. She suffered from depression, was subject to self-harming incidents, became dependent on alcohol / pills and had a number of relationships with women whilst trying to keep her private life private. One partner, American singer Norma Tanega (who had a hit with the bizarrely titled 'Walking My Cat Named Dog') was her companion for a few years during the height of her successes but later liaisons were anything but stable.

In the fickle world of showbiz, Dusty's legacy is there for all to hear but she is yet another example of a singer who never quite achieved or was recognised for her potential.

Cancer was also the cause of death of respected guitarist Bert Jansch who lost his fight in 2011 at the age of 67.

Although his popularity and talent did not cross into major record sales, Jansch's musicianship was not confined to the folk world where he was mentioned in legendary terms but rock artists from Neil Young to Johnny Marr counted him as an influence. As a member of Pentangle, Scottish born Bert Jansch had experienced the 'pop' scene but was more at home with an acoustic guitar and an appreciative audience irrespective of folk club or rock festival setting.

Another Scot, Graeme Kelling, guitarist from the band
Deacon Blue, succumbed to pancreatic cancer after a
four year battle and Jon Lord, best known as
keyboardist with Deep Purple also lost his battle with
pancreatic cancer and passed away in July 2012.
Lord was aged 71 and Kelling only 47 when he died in
2004.

Also passing away at the age of 47 after battling
cancer for a few years, was Adam Yauch, onetime
Beastie Boy.
Yauch's stage persona as a rapper and controversial
musician was at odds with his serious activism in
support of feminism, gay rights and the cause of
Tibetan independence.
He suffered from salivary gland cancer which ended
his life in May 2012.

Another musician with a bit of a reputation was
Arthur Lee, writer, singer, guitarist and vocalist from
the psychedelic era American band 'Love'.
Lee was at the helm for the band's best known album
'Forever Changes' in 1967, which he would recreate in
its entirety thirty-five years later in concert.
Having collaborated with Jimi Hendrix and followed
his 'Love' releases with a few solo albums, many
thought his potential would again be realised but all
stopped in 1996 when he was given a 12 year jail
sentence for a firearms offence. Released early and
with much to prove, he surrounded himself with

younger musicians and toured successfully as Love with Arthur Lee.

Unfortunately the touring stopped in 2006 when, despite aggressive treatment for acute myeloid leukemia, Arthur Lee died at the age of 61.

The following year singer songwriter Dan Fogelberg succumbed to prostate cancer, aged 56. Fogelberg had a string of top 50 albums in his native US and a number in Canada with his best known being 'Souvenirs' and the single 'Longer'

Dee Murray was a bass player who made his name as a member of Elton John's band for years and also played with the Spencer Davis Group and Procul Harum but his time was limited as he fought skin cancer and passed away from a stroke in 1992 when he was 45.

Bruce Springsteen's E Street organist / accordionist for more than 30 years, Danny Federici, had a 3 year battle with melanoma that he lost in 2008, aged 58.

2008 was also the year another influential keyboard player passed away as a result of cancer. 65 year old Richard Wright whose improvisational skills guided Pink Floyd towards the epic 'Dark Side Of the Moon' for which he composed 'Us and Them' and the unique 'Great Gig in the Sky'.

The quietest member of the innovative foursome, Wright's contribution was often understated but despite very public estrangements, he joined his 'Wish you were Here' band mates for the finale of Live 8 three years prior to his death, allowing a new generation to get a flavour of one of the best-selling bands of all time.

Wright's one time Pink Floyd colleague and co-founder Syd Barret had a troubled life following the band's initial success in 1967.
While the musical careers of Richard Wright, Roger Waters, Nick Mason and David Gilmour ascended beyond expectation, Barrett's condition and mental health descended the depths and the once enigmatic innovator became reclusive and distant from the world of rock music.
There was much speculation as to the cause of his irrational behaviour and it may have been a deep routed condition which was exacerbated by his experimentation with hallucinogenic drugs, but his musical output 'The Madcap Laughs' was recorded under trying circumstances and was only completed because of the perseverance of Barrett's musician friends.
He may well have been the 'Crazy Diamond' urged by his ex-colleagues to 'Shine On' but Syd Barrett remained in the shadows dogged by psychological difficulties and diabetes, eventually succumbing to pancreatic cancer in 2006 at the age of 60 and although his existence had been supported by

royalties from 'Floyd's early work, his actual input to the world of music since 1968 was minimal.

Another innovator from mid-1960's who created music that was not altogether commercial but unquestionably influential had died three years previously at the age of 52.
Frank Zappa passed away in 2003 having battled prostate cancer for three years. Zappa released more than 60 albums and in addition, there have been numerous compilations and posthumous releases. Not easy to pigeonhole, Frank Zappa's music is often referred to as avant-garde and throughout his career he experimented with sounds from full orchestration to his use of the 'synclavier' (an early synthesiser). He achieved some commercial success but became as well known for his outspoken views as his music, even testifying before a US Senate Committee against censorship and for artistic freedom and was acknowledged as cultural attaché to Czechoslovakia. Zappa suffered from a few ailments as a child, was seriously injured in the 1970's when he was pushed offstage into an orchestra pit and had not reached 50 when he was diagnosed with terminal cancer.

The year after Zappa's death, 55 year old Ramones' guitarist Johnny, passed away from prostate cancer following a five year fight against the condition. Fellow Ramones, singer and songwriter Joey, had previously battled against the cancer lymphoma for seven years, losing in 2001 at the age of 49.

Drummer Bruce Garry had played with The Knack (My Sharona) but he died at the same age 55, as Johnny Ramone and from the same disease, lymphoma as Joey Ramone.

Another drummer, Paul Caravello, assumed the name Eric Carr and adopted the stage persona as 'The Fox' when he joined the heavily made up American 'glam – rock' band 'Kiss' in 1980.
Caravello remained popular with 'Kiss' followers when the band came out from behind their stage make up and revealed themselves and the drummer's passing in 1991, at the age of 41 from a brain haemorrhage following an aneurysm brought on by aggressive treatment for heart cancer, was a shock for many fans.

Back in the seventies, the easy listening melodic sound of the group 'Bread' graced the airwaves but in 2005, two members of the band guitarist Jimmy Griffin and drummer Mike Botts died from cancer. They were both 61 years old.

Also in the seventies the glam image was in full swing in the UK and one of the groups at the forefront of this was The Sweet. Drummer Mick Tucker died from leukemia in 2002 at the age of 54.

Contemporaries of Sweet were The New Seekers which was a group formed by Keith Potger who had been a member of the original 'Seekers' and intended that the 'new' version would continue with the melodic and harmony pop sound which would appeal to the same audience.

The idea certainly worked and the sing-along 'I'd Like to Teach the World to Sing' gave The New Seekers global recognition. Alternating between two female lead vocalists as well as showcasing the three male members vocal talents, the group's clean cut image and catchy songs proved popular for the first half of the 1970's after which there were various personnel changes and attempted solo careers.

Singer / guitarist Peter Doyle had already tasted chart success in his native Australia prior to joining Eve Graham, Lyn Paul, Marty Christian and Paul Layton in the most popular New Seekers' line-up.

Doyle returned to Australia and died from throat cancer aged 52, in 2001.

Also in 2001, two-thirds of the band who performed 'Resurrection Shuffle', keyboard player Tony Ashton and bass player Kim Gardner, both succumbed to cancer in their early fifties.

Songwriter and half of the Duo Ashford and Simpson, Nick Ashford passed away from throat cancer in 2011.

A friend of Ashford's wife Valerie Simpson was Gwen Guthrie and the pair had occasionally sung together. Guthrie's biggest hit was 'Ain't Nothing Going on but the Rent' in 1986 and she also had some success as a songwriter but passed away in 1999 from uterine cancer, aged 48.

Unfortunately, and as expected, the number of cancer victims among musicians mirrors the proportion of those not involved in the industry and although there can be miraculous recoveries in some cases, there are also examples where the disease can spread aggressively.

Along with her sisters, June Pointer had enjoyed the heights of 'pop' stardom across many genres during the 1970's and 80's. She was a member during the Pointer Sisters biggest successes and had minor hits as a solo artist. June was more rebellious than her siblings, posed for Playboy magazine and had alcohol and drug issues.
Diagnosed with cancer early in 2006 when she was admitted to hospital with a stroke, the disease rapidly

spread from her breast, liver, colon and bones and she died within a couple of months of diagnosis, aged 52.

Marion Ryan was a popular singer in the UK in the fifties featuring more as a television vocalist than in the charts but the Ryan name did chart when twin sons Paul and Barry came to prominence in the mid-1960's.

Following early duets, Paul concentrated on writing giving brother Barry major success with 'Eloise' and a string of other 'melodramatic' hits particularly in Germany. He also composed 'I will Drink the Wine' which became a standard for Frank Sinatra and released his own album 'Scorpio Rising' but passed away from cancer in 1992 at the age of 44.

One of the most sarcastic, sardonic and even ironic lyricists of the rock era was Warren Zevon. The American pianist, guitarist and vocalist was on the verge of mainstream success for years but never quite made the big time although he was appreciated in the US. However, if it could be said that he had a cult following, it was a big cult. Zevon played in the Everly Brother's back-up band, was championed by Jackson Browne, had a number of his songs covered by Linda Ronstadt and could count on the cream of rock players to help out on his albums.

Having burned the candle at both ends for much of his career, Warren Zevon was enjoying a healthy lifestyle and renewed success in his early fifties when he was diagnosed with an inoperable form of lung cancer. With limited time and ailing health, the composer of 'I'll Sleep When I'm Dead' recorded a final set of songs on CD with the process being filmed for DVD release and with Bruce Springsteen, Don Henley, Joe Walsh, Billy Bob Thornton and others helping out, the project was a success both musically and from the documentary perspective of following the deterioration of the physical body while the talented mind continues to operate.

Warren Zevon stopped breathing at the age of 56 in September 2003 and three months later his final opus, The Wind was certified gold.

Levon Helm was 71 when he succumbed to cancer in 2012.

He was one of the few rock drummers who also performed lead vocals whilst drumming (Phil Collins, Don Henley, Karen Carpenter, Dave Grohl, Sheila E all played percussion and sang, but Helm was at the helm).

Levon was the only American in The Band, the others being from Canada and his Arkansas drawl was prominent on many numbers such as 'The Night They Drove old Dixie Down', 'Up on Cripple Creek' and 'The Weight'. He was also a successful movie actor, fronted his own band and collaborated with many other musicians across musical genres.

The final icon to be mentioned on the list of musicians who died from cancer, had an extraordinary life which ended in 1963 prior to the pop / rock boom, but the influence of this 142cm tall French singer is still apparent today.

Edith Piaf had been given the stage name 'little sparrow' and the diminutive singer's strong voice and choice of emotionally tinged songs helped her reputation and took her to the top in France throughout the war years and beyond.
Classic renditions of songs from her repertoire such as 'Non, je ne Regrette Rien' and 'La Vie en Rose' spread far beyond the Gallic border and featured in contemporary movies as does the biography of the singer herself, and modern artists such as Martha Wainwright have performed tributes to the French chanteuse.
By the time of her death from liver cancer at the age of 47, Edith Piaf had led a life impacted by tragedy.
Piaf's life story contains some speculation due to conflicting reports but dramatic highlights indicate that she was abandoned as a child and cared for, for a time by prostitutes, she herself gave birth at the age of seventeen but the child died two years later. She was once charged as an accessory to murder, accused of being a Nazi collaborator during World War 2, her lover was killed in a plane crash and she was involved in a number of car crashes, sustaining serious injuries and subsequently becoming to an extent alcohol and

drug dependent.

An alternative slant on her life suggests that she may have been working for the French Resistance and despite failed relationships Edith Piaf achieved star status in the USA and became the major French celebrity during her life.

Anyone Who Had A Heart

"Once I had a love and it was a gas, soon turned out had a heart of glass……   once I had a love and it was a gas, soon turned out to be a pain in the ass" (xvi)   'Heart of Glass' by Blondie

The heart is the organ of the body that has assumed romantic connotations and is often used in song lyrics to portray love or in the case of heartache or broken heart, the end of affection. Less metaphorical are the terms heart attack and heart failure but unfortunately in many cases these can refer to musicians rather than their lyrics.

The introduction to this journey through the connections, coincidences and similarities in musicians' lives and deaths introduced the reader to Harry Nilsson.

The singer and composer's life had the highs of success, Grammy wins and the acclaim of fellow musicians as well as the public. Nilsson's lows, however, took their toll, from the abandonment by his father, deaths of close friends, overindulgence in alcohol, a couple of broken marriages and ill health.

In 1993 he had a massive heart attack and a year later died from heart failure at the age of 52.

Some people have heart complaints and perhaps their life expectancy is expected to be reduced but in certain cases, lifestyle can exacerbate the problem. In the case of some musicians who left the stage early due to failed hearts, it is difficult to determine whether overindulgence in certain behaviours, specifically illegal drug consumption, was the real cause of death.

While still at school, a promoter heard Florence Ballard singing and asked if she knew other singers. Ballard called friend Mary Wilson who brought school friend Diana Ross along and the Supremes were born. Beginning with the 1964 number 1 'Where Did our Love Go', the girls went on to have further success with 'Baby Love', 'Stop in the Name of Love', 'You Can't Hurry Love' and many more but despite the recurring use of the word love in many of their songs, there was no love lost between Florence and label Boss Berry Gordy.
He had been pushing Diana Ross to the front of the trio, changed the name to The Supremes with Diana Ross and eventually fired Ballard from the group. She became depressed, turned to alcohol and tragically died in poverty at the age of 32 from cardiac arrest while diva Diana became a superstar.

Ellen Naomi Cohen was known in the music world as Cass Elliot and her group name, Mama Cass from the Mamas and Papas in which she shared vocals with 'friend' Denny Doherty, John Phillips and his then wife Michelle.

Cass passed away in Harry Nilsson's London flat also at the age of 32 and left as a legacy, the smooth vocal sound of 'California Dreaming', Monday Monday' and 'Dream a Little Dream of me' as well as a reputation among the 'hippie culture' of the time as a fun loving girl with a sense of humour. Cass Elliot always had a weight problem and this coupled with drug intake no doubt contributed to her death from heart failure.

Papa John Phillips also died of heart failure having lived double the time that Cass had which is surprising due to his legendary consumption of illegal substances. Nevertheless, the main songwriter from the harmonising foursome lasted until 2001 when his heart gave out at the age of 65.

Another singer who died young, a few days after turning 30 in 1988, reportedly from a heart complaint, was Andy Gibb. Never officially a Bee Gee, the youngest of the Gibb brothers had US number ones with his first three single releases and was a popular entertainer in the late 1970's. Pressures, drug problems and bankruptcy gave Gibb bad press but he attempted to clean up his act and his outlook was more positive when the young vocalist died suddenly and was found to have suffered from inflammation of the heart, myocarditis supposedly exacerbated by previous cocaine use.

One year older at 31, blues harmonica player, musical and business partner of Alexis Korner in Blues Incorporated and the club scene that spawned the London R&B sound, Cyril Davies did not live to see or hear the careers of Charlie Watts, Ginger Baker, Rod Stewart or Long John Baldry, with whom he played, take off.

He died in 1964, not from leukemia as has been suggested, but from endocarditis.

Scottish rocker Alex Harvey showed his humour by prefixing his eponymous band with a superlative adjective and we were treated to the Sensational Alex Harvey Band.

SAHB's act was humorous, theatrical, musical and entertaining. Songs were sung, shouted and growled with lyrics about venereal disease to gang bangs and anything in between. Album sales were reasonable in the UK but moderate elsewhere and the band's token big hit single was a remake of the Tom Jones' standard 'Delilah'.

However, SAHB's live shows were an experience which unfortunately ended in 1976, were briefly reprised in 1978 but when 46 year old Alex suffered a fatal heart attack in 1982, the 'sensational' show was over.

56 year old bass player and emotive vocalist with one time Bob Dylan's backing group and influential band, named The Band, Rick Danko died from heart failure caused by drug taking.

57 year old bass player with The Who had a similar cause of death.   John Entwhistle aka The Ox, Boris the Spider was the unassuming character in the otherwise gregarious foursome that progressed from The High Numbers to become global sensation that was The Who. Moon's arms flailed about with his overt drumming style, Townsend's arms produced the windmill motion as he struck the power chords and Daltrey's arms controlled the swinging microphone as he swirled the lengthy cable but when it came to the bass player, Entwhistle's arms barely moved but his fingers were the opposite of his static pose as they walked all over the frets and plucked away in his unique style reminiscent of lead guitar playing.   Often topping polls as the best rock bass player, John died of a heart attack in 2002.

Having lived the rock and roll lifestyle for most of his life, Englishman Entwhistle exited in typical rock fashion, on the eve of a reunion gig, in a Las Vegas hotel bed with a stripper / groupie having consumed cocaine.

58 year old talented axeman Gary Moore also died from a heart attack in a foreign hotel room, but in different circumstances.

The Belfast born session guitarist, member of Thin Lizzy and solo blues player extraordinaire was in Spain on holiday with his family in 2011, when he passed away. Having released a score of solo albums, his final output 'Bad for you Baby' was advisably prophetic as Moore died following consumption of a vast amount of alcohol.

Whether a musician or not, excess partaking of uppers, downers or room spin around us, puts strain on the vital organs and they, unlike the musical organs cannot be repaired by a retune.

In the case of Turkish born John Mellor, who died at the age of 50 due to a congenital heart disease, it is was non diagnosis rather than over indulgence that was the cause.
However, the lifestyle of a man who supposedly ran the Paris marathon at the age of 30, having reportedly drunk 10 pints the night before, was not without rock and roll cliché.

Better known in musical circles as Joe Strummer, the singer / guitarist contributed songs to films, was a broadcaster, was a Mescalero and for 10 years an outspoken, social commentator and angry member of one of the best bands to come out of the punk era, The Clash.
He certainly 'Rocked the Casbah' and made sure we all

knew that 'London's Calling' but Strummer's energetic live performances epitomised the image of UK youth in the early 1980's and did not hint at any underlying cardiology problem.

A congenital heart defect was also the cause of death of 33 year old singer Stephen Gately. The Irishman rose to fame as a member of one of the most popular 'Boy bands' during the 90's in the UK and Ireland. Gately shared lead vocals with Ronan Keating and following the initial break-up of the group had a brief successful solo career. With much of his admiration coming from young female fans, it was a shock to some when he came out openly as gay but his honesty earned the praise of many and a reunion of Boyzone maintained Gately's and the rest of the group's popularity. Young fans did however, have to deal with the tragic death of one of their idols when a pulmonary oedema caused the early demise of the singer.

Only 34 years old, Lowell George had collapsed and died of heart failure in 1979. George was a respected slide guitarist, songwriter and one time member of Frank Zappa's Mothers of Invention. He rose to fame and acclaim in his native US as founding member of 'Little Feat' and his co-written laid back soft rock numbers 'Dixie Chicken', 'Willin' and 'Rock & Roll Doctor' are still given regular airplay.

It would not be overstating to point out that Lowell George's heart suffered the strain of substance intake.

Similarly, another American guitar legend was as famous and infamous for his extended live show playing, guesting on other artist's recordings and consumption of hallucinogenics and more.

The fans were called 'Dead Heads' but head dead Jerry Garcia was only 53 when he succumbed to the combined rock and roll excesses and his heart gave out in August 1995.

The third in this trio of American exponents of electric guitar was fittingly christened Johnny 'Guitar' Watson'.

John Watson was born in 1935 and less than 20 years later released the record 'Space Guitar' which reputedly featured the first use of feedback and reverb. He wrote the oft covered 'Gangster of Love' and had a number of minor hits and continued to tour right up to the time of his death in 1996 at the age of 61 when performing at a gig in Japan, J 'Guitar' W collapsed whilst playing a lead break and is said to have quoted the name of his most successful album as the cardiac arrest ended his solo, 'Ain't That a Bitch'.

Two lead singers from early 70's UK Glam rock bands suffered illnesses and died from heart attacks in their fifties.

'Blockbuster', 'Ballroom Blitz', 'Fox on the Run' and 'Love is Like Oxygen' were hits for the flamboyant 'Sweet' fronted by blond Brian Connelly. When the band broke up Connelly's health deteriorated as his alcohol dependency increased.
He had a few heart attacks, liver and renal failure before his final cardiac arrest in 1997 at 51 years of age.
Contemporary Les Gray was vocalist for the rock and roll pastiche outfit 'Mud' best known for the catchy dance number 'Tiger Feet' and the Elvis Pressley festive impersonation that is 'Lonely This Christmas'. When Mud disbanded in 1980, bassist Ray Stiles joined The Hollies, guitarist Rob Davis wrote hits for Kylie Minogue among others while the other two members kept a low profile. Drummer Dave Mount died in 2006, two years after singer Les Gray had passed away from a heart attack whilst fighting throat cancer.

Vying for positions in the charts with Mud and Sweet in the early seventies was the Geordie folk / pop sound of Lindisfarne. Their principal songwriter and vocalist who went on to have a couple of popular solo albums was Alan Hull. The writer of 'Lady Eleanor',

'We can Swing Together' and 'Run for Home' died from a heart thrombosis aged 50 in 1995.

In 1973 while these bands were beginning to get recognised, a singer who had begun to scale the heights of popularity 15 years previously passed away. Bobby Darin' rendition of 'Mack the Knife' co-written breakthrough 'Splish Splash' and self-penned chart topper 'Dream Lover' had made the young American a favourite of the late fifties record buying public. However, his health was always suspect and having battled with rheumatic fever since childhood, he died aged 37 following a heart operation.

In 1965 the American boogie / blues band Canned Heat was formed and a version still plays more than 45 years later. However, the original vocalists did not last the pace with Al Wilson's suicide in 1970 and the death of big Bob 'the bear' Hite, eleven years later at the age of 38 from a heart attack.

One year older at 39, Van McCoy of the 1975 dance favourite 'The Hustle' fame had a fatal heart attack four years later.

Ian Stewart was a boogie-woogie pianist and founder member of the Rolling Stones. Because his image didn't fit the band he was 'demoted' to road manager

and occasional piano player. Examples of Stewart's keyboard skills can be heard on 'Honky Tonk Women', Let it Bleed' and 'Brown Sugar' as well as Led Zeppelin's 'Rock and Roll' on which he featured.
In 1985, the 47 year old Scot had difficulty breathing, went to have the problem checked out but had a fatal heart attack in the waiting room.

Bryan MacLean was a singer / songwriter who played in LA's legendary 'Troubadour' club in the mid-sixties, was friendly and worked with The Byrds and failed to become a Monkee. However, his 'on the fringes' of the music scene materialised into something more when he teamed up with Arthur Lee in the ground breaking band 'Love'.
The group's output has been recognised years later as innovative and their album 'Forever Changes' featuring MacLean's opening track 'Alone Again Or' has garnered a reputation as a classic.
After the break-up of 'Love' Bryan MacLean released some Christian material and ironically died at the age of 52, from a heart attack on Christmas Day 1998.

On Christmas Day 1985, the writer, bass player and lead singer with the popular rock band Thin Lizzy collapsed due to persistent drug and alcohol consumption. Ten days later 36 year old Phil Lynott died from heart failure, pneumonia and septicaemia. Although brought up in Ireland, Lynott was actually born in England. He fronted the band from initial breakthrough with a rocked up version of the traditional song 'Whiskey in the Jar' through 'The Boys are Back in Town' and albums 'Jailbreak' and 'Chinatown' as well as solo and collaborative success. However, he had a penchant for drink and drugs that impacted on his performance and ended his promising career and life prematurely.

Tim Rose died aged 62 from a heart attack during an operation in 2002. The American singer was better known in Europe and after splitting from The Big Three which featured Cass Elliot prior to becoming Mama Cass, Rose became a solo artist.
Although he never had major success, he was responsible for bring to prominence the much covered songs 'Hey Joe' and 'Morning Dew', neither of which he actually wrote but claimed credit.

Rose had battled with alcoholism which aggravated health problems as did another American singer / songwriter Gene Clark.

Clark had been a member of the original Byrds and was first to capitalise on song writing royalties from the early days when the group mostly recorded Bob Dylan material or shared co-writing credit. Of the many songs he composed, Clark wrote 'I'll Feel a Whole Lot Better' which gave him a second financial return years later when Tom Petty recorded a version. Ironically at the time Clark's post Byrds career was at a low point and the payback enabled him to go back on the juice which exacerbated an already serious stomach problem.   Ill health continued and at the age of 46 Gene Clark died from a heart attack in 1991.

Another American singer called Gene passed away as a result of heart problems.

Gene Pitney was known for his melodramatic vocals on such 60's hits as '24 hours from Tulsa', 'Backstage', 'I'm Gonna be Strong' and 'Something's Gotten Hold of my Heart' but he was also a songwriter and was responsible for 'Rubber Ball' a hit for Bobby Vee, 'Hello, Mary Lou' for Ricky Nelson and The Crystals 'He's a Rebel'.
Pitney was 66 when he was found dead in a hotel room in Wales, following a concert, the cause of death being atherosclerosis.

The same condition caused the death at the same age of one-time teen heartthrob Davy Jones, the diminutive singer from the Monkees.
The ex-trainee jockey and actor still pursued his interest in horses and had just completed a ride in February 2012 when he had a severe heart attack.

Also a singing star in the sixties, was Billy Fury, who although never having a number one record, did have 24 hits and appeared in the rock 'n roll film 'That'll be the Day'.
Having suffered from rheumatic fever as a child, his

heart was damaged and Fury collapsed in January 1983 and died at the age of 42.

A contemporary of Fury's was Adam Faith who followed his early sixties pop career as a manager for Leo Sayer, a few movie appearances and credible performances on British television, notably starring in the series 'Budgie' prior to fronting financial programmes. When the Decca record label famously turned down The Beatles, in favour of The Tremeloes, Parlaphone took on the 'four' and enjoyed their progression to the 'Fab four'. However, they were not the first pop act to find success on the label as Adam Faith gave Parlaphone its first number one in 1959 with 'What do you Want'.

Faith had undergone open heart surgery in 1986 and had a fatal heart attack whilst touring in a play in 2003 and was dead at the age of 62.

Popular singer from the fifties and sixties, Little Willie John died in prison at the age of 30 and the official verdict was a heart attack but this has been claimed to be untrue and is another of the alleged conspiracies in the biographies of musicians.

Richard Turner was a trumpet player who had played along with the band 'Friendly Fires' at many of their live gigs for the three years prior to his death in 2011.

Turner was a keen and strong swimmer who suffered a cardiac arrest whilst swimming in an outdoor swimming pool. He was yet another musician who died at 27.

Singer and recording artist Robert Palmer had a very successful, if understated career.
Best known due to the video for his hit single 'Addicted to Love' which portrayed him fronting a band of sensuous pouting females and his short-lived 'supergroup – Power Station', Palmer also worked with an eclectic list of musicians over the years.
Briefly in the jazz / rock fusion outfit 'Dada', Palmer and female singing partner Elkie Brooks moved to form the rockier and edgier 'Vinegar Joe' which lasted three years before they parted company on diverging successful paths.

Robert Palmer covered rock, blues, soul, electronic, jazz and pop influences on his dozen plus studio albums, many of which made top 50 in both sides of the Atlantic as well as his global top 10 singles.
Robert Palmer's image was the well dressed, suave and cool singer who could croon, rock and smile in the same performance and having lived for a time in the Bahamas followed by 15 years in Switzerland, he gave the impression of fitness but a lifetime of smoking took its toll and the singer died of a heart attack in 2003 when he was 54 years old.

Another respected singer who passed away from a heart attack at the age of 54 was Luther Vandross. His soulful R&B voice and song writing skills were rewarded with 8 Grammy's including a best song award for his version of 'Dance with my Father' which he co-wrote with Richard Marx. Vandross' voice was sought after as backing vocalist with many major artists including Barbra Streisand, Diana Ross, Roberta Flack, Donna Summer, Stevie Wonder and David Bowie for whom he co-wrote the track Fascination. With numerous top 20 albums, singles and collaborations Luther Vandross had the potential of a long and successful career but ill health dogged him as a diabetic and subject to hypertension, he had a stroke in 2003 and died two years later of heart failure.

The single 'Reet Petite' was released in 1957 by Jackie Wilson but was not a major hit and ten years later his version of 'I get the Sweetest Feeling' had the same fate.
However, both of these records became massive sellers when re-released and along with others such as ('You're Love keeps Lifting Me) Higher and Higher' and 'Lonely Teardrops' as well a lively stage show, earned Jackie the name 'Mr Excitement'.
His stage moves influenced Elvis Presley and Michael Jackson but whilst performing in 1975, he had a

massive heart attack as he sung the lines "my heart is crying" and the audience thought his antics were part of the act.   However, the 41 year old slipped into a coma which lasted for almost nine years prior to his death in 1975.

Slip Sliding Away

"Tip-toes in silence round my bed and quiets the raindrops overhead, with her everlasting smile she still my fever for a while, oh nursie dear I'm glad you're here, to brush away my pain" (xvii)   -   'Nursie' by Jethro Tull

A few musicians actually died in hospital in differing circumstances.

One of the talented singing songwriter brothers from the Bee Gees and the group's multi-instrumentalist, Maurice Gibb suffered a heart attack during surgery for a twisted intestine and never recovered.   He was 53 when the tragedy occurred in 2003.

Popular session singer who had a few country hits, top 10 in the US charts with Neil Young's 'Lotta Love' and top 50 album placings, Nicolette Larson was admitted to UCLA Medical Centre in December 1997 suffering from cerebral edema and liver failure. She died within days at the age of 45.

Another respected female vocalist had died in hospital back in 1978 following an accident when she fell down stairs hitting her head on concrete.
Sandy Denny had been a singer, very briefly in The Strawbs, Fotheringay and is best known for her time with Fairport Convention. Denny also appeared on Led Zeppelin's 'The Battle of Evermore' and as a songwriter her most covered work is 'Who Knows Where the Time Goes'.

Having suffered headaches since the fall, a few weeks later, she collapsed and lapsed into a coma from which she never recovered.

Dave Alexander, original bass player with The Stooges was a 27 year old victim of pulmonary edema linked to pancreatitis in 1975.

Two years previously, also 27 when he suffered a fatal gastrointestinal haemorrhage, was Grateful Dead's Ron McKernan aka 'Pigpen'.

Yet two more on the members book for the infamous fictitious '27 club'

Gar Samuelson was drummer for thrash metal band Megadeth from 1984-87 and played on the band's first two albums.
He died from liver failure, aged 41 in 1999.

The following year, 42 year old Rob Buck, guitarist and co-writer along with Natalie Merchant of 10,000 Maniacs, passed away, also from liver failure.

The list goes on.

Pete Quaife, original bass player with iconic group The Kinks, passed away from kidney failure in 2010. He was 66 but had been on dialysis for ten years following renal problems.

Funk bass player per excellence Bernard Edwards had an instantly recognisable style as showcased in the many hits of 'Chic'.   He produced the 'supergroup – Power Station' album and the lead vocalist Robert Palmer's follow up as well as playing on tracks for Diana Ross, Sister Sledge and Debbie Harry. Whilst touring Japan in 1996, Edwards died from pneumonia.

Newcastle born Chas Chandler returned to his roots in the area and contributed to the building of the Newcastle Arena and died at the age of 57 from an aortic aneurysm in Newcastle General Hospital. Although associated as being the bass player with the Geordie group The Animals, Chandler's entrepreneurial skills took him further than his musical ability.   He 'discovered' Jimi Hendrix, brought the guitarist to the UK and recruited Mitch Mitchell and Noel Redding to form The Jimi Hendrix Experience. Chas Chandler became Hendrix' manager and then went on to manage and produce Slade during the band's successful twelve year career.

Canadian born, but very much exponent of the California sound, Denny Doherty was one quarter of the harmony singing Mamas and Papas. He died in 2007, 40 years after his peak success, having had an abdominal aortic aneurysm removed, he died from a second.

English born, but having taken Canadian citizenship in the late 1970's, Long John Baldry settled in Vancouver until his death in 1985 from a lung infection at the age of 64.

Back in sixties UK, Baldry was given the epithet 'Long' due to his height of 6 feet 7 inches and became a stalwart of the booming blues scene and his bands the 'Hoochie Coochie Men' and 'Steampacket' were where Rod Stewart and Elton John, among others, served their apprenticeships.

Long John reached the top of the UK charts in 1967 with the ballad 'Let the Heartaches Begin' and charted the following year with the theme for the 'Mexico' Olympics.

Being gay during the era when it was still considered a criminal offence, Baldry was well placed to provide understanding and support to Elton John when the latter was stressed about the perception of his sexuality following a failed relationship with a woman.

However, Baldry was also institutionalised for a time in the seventies due to mental health difficulties. As laws were modified to reflect society's recognition of same sex relationships, both Elton John and Long John found long term partners and as Baldry reduced his musical activities, he continued to perform voiceovers.

Pianist Nicky Hopkins suffered from Crohn's Disease and required regular hospitalisation which prevented him becoming a permanent member of major touring bands.

His musical legacy is astounding in that he played keyboards for an endless list of popular music's main acts. Starting out in Screaming Lord Sutch's Savages, Nicky progressed to work with the Kinks, The Beatles (together and all four individual members), Jefferson Airplane, Steve Miller Band, Harry Nilsson, David Bowie, Peter Frampton and appeared on many Rolling Stones tracks. He worked with Donovan, Rod Stewart, Jeff Beck, Joe Walsh, Joe Cocker, Carly Simon and others and still found time to record four albums under his own name and create three movie soundtracks, but complications set in following surgery and he died in 1995 at the age of 50.

Chapter 8

Eight Miles High

"Eight miles high and when you touch down, you'll
find that it's stranger than known" - (xviii)

Clark, McGuinn & Crosby

'Eight Miles High' was a 1966 single by American band
The Byrds that was innovative in its complexity for a
'pop' single combining the Eastern influence of Ravi
Shankar and the Jazz style of John Coltrane. It did
manage to make the top 20 in the US and UK despite a
radio ban in the band's home country.
Censorship in pop / rock music was not widespread
but did occur on occasion.

Silence Is Golden

 In 1969 the influential BBC did not allow the Jane
Birkin & Serge Gainsbourg song 'Je t'aime…Moi Non
Plus' to be played on television or radio, which despite
being sung in French was thought to be too blatantly
sexual complete with heavy breathing.
Nevertheless, the song was a number one hit in the
UK as well as Austria, Switzerland and Norway and top
3 in Germany, Holland and Ireland.

Therefore the institution could silence the airwaves but could not prevent the record becoming a 'gold' seller.

Other songs that were banned for sexual connotations include 'Wet Dream' by reggie artist Max Romeo, 'Relax' by Frankie Goes to Hollywood, 'Hi Hi Hi' by Paul McCartney and Wings and much of the output by Judge Dread.

Perhaps the strangest ban was the Cliff Richard single 'Honky Tonk Angel' which was banned and withdrawn by the singer himself after he found out that the lyrics referred to a hooker and he did not wish to tarnish his image by singing about such a subject.

A number of records were banned for 'political' reasons such as 'Give Ireland back to the Irish' by Paul McCartney and Wings and 'Invisible Sun' by The Police – both due to references to the UK and Northern Ireland problems but at the time of the Gulf War many more songs were banned from airplay such as 'Brothers in Arms' by Dire Straits and The Doors' 'Light My Fire' even although they were not overtly militaristic or jingoistic.

In the sixties, The Ed Sullivan show was one of the few television shows in America that enabled national exposure for modern acts, even although the format and Ed himself were old fashioned establishment.

Sullivan was not enamoured with the unkempt appearance of The Rolling Stones and insisted that the band members wash their hair before appearing but the most notorious incident was his insistence that singer Mick Jagger change the lyrics of 'Let's Spend the Night Together' to 'Let's Spend Some Time Together' or they would not be allowed to perform the song due to its sexual overtones.

Even commercial references lead to record bans for Paul Simon, The Kinks and Dr Hook and the Medicine show for mentioning a photographic company, soft drink and magazine by brand names.

Bad language and bad taste resulted in bans for numerous songs containing the 'F' word or the 'Mother F' words from such artists as Martha Wainright, Arctic Monkeys, Rolling Stones, John Lennon, Teenage Fanclub, Amy Winehouse and Prince.
Even the original Monty Python Eric Idle's humorous take on the Crucifiction was banned, not for any moral reason other than the line 'life's a piece of shit, when you think of it'.

With such prudish approach to standards, the lyrical expert that was Warren Zevon had little chance with his ironically autobiographical 'My Shit's Fucked Up' or even his use of 'The Hollywood Hawiian Hotel', The Hyatt House' or the alliteration that described his mixed up love 'like a Waring blender'.

The sixties had numerous '3 minutes' of tragedy from 'Twinkle's Terry, 'Shangri-La's Leader of the Pack, Jan and Dean's 'Dead Man's Curve' and an early ban for the stock car crash that featured in 'Tell Laura I Love Her' but the witty 'They're Coming to Take Me Away Ha Ha' a 1966 hit for Napoleon XIV was considered too close to the bone in its take on the mentally deranged and it too received a ban.

Jagged Little Pill

When it came to banning records for drug references, the powers that be had more difficulty determining which songs should or should not be played.
The Beatle's 'A Day in the Life', 'I am the Walrus' and 'Lucy in the Sky with Diamonds' could have been created under the influence but so too could 'Yellow Submarine'.
Although the Mamas and the Papas songs were harmoniously happy, their writer John Phillips was a serious drug taker, as was Eric Clapton and his Cream compatriots and of course, David Crosby. Fast forward to Pete Docherty and not much has changed.

However, although the behaviour of musician's and writers could not be influenced by the authorities, where possible, their exposure would be curtailed. The difficulty was deciding what constituted an overt drug reference and taking action.

This was agreed in respect of Crosby and CO's 'Eight Miles High' despite the group's protestations at the time that the song was about their visit to the UK and the plane journey. In fact one of the writer's, Gene Clark' quit the band shortly after the song's release, citing fear of flying as the main reason.

With the passage of time, the writers did admit that there was an element of drug reference in the lyrics, but it all seems tame now. In hindsight, the 'hippie' era of drug consumption has had too many victims to suggest it was 'tame'.

Whether the eight miles was a flying height (normally seven miles) or a drug high, as the lyrics elucidate, what goes up, needs to touch down. One musician, Paul Kossoff had achieved success as guitarist with the band 'Free' and although they declared that they were 'Alright Now', Kossoff was anything but alright as he became more dependent on hard drugs.
As a musician, his talent was praised by his contemporaries but as a functioning human being, his actor father, David watched helplessly as his son slipped deeper into addiction (eventually using his experience to educate others about the problem).
At the age of 25, Paul Kossoff was literally eight miles high when during a flight between Los Angeles and New York in 1976 he died of cardiac arrest caused by drug intake.

Drug deaths of musicians are not always reported as such because the actual cause of death is usually a medical condition exacerbated by an overdose or an accumulated drug lifestyle.

Country rock exponent Gram Parsons was only 26 when he overdosed in September 1973 on morphine, ending another promising career. Although Parsons' legacy is in the recordings he made with The Byrds, Flying Burritto Brothers and his solo work featuring a young Emmylou Harris, he partied with the Rolling Stones and was influential on Keith Richards interest in country music and is also cited as a pioneer of the music genre known as country rock.

However, Gram Parsons' death was not the end of his short controversial story as there was a family dispute over his estate and repatriation of his remains between States. The matter was resolved in an unconventional and highly illegal manner when his ex-roadie and friend Phil Kaufman stole the body from Los Angeles Airport and drove it to the Joshua Tree National Park where they set fire to the coffin. This arrangement was supposedly agreed between the deceased and the perpetrator 'just in case'.

Another promising musician had OD'd less than a year previous at the age of 29.

Danny Whitten was a member of Crazy Horse and had served as second guitar and vocals to Neil Young but the relatively unknown songwriter did leave a well-known legacy in his self-penned and much covered ballad 'I Don't Want to Talk About it'.

Whitten's drug habit was also the inspiration for Young's anti-drug song 'Needle and the Damage Done' and in his liner notes Young elucidates (b) "I am not a preacher, but drugs killed a lot of great men".

From Whitten to Whitney and the much publicised demise of one of the best-selling recording artists of all time.

Whitney Houston rose to prominence in the second half of the eighties with her debut album 'Whitney Houston' and the follow up 'Whitney' both reaching 25 million sales.   The ex-model whose mother was gospel singer Cissy Houston, cousins Dionne and Dee Warwick, godmother Darlene Love and with soul legend Aretha Franklin as family friend, was surrounded by music and destined to become a singer. In addition to her major hits, 'I Wanna Dance with Somebody', 'I will Always Love You', 'Saving all my Love for You', 'Greatest Love of All', 'I'm Your Baby Tonight' and 'All the Man that I Need', Whitney duetted with Stevie Wonder, appeared at the Nelson Mandela tribute concert, won Grammy's and many other awards and became a successful actress in The Bodyguard, Waiting to Exhale and The Preacher's Wife.

Houston married R&B singer Bobby Brown in 1992 and by the mid-1990's her reliability and appearance progressively deteriorated. There were rumours of marital violence and drugs and Brown spent some time in jail but by 2007, the couple had divorced with Whitney being awarded custody of their daughter. Despite releasing new material and embarking on a major tour in support, the singer could not perform to her previous standards, reviews were poor and some dates cancelled. Whitney Houston was found dead in a hotel bath on 11 February 2012, she was 48 years old. The cause of death was listed as an accident, initially thought to be a mistaken drowning but confirmed as atherosclerotic heart disease and cocaine use.

Public reaction and response from fellow musicians was emotive because the girl who had achieved so much, had so much to lose and sadly lost it all too early.

One young Scottish guitarist had a CV to die for and unfortunately he did, prematurely at only 26 years of age. Prior to a heroin overdose that caused a fatal heart attack in September 1979, Jimmy McCulloch had been in the band 'Wild Horses' with fellow Scots ex-Thin Lizzie guitarist Brian Robertson and ex-Rainbow bassist Jimmy Bain as well as future 'Who', ex-Faces and Small Faces drummer Kenney Jones. McCulloch had also been in the short lived reformed Small Faces with Jones, played on session work and had previously replaced Les Harvey in Stone the Crows.

He first came to prominence as part of the Pete Townsend produced outfit called 'Thunderclap Newman' featuring on their number 1 Single 'Something in the Air' when he was only 16.

Jimmy McCulloch's career high spot was as an official member of Wings alongside Paul McCartney from 1974-77 and he even co-wrote and sung a couple of songs on Wings' albums, one of which 'Medicine Jar' was ironically an anti-drug song.

Also 26 when he overdosed on heroin was Hillel Slovak, the Israeli born guitarist from The Red Hot Chilli Peppers, who appeared on the band's first two albums prior to his death in 1988.

Tragically the list of deaths of young musicians continues to grow.

Another 26 year old guitarist and screaming vocalist, Casey Calvert from the Ohio rock band 'Hawthorne Heights' became a victim of drugs but his accidental death was not due to substance abuse. He had apparently taken two types of prescription drugs that had reacted as a combination and he died in his sleep, the chance of which happening, a pharmacologist described as being so rare that he could not put a number on it.

Tim Buckley was a wayward singer songwriter in the mid 60's whose recordings began as a folk sound and altered to include psychedelia, jazz and even funk but he never quite gained commercial acceptance.

Having fathered a son, Jeff who would become a respected musician in his own right, Tim took no part in the boy's upbringing. Tim Buckley died of a combination of drugs and alcohol, at the age of 29 and the 'friend' who provided him with the drugs was charged with manslaughter.

Prior to Marc Bolan's glam success with T.Rex, he played as a duo in the elongated named Tyrannosaurus Rex with the 'Lord of the Rings' monikered Steve 'Peregrin Took' (real name Stephen Ross Porter).

This arrangement lasted from 1967-69 when the pair split due to musical and personal differences, the latter mainly being Took's drug habit. Although the bongo playing drummer tried further collaborations, he never met with much in the way of positive reactions and his continued drug use did not help the situation.

At the age of 31, SPT died, reportedly from asphyxiation after inhaling a cocktail cherry but it was understood that he had recently injected morphine.

Drummer Robbie McIntosh was enjoying the success of the Average White Band in the USA where the band's 'white album' AWB had reached the top. The year was 1974 and the Scottish band had just broken through into the big time when 24 year old McIntosh and founding member Alan Gorrie were at a post gig party and took what they thought was cocaine but was in fact heroin. The dose was fatal and Robbie died but Gorrie was reportedly kept conscious by singer Cher, until medical assistance arrived to save him.

As The Pretenders were starting to make a name for themselves in the early eighties, bass player Pete Farndon was fired for his drug problem.
Ironically, two days later, guitarist James Honeyman-Scott, who was only 25, died of cocaine induced heart failure.
Less than one year later, 30 year old Farndon was also dead having drowned in his bath following a heroin overdose.
The original Pretenders line-up made only two albums prior to losing half its members to drugs, but Chrissie Hynde maintained the success and recruited others to replace the deceased vacancies.

An accidental overdose killed one of the rappers from New York outfit Wu-Tang Clan in 2004. Legal problems and a spell in jail as well as drugs had troubled Russell Tyrone Jones whose stage name was an indication of his lyrical style, Ol' Dirty Bastard.

Jason Rae was in his early 30's when he was found dead from an accidental overdose of alcohol and drugs in 2008. Rae was a saxophonist who had played with a few artists including his wife Corinne Bailey Rae.

Other musician deaths by accidental overdose include Tommy Bolin, 25, guitarist and one time member of Deep Purple, 50 year old Douglas Colvin aka Dee Dee Ramone bass player with The Ramones, and keyboardist Jonathan Melvoin 34, who had played with Prince and the Revolution and was on tour with The Smashing Pumpkins at the time of his death

.Also 34 when he died of an overdose was 'Alice in Chains' vocalist Layne Staley. He was found dead in 2002 after a long addiction that he knew would eventually kill him. The 'grunge' band had achieved top 10 album position and Grammy nomination but Staley's drawn out deterioration and reclusiveness prevented further success.

Songwriting collaborator with Guns N' Roses West Arkeen was 36 when a drug overdose, reportedly taken to diminish the effects of severe burns following a barbecue accident, killed him.

Sadly the lessons that could have been learned from early deaths due to the rock 'n' roll lifestyle were not acted upon and the premature burn outs of examples like Janis Joplin did not prevent the many accidental overdoses or overindulgences overtaking the takers.

Joplin had a five year singing career including five chart singles and four album releases (including 'Pearl which was posthumous) as a solo performer and as part of the sixties interestingly named bands 'Big Brother and the Holding Company', 'Kozmic Blues Band' and 'Full Tilt Boogie Band'.
Janis Joplin came to prominence at the Monterey Pop Festival in 1967 and was one of the major acts two years later at Woodstock but her performance at the latter was not up to par and did not feature in the movie or soundtrack. Having been a rebellious character for most of her formative years, including excessive drinking at a young age and an appetite for a variety of substances, Janis Joplin's drug addiction had begun to impact on her singing and reliability. In October 1970, she was found lying on the floor of a hotel room, victim of a heroin overdose exacerbated with alcohol intake. Joplin, along with Jefferson

Airplane singer Grace Slick broke the stereotype female vocalist image and her impact and death at 27 was a precursor to the similarly troubled performer Amy Winehouse more than 40 years later, also at the age of 27.

Two weeks after Janis Joplin's death Jimi Hendrix was dead at the same age and having already lost Brian Jones 3 July 1969 and then exactly two years later to the day, Jim Morrison, the 27 Club was born.

A few more victims of drugs increased the membership of the 27 club and sadly it is probable that others will join in the future. .

Just a couple of months after Courtney Love witnessed boyfriend Kurt Cobain's death at 27, the bass player in her band 'Hole' Kristen Pfaff overdosed and died at the same age.

Bryan Ottoson, guitarist with 'American Head Charge' died from a mixture of prescription drugs and Jeremy Michael Ward vocaliser with The Mars Volta / De Facto overdosed.

Rudy Lewis had been one of the main vocalists in the harmony group The Drifters, singing lead on a number of songs including the hits, 'Up on the Roof' and 'On Broadway' but he was troubled with drug dependency and died of a drug overdose in 1964, at the height of the group's success, when he was only 27 years of age.

In 1969, 10 years after his only top 30 hit, English singer Dickie Pride, who suffered from mental problems, died of an overdose of sleeping tablets at the age of 27.

New Zealand born Gary Thain was best known as bass player for rockers Uriah Heep over a four year, four album period which ended in 1975 following his expulsion due to his drug consumption. His life also ended at the end of that year when his breathing stopped as a result of a heroin overdose; he was also 27 years old.

21

Although not quite in the same league as the 27 club, the 21 club can count in its number, an idol from the rock 'n' roll era, a country singer, a member of the most famous band ever, a glam-rock star, alternative pop drummer and a punk icon.

Six musicians did not live to fulfil their potential in the various eras and musical genres, passing away at the very young age of 21.

American Rocker Eddie Cochran was killed in a car crash on a visit to the UK and country singer Amie Comeaux's car aquaplaned on a wet road and hit a tree killing her outright.

Enigmatic and artistic early Beatle Stuart Sutcliffe died of a brain haemorrhage when the 'fab four' were a five piece in Hamburg. Sutcliffe was influential on the group's developing image but his interest had already moved from music to art prior to his sad demise.

Original New York Doll drummer Billy Murcia accidently overdosed whilst on the bands' first UK visit and another beat provider, Andy McVann the original drummer with The Farm was killed following a Police chase.

The troubled final year of controversial punk bassist Sid Vicious ended with his death by overdose when he was 21 years of age.

Chapter 9

SUICIDE IS PAINLESS

"The game of life is hard to play, I'm gonna lose it anyway, the losing card I'll someday lay, so this is all I have to say, that suicide is painless, it brings on many changes, and I can take or leave it if I please" (xix) by Mike Altman & Johnny Mandel

At the beginning of the 1970's an American film and television show based on a medical team's experience in the Korean War achieved great popularity. Although the subject matter was serious, especially as America was still engaged in the Vietnam War at the time, the theme was played for laughs and the characters from the black comedy 'Mash' became household names.

Robert Altman directed the film version and his 14 year old son Mike wrote the lyrics for the title song used in both the film and television versions. With music by composer Johnny Mandel and performed by unknown session singers, the song 'Suicide is Painless' was a major hit beyond the confines of TV and soundtrack to the extent that Altman Snr. announced on a Johnny Carson TV show that he earned about $70,000 for directing the film whereas Altman Jnr. got $1million from royalties for writing the song's words.

The irony of the lyrics suited the mood of 'Mash' but away from that context, the legacy of suicide is anything but painless.

The deaths of a number of musicians have been attributed to suicide and speculation surrounds many others.

Bang Bang

One of the first questionable deaths was on Christmas Day 1954 when R&B singer Johnny Ace (25) shot himself in the side of the head with a handgun.
Some friends and fellow musicians, including renowned singer Big Mama Thornton, witnessed the 'accident' and maintain that he had been playing with the gun and thought it was not loaded when it 'went off' killing the vocalist.
The Press embellished the story and suggested he had been playing 'Russian Roulette' but this was never substantiated.

Similar circumstances led to the death of 31 year old singer and guitarist Terry Kath from the band Chicago in 1978.
He too was waving a gun around and pulled the

trigger a few times to prove it was empty but put it down, picked up a different gun, pointed it at his head and fired.

The influence of alcohol and drugs confuse the picture even more as the state of mind of the perpetrator could be affected arguably distorting reality and the spur of the moment act could well have been a mistake.

When Kurt Cobain ended it all, traces of drugs were found in his bloodstream following his death by self-inflicted gunshot, however in this case, also found at the scene was a suicide note.

Cobain was a singer / songwriter / guitarist from Seattle who founded the 'grunge' band Nirvana in the late 80's. His moody, laconic vocals, mix of covers such as Leadbelly's 'Where Did You Sleep Last Night' and original material, most notably 'Smells Like Teen Spirit' proved popular with 1990's youth and the band's televised unplugged debut is still viewed today as a classic of the era.   However, spiralling drug misuse and an erratic relationship with Courtney Love halted Nirvana and Cobain's careers.

It was alleged that he had previously attempted suicide prior to the fateful day in early April 1994 when the 27 year old pointed a gun to his chin and fired.

Access to drugs by musicians is commonplace and often where illegal drugs are involved, firearms are also available.

Other apparent gunshot suicides by musicians include twenty eight year old 'Pennywise' bass player Jason Thirsk.
Songwriter Tommy Boyce (55) who co-wrote 'The Monkees' theme and 'Last Train To Clarksville' shot himself as did Country singer Faron Young (64) best known for 'Hello Walls' and 'Four In The Morning'.

A similar farewell was made by rock guitarist Ronnie Montrose (64) who fronted the eponymous 'Montrose' with Sammy Hagar and played with The Edgar Winter Group.

33 year old Tommy Marth killed himself by a gunshot to the head in April 2012. He had played and toured as saxophonist with 'The Killers'

As the American group the 'Gin Blossoms' were getting recognition and record sales, even achieving a gold disc for the single, 'Hey Jealousy' the band's writer and guitarist Doug Hopkins was battling alcoholism and depression.
Whilst in rehab in 1993, the 32 year old shot and killed himself.

In the case of songwriter, producer and engineer Joe Meek, recognised as a pioneer of electronic sounds as exemplified on The Tornados 1962 instrumental 'Telstar' (which he produced), not only did he kill himself by blasting his face with a shotgun, he first killed his landlady with the same weapon.

Meek's involvement with hits such as 'Johnnie Remember Me' sung by Johnnie Leyton and The Honeycombs 'Have I the Right' ensured his popularity but when the music stopped, he also sunk into depression resulting in the double death in 1967 when the perpetrator was 37 years old.

Another self-inflicted gunshot fatality was 22 year old Per Yngve Ohlin previously of the Swedish band Morbid and latterly vocalist with Norwegian black metal band Mayhem. Ohlin's stage same was 'Dead' and he appeared in 'corpse make-up'.

The singer had been obsessed by death since childhood when he suffered internal bleeding and for a time was pronounced clinically dead before being resuscitated. He frequently self-harmed, even onstage but on the fateful day in April 1991, the introverted and delusional shock rock artist slit his wrists, throat and then shot himself leaving a suicide note apologising for using the gun indoors and ending with the words, "excuse all the blood".

1950's classic dance song 'At the Hop' was credited to Danny and the Juniors with lead vocal by 16 year old Danny Rapp. The song was again a hit in 1976 but Rapp did not enjoy any long term benefits from this shot at stardom because seven years later the singer shot himself.

The Dickies were formed in the late 1970's, marketed as California's first punk band but achieved success in the UK charts with 'Banana Splits (the tra la song)' in 1979. Keyboardist Bob Davis who went by the stage name of 'Chuck Wagon' was only 24 when he shot himself two years later.

Even younger at only 18 years of age when he shot himself dead in 1987 was founding member, along with Gwen and Eric Stefani, of ska band 'No Doubt'. John Spence who was the group's initial energetic lead vocalist named the band but tragically killed himself before they broke through.

Paul Williams was the baritone voice in the original incarnation of soul vocal group The Temptations and also acted as choreographer for the first Tamla Motown act to win a Grammy award.
Through the extensive career of the group there were personnel changes but six long serving members of The Temptations, including Paul Williams, were inducted into the Rock and Roll Hall of Fame in 1989.

However, this was a posthumous accolade in respect of Williams who had left the group in 1971, officially for health reasons as he had sickle-cell anaemia, but unofficially his alcohol consumption was causing concern.

His condition declined and two years later the 34 year old shot himself in an alley.

Fleetwood Mac are a band with a history of highs and lows and during the transitional period in the early 1970's when the English based blues band were at an end and the remnants of that group were about to morph into the Anglo-American multi-million selling 'new Mac', they made 3 albums with Guitarist Bob Welch, whose leaving the band was the catalyst to enrol Lindsey Buckingham and Stevie Nicks.

Welch's contribution was important and helped maintain the name Fleetwood Mac in the lower regions of the charts prior to their classic popular line-up.

Welch then had reasonable success as a solo artist, notably with the single 'Sentimental Lady' and albums 'French Kiss' and 'Three Hearts' aided by ex-Mac colleagues but relations became soured when he was omitted from the list of Fleetwood Mac inductees into the Rock and Roll Hall of Fame, a controversial decision that he could not come to terms with.

Having undergone surgery for an irreparable spinal problem, 65 year old Bob Welch did not wish to become a burden on family or friends and leaving a suicide note, died of a self-inflicted gunshot wound on 7 June 2012.

Del Shannon, who scored major hits in the early 1960's with 'Runaway' and 'Hats Off To Larry' was tipped as a possible replacement for Roy Orbison, who had died in December 1988, in The Traveling Wilburys. Shannon had been recording with 'Wilbury' Jeff Lynne but in February 1990, the 55 year old veteran singer shot himself dead whilst suffering from depression.

Previously, Howie Epstein had been bass player in Del Shannon's touring band and when Tom Petty was producing an album for Shannon in the early 1980's, he offered Epstein a place in his group, The Heartbreakers to replace the retiring Ron Blair. Howie Epstein was bass player with Tom Petty and The Heartbreakers for 21 years but also played with many American musicians such as Stevie Nicks, Roy Orbison and Bob Dylan and produced John Prine's Grammy award winning album 'The Missing Years' and albums for Carlene Carter with whom he was romantically involved for a time.

However, Howie Epstein's use of drugs resulted in his death and it has been suggested by some that his increasing use of heroin, altered personality and depression points to an overdose but he had been unwell and was on prescription drugs when he collapsed and was taken to hospital.

The verdict was that he died from complications due to drug use and his friends and the rest of The Heartbreakers had watched helplessly at his deteriorating state through his drugs misuse. Coincidently his replacement in Tom Petty's band was Ron Blair, previously 10 years as Heartbreaker's bassist before the position was filled by Epstein.

Another questionable suicide was the death of 34 year old American singer songwriter Elliot Smith which was caused by two stab wounds in his chest. The initial verdict was suicide but this was altered later to include possible homicide.

Although he never hit the big time, Smith made five albums prior to his death in 2003 and a further three have been released since. His material often referred to depression, drink and drugs, all of which he battled with and his highest point was as an Oscar nomination for his song 'Miss Misery' which appeared on the soundtrack of 'Good Will Hunting'.

Jumping Jack Flash

While many suicides are quiet, lonely affairs, occasionally musicians end their lives with more of a theatrical farewell.

Israeli singer Mike Brant had a number of hits in France in the early 1970's but depressed, he attempted suicide by jumping from a hotel window in Geneva in November 1974. Although he survived that attempt, 28 year old Brant, jumped to his death 5 months later from an apartment in France.

Another European entertainer died as the result of a fatal leap.
Herman Brood was a Dutch (Hairmon Broat) rock star of the 1970's into the 80's who was also a proficient artist. Brood had been jailed for drug dealing, was a user and many of his songs were about the drug lifestyle.
A 'bad-boy' star in his native Holland, he became romantically linked to German singer Nina Hagen and almost broke through into the English speaking music world with his American top 40 hit 'Saturday Night'. Unable to shake off his drug habit, at the age of 54, Herman Brood jumped to his death from the roof of the Amsterdam Hilton Hotel.

American soul singer Donny Hathaway was 33 when he removed the glass from a window in his 15th floor apartment building and leapt to his death.

Diagnosed with paranoid schizophrenia, he was required to take strong medication to stabilise the condition but was not disciplined to control his intake and regularly got depressed.

Musically Hathaway's biggest successes were his duets 'Where Is The Love' and 'The Closer I get To You' with Roberta Flack but he also wrote material, the best known being his much covered co-composition 'This Christmas'.

Hang On Sloopy

The most common suicide method by musicians is hanging and as mentioned in the introduction both Pete Ham and Tom Evans from the group Badfinger ended their lives in this manner.

So too did Joy Division's singer Ian Curtis.

Joy Division were a post-punk four piece band from Salford in England, signed to the fledgling Factory Records, their popularity was growing, when on the eve of the group's first American tour, the singer hanged himself in his kitchen.

Ian Curtis suffered from depression and had an increasing medical problem with epilepsy which caused him to have seizures, in some cases whilst performing.   He was also having marital problems and had previously attempted suicide by overdose.

Ironically Joy Division's biggest success with the single 'Love Will Tear Us Apart' and album 'Closer' were posthumous hits in respect of Curtis, while the other members Peter Hook, Bernard Sumner and Steven Morris changed their name to New Order and eclipsed the achievements of Joy Division.

Roy Buchanan was a critically acclaimed guitarist prominent in the 1970's who had been playing since the late 1950's and at the time of his death in 1988 at the age of 48, had released 12 albums, some of which earned gold sales status.   He had a problem with alcohol and following arrest for drunkenness, he reportedly hanged himself in a jail cell by using his shirt as a noose, however, this was disputed by some members of his family and friends who allegedly claimed that they witnessed bruising on his head. Some journalists referred to Buchanan, who ranked number 57 on Rolling Stone magazine's 2003 poll of 100 greatest guitarists of all time as "the best unknown guitarist in the world".   This same title was also bestowed on the player who ranked number 63 in the same poll.   Danny Gatten had apparently shared a room with Buchanan in Nashville in the 1960's and they had jammed together. Gatten's virtuosity was recognised by his peers but never achieved commercial acknowledgement and ironically, like Buchanan, he took his own life, in 1994 at the age of 49, Danny Gatten locked himself in his garage and shot himself.

Richard Manuel was one of the singer / keyboard players in the band that was called The Band. From backing Ronnie Hawkins they moved to provide live accompaniment for Bob Dylan when he infamously 'went electric'. The Band also had a respectful career in their own right with eclectic albums and singles such as 'The Night They Drove Old Dixie Down', 'Up on Crickle Creek' and 'The Weight'. Manuel's fragile vocals can be heard on the cover of Dylan's 'I Shall Be Released' and 'Tears of Rage' which Dylan and he co-wrote.

Addiction to alcohol and drugs robbed him of his musical quality and his career and condition deteriorated. Despite a hiatus from stimulant dependency in the early 1980's, he lapsed into his old ways and became depressed.
After a performance in March 1986 Richard Manuel (48) hanged himself in his hotel room, whilst intoxicated.
Ex Band bass player Rick Danko was of the opinion that his death was a 'silly accident' and drummer Levon Helm had played cards with him after the gig and they had talked about music but strangely Manuel had thanked keyboard maestro Garth Hudson for "twenty-five years of incredible music".
Band guitarist Robbie Robertson wrote 'Fallen Angel' as a tribute to Richard Manuel, Eric Clapton wrote 'Holy Mother' as his tribute and lesser known acts have recorded songs with his name in the title.

Canadian Manuel was far from home when he hanged himself in a hotel room in Florida USA and another musician was far from his English birthplace when he hanged himself in a hotel room in Hawaii.

Born in Manchester of Scottish parents and raised in Fife, Stuart Adamson was 18 when he formed The Skids who quickly gained popularity, their biggest hit being 'Into the Valley' in 1979.

Leaving this group behind, Adamson and friend Bruce Watson started a new band that they named 'Big Country' and the single 'In a Big Country' with its recognisable twin guitar sound was a hit on both sides of the Atlantic as was the album 'The Crossing'. The group enjoyed success for a few years with Adamson being the main writer, singer and provider of the distinctive guitar sound and although he appeared grounded and secure, he admitted to having had a nervous breakdown.

In the mid-1990's the musician divorced and settled in Nashville where he continued to pursue a musical direction but dejected in 2001, at the age of 43, Stuart Adamson ended his life by hanging.

In March 2005, 46 year old Paul Hester hanged himself from a tree in a public park in Melbourne in his native Australia.

Hester was a popular radio and television personality in his home country but was known in international music circles as drummer with both Antipodean groups Split Enz and Crowded House. Depression and personal problems were cited as the causes that lead to his death.

Another drummer hanged himself in his parent's house in 1996 at the age of only 30. Chris Acland had been sticks man with English Brit-pop band Lush.

The Welsh band 'Feeder' had progressed from the 2001 hit single 'Buck Rogers' to top 5 UK album position with 'Echo Park'.
Early in 2002, the band's drummer Jon Lee, now living in the USA, hanged himself with a metal dog chain.

Steve MacDonald, 31 year old drummer for Quebec heavy metal band 'Gorguts hanged himself during one of many bouts of depression.

Yet another drummer, Kevin Wilkinson one time skin thumper for The Waterboys, China Crisis and Squeeze as well as session player, hanged himself at home, aged 41.

There is no link to percussion and suicide even although there appears to be quite a few drummers who exited their kits early, nor does the amount of fame sought or acquired have any bearing on the decisions to commit the most final of acts.

In some cases alcohol and or drugs have a part to play but the often misunderstood word 'depression' is apparent in the great majority of all suicides.

Brian O'Hara was co-founder, lead singer and guitarist with 1960's band The Fourmost.   They played at The Cavern and had a top 10 hit in 1964 with 'A Little Lovin' but further success eluded the group.   O'Hara was found hanged in 1999, aged 58.

In 1994, a new band called 'Hope of States' were recording their debut album in Peter Gabriel's studio in Bath, England, on the back of a moderate single success, a Top of the Pops appearance and a record deal from Sony .
All seemed positive until band members discovered 26 year old guitarist James Lawrence hanging from the rafters in the studio having taken his own life. Lawrence was attractive, a gifted academic, humorous and had shown no signs of depression which made the act even more difficult to comprehend.

Depression can beset individuals in many backgrounds and having musical talent, receiving acclamation and being paid for what is as much a hobby as a chore does not eradicate innate personality disorder.   The demise of depressives cannot be halted by any element of fame nor does it discriminate by age and although drink and / or drugs feature in a number of the suicide musician's stories, depression is the most common trait in the personalities of these victims and in many cases their final act is not the first attempt at ending it all.

Stuart Wolstenholme battled with depression for years and at the age of 63 committed suicide. 'Wooly' Wolstenholme was known for his mellotron sound which was integral to the progressive rock image of Barclay James Harvest with whom he played from the mid-1960's until 1979 when disillusioned, he quit the music business. He did venture into some solo work and toured again with members of the original BJH but his mental health was unstable resulting in the taking of his own life in 2010.

Hey, That's No Way To Say Goodbye

Some deaths involving drugs are questionable as to whether the user meant to overdose or whether their deaths were tragic mistakes.

Alan Wilson overdosed at the age of 27, Vincent Crane 47, Steve Clark was 30 and Nick Drake was only 24.

Wilson was referred to by fellow musical aficionados as 'Blind Owl' due to his very poor eyesight. However, restricted vision did not prevent him becoming a very accomplished blues guitarist and harmonica player. As a member of Canned Heat, his voice can be heard on the hit single 'Going Up The Country', often cited as the theme from Woodstock the Movie (at which the band played) and he also wrote another of their hits 'On The Road Again'.

Having supposedly attempted suicide on previous occasions, it was accepted by some that he overdosed on purpose but others dispute this and there is no substantiating evidence to prove that he meant to take his own life.

Vincent Crane was a keyboard player who was with the Crazy World of Arthur Brown when the single 'Fire' was popular in 1968 and then Crane moved on to Atomic Rooster for the hits 'Tomorrow Night' and 'Devils' Answer'. Crane battled with depression and had been treated in mental institutions over the years before overdosing in 1989.

Def Leppard guitarist Steve Clark overdosed on drink and prescription drugs at the age of 30 and although he was on a 6 month break from the band with which he had found success, there was no indication that the overdose was anything but a mistake.

The enigmatic Nick Drake made four albums in his short career and at the time they did not sell particularly well, one of the reasons given for his depression, however he was naturally shy and also suffered from a form of stage fright and he used stimulants to help overcome fear of playing in public. At the time of his death, Drake was taking prescription drugs to assist with his condition and died from an overdose that many consider could have been a mistake rather than a purposeful decision to die. Ironically his legacy has resulted in steady sales since his death in the mid-1970's and his mellow voice, introspective lyrics and open tunings have earned him cult status.

In contrast to Nick Drake's introverted image, Michael Hutchence appeared to be the confident extroverted front man. As lead singer of the Australian outfit INXS Hutchence lived the rock star lifestyle acting in movies and dating attractive women including a five year romance with ex-Miss Denmark and international fashion model Helena Christensen and the much publicised affair with UK TV presenter and wife of Bob Geldof, Paula Yates with whom he had a daughter.

Musically INXS were in their prime in the late 1980's with the release of the album 'Kick' and worldwide single success with songs such as 'The Devil Inside', 'I Need You Tonight' and 'Suicide Blonde'. A recipient of many awards, Hutchence and band member Andrew Farris wrote most of the material and some of their songs also featured in soundtracks.

Whilst in the midst of an Australian tour in 1987, Michael Hutchence was found dead in his hotel room and the official verdict was suicide, the reasons given being depression but at the time, under the influence of drink and drugs.

Again, this statement was disputed by some and the Press had a field day with articles about the relationship between Hutchence and Yates, custody battle for their daughter, the views of Geldof, drug use and the claim that his death was autoerotic asphyxiation.

Being a rock musician in 1980's Soviet Union had additional pressures due to Government imposed censorship but public events did progressively take place such as the Leningrad Rock Festival which attracted hundreds of concert goers as opposed to the many thousands normally attending rock festivals. One act that performed at this event was singer songwriter Alexander Bashlachev, a journalism graduate.

A few months before the birth of his daughter, the 27 year old mysteriously 'fell' from a ninth floor window in his apartment. There was no explanation for the 'accident' and suicide was suspected.

Whilst all suicides could be considered tragic events, often deterioration of mental and behavioural characteristics can result in only one conclusion, as was the case with Phil Ochs. Ochs was a writer and performer of protest songs throughout the 1960's, with anti-establishment sentiments like 'I Aint Marching Anymore', 'Draft Dodger Rag' and his most famous composition which became a hit for Joan Baez 'There but for Fortune'.

He played the Newport Folk Festival twice as well as Carnegie Hall, released 8 albums and has featured in many compilations and although he was an early rival to Bob Dylan, Ochs career never progressed into commercial recognition.

Since his death, there have been many covers of Phil Ochs material and like Richard Manuel, tribute songs by fellow musician name check or are about the troubled singer.

Ochs father was a medical doctor who had been diagnosed as bipolar and suffered from depression, conditions that Phil also battled for most of his life, in addition to alcohol dependency.

Throughout the 1970's, Ochs mental state deteriorated and he became delusional claiming that his persona had been taken over by someone by the name of John Butler Train who he maintained had murdered the original Ochs.

Talk of suicide worried his family but ominously, even in the late 1960's, on the cover of his album

'Rehearsals For Retirement' a picture of a gravestone had the inscription -
'Phil Ochs (American) born El Paso, Texas 1940 ; died Chicago, Illinois 1968.
Although this was premature, in New York 8 years later, 35 year old Phil Ochs hanged himself.

Most people are familiar with the song 'More Than A Feeling' from the mid-1970's with its high pitched vocals and harmonies, some may even know the band's name was Boston, those with more interest could even name the writer as Tom Scholz and the singer of both lead and harmony backing as Brad Delp.

Boston had further popular songs sung by Delp who enjoyed the music of The Beatles to the extent that he also played in a tribute band called Beatlejuice. With a reputation as a 'nice guy' it was a shock to everyone when news of his suicide was announced in 2007.

A planned act, 55 year old Brad Delp left 'farewell' messages for those close to him and died from carbon monoxide poisoning in his own home, even warning anyone who entered the premises to be careful of the fumes. With signs of an attempt at poisoning from his car exhaust, a message on the garage door ominously lead to his 'plan B' where burning charcoal grills in his bedroom, gave off the fatal noxious fumes.

A final telling note pinned to his shirt confirmed that he was "Mr Brad Delp" with a further message in French stating that he was 'a lonely soul'.

An innovative Hammond organist and mellotron player from the mid 1960's with a pre-Cream rhythm section of Ginger Baker and Jack Bruce along with respected guitarist John McLaughlin, Graham Bond is another casualty of the 'nearly made it' musician syndrome. From auspicious beginnings as a jazz saxophonist, he featured briefly in Alexis Korner's Blues Incorporated prior to forming The Graham Bond organisation with some of rock's aspiring heavyweights.
However commercial success never materialised and Bond battled with depression and drugs.
Again, although some acquaintances dispute that he planned to commit suicide because he was off drugs at the time of his death and had plans to get back to music, having dabbled for a time with the Occult, nevertheless on 8 May 1974 Graham Bond died under the wheels of a train – did he jump or did he fall ?

The list of musicians who committed suicide is potentially endless as many people play an instrument and many disillusioned beings follow their own destiny but the point to be made is that success does not preclude depressive states of mind.

Even without the added pressures of fame, some aspiring musicians have performed this final act.

Adrian Borland was an English singer / songwriter and record producer, erstwhile member of The Sound who never achieved widespread recognition for his talents, had battled with depression for years and had attempted suicide on previous occasions prior to the fatal occasion when the 41 year old jumped in front of a train.

Greg Guidry was an American songwriter who had minor success as a singer and at the age of 53 died in a fire in his garaged car, official verdict suicide.

Peter Bellamy was a traditional English folk singer who was a stalwart of the movement through the 1960's /70's, and with The Young Tradition attempted to popularise the genre but throughout his career would not compromise his style for the sake of commerciality.   At the age of 47 he took his own life with the aid of whisky and pills.

John Bottomley was a singer / songwriter who had recognition in his native Canada in the 1990's. He committed suicide at the age of 50 in 2011.

Dave Lepard from Swedish metal band Crashdiet was only 25 when he ended it all.

Darby Crash was the singer in the Californian punk band The Germs from 1977-80 as they disbanded following his death in that year, but reformed 25 years later with Shane West, who was hired to play the part of Darby Crash in a movie about the band, now on vocals. At the age of 22, Crash had entered a suicide pact and overdosed on purpose, while the girl in the agreement lived to tell the tale.

His death occurred on 7 December 1980 and had minimal press coverage due to the murder of John Lennon the next day.

Nick Traina was the son of romance fiction writer Danielle Steele and although the family's wealth allowed what many would consider a privileged upbringing including playing in his first band at the age of 13 and touring with working punk outfit 'Link 80' for three years from the age of 16, Traina suffered depression and bi-polar syndrome.

He had reportedly attempted suicide a few times but despite his mother ensuring he was offered the best medical intervention, Nick Traina killed himself with an overdose of morphine at the tragically young age of 19.

The Last Farewell

Speculation about musicians taking their own lives is not confined to situations where no suicide note can be found but in the case of Richey Edwards, no body has been found either.   Edwards involvement in musical circles began when he was driver and roadie with Welsh group The Manic Street Preachers but soon progressed to be the band's main lyricist.
A University graduate, he was both articulate and artistic but suffered from depression and had a history of self-harming, conditions that he discussed publicly with candour.   Edwards disappeared on 1 February 1995 and his car was found abandoned a couple of weeks later with signs that someone had been living in the vehicle. The location was a Service Station in close proximity to the Severn Bridge, a notorious suicide spot, giving rise to the suggestion that he had ended his life.
Family and friends criticised Police attempts to locate Richey Edwards and it was not until 2008 when his status was recognised as 'presumed dead'.

An equally bizarre disappearance was the case of one time 'Iron Butterfly' bassist Philip Taylor Kramer. Iron Butterfly was most famous for the album 'In-A-Gadda-Da-Vida' a popular record from the end of the psychedelic era in 1968.

Kramer's musical involvement was brief 1974-75 and he then had a career in aerospace engineering working on US Govt. missile systems and later in the computer industry along with Michael Jackson's brother, Randy.

In 1995, the 42 year old went missing having been last seen at Los Angeles International Airport and in telephone contact with the Police, with whom it is alleged he claimed that he was going to kill himself. His wrecked minivan and skeletal remains were found 4 years later at the bottom of a canyon and there have been numerous conspiracy theories about the ex-musician's death particularly because he had previously been involved with US missile systems and also worked on facial detection processes.

Goodbye

To conclude the depressing list of dead musicians who can be considered as possible suicides, are three very different characters of whom there is no doubt that their demise was of their own doing.

David Sutch was a flamboyant individual, Jeanine Deckers had a serene personality and Wendy O'Williams portrayed an image of anti-establishment shock.

As Screaming Lord Sutch and The Savages, David Sutch fronted an early 1960's incarnation of theatrical rock and roll dressing up as Jack the Ripper and emerging from a coffin, years before the likes of Alice Cooper adopted the style. Musically the band's recordings were not well received despite the presence of guitarist Richie Blackmore for a time and the reputation that Sutch gained was more for his stage show than singing.

In 1963, David Sutch stood in his first election for the UK Parliament and contested many more throughout his life, winning none but gaining notoriety and bringing a sense of fun to the process. In 1983, he created The Monster Raving Loony Party which did actually succeed in having candidates elected at local Council level.

Despite the public image portrayed by the self-titled Screaming Lord Sutch, 3rd Earl of Harrow, David suffered from depression for most of his life. In 1998, his mother died and the following year, at the age of 58, he hanged himself in her house.

Although his musical records did not do well, one record that will be hard to beat is that David Sutch was the longest serving leader of a UK Political Party who stood for Parliament on more than 40 occasions and although always considered a fringe candidate, his political legacy could be that policies proposed by his Party in its manifesto did indeed become law at a later date such as lowering the voting age to 18, all day pub opening and having passports for pets.

Jeanine Deckers was the real name of a unique act who had an international hit record in 1963, making number one in the US, Canada and New Zealand charts, prompting an appearance on the Ed Sullivan Show.
The song was called 'Dominique' and was performed by Sister Luc Gabriel of the Belgian Dominican Convent, credited on record as The Singing Nun and referred to as Soeur Sourire (Sister Smile).
Although she achieved initial fame, Ms Deckers did not receive royalties for the success as they went to the Convent. She left the monastery in 1967 to try and pursue a career in music but remained a one hit wonder.

Becoming disillusioned not only with musical fame but also with Catholic teachings, the ex-nun spoke out in support of contraception.
Having retired from the music business from which she claimed she made no financial gain, Deckers was charged with a large tax bill by the Belgian Government and in a suicide note in 1985, the one-time Sister Smile at the age of 51 and her partner of 10 years Annie Pecher claimed that their financial problems was the reason for both their deaths by overdosing on pills.

Wendy O'Williams was lead singer with American anarchic punk band known as The Plasmatics whose outrageous stage act included risqué revealing costumes, simulated sex acts and the use of chainsaws. Williams continued the rebellious image after leaving the confines of the group and despite her controversial persona, was nominated for a Grammy for Best Female Rock Vocal in 1985.

However, away from the spotlight, she was a deep individual with a passion for animal welfare and a nihilistic perception of her own life. Wendy O'Williams withdrew from public performing in the early 1990's and shortly after attempted suicide by hammering a knife into her chest. This bizarre action was unsuccessful when the blade hit bone and she abandoned the attempt and called for help but a few years later failed in a second attempt by overdosing on prescription drugs.

Nevertheless, the following year, Williams ensured her death would be the outcome when she shot herself, leaving an explanation for her action. The content of her suicide note, while not justifying the rights of suicide, which many consider a selfish act, does however articulate the thought process of someone with that intent.

"I don't believe that people should take their own lives without deep and thoughtful reflection over a considerable period of time. I do believe strongly, however, that the right to do so is one of the most fundamental rights that anyone in a free society should have. For me, much of the world makes no sense, but my feelings about what I am doing ring loud and clear to an inner ear and a place where there is no self, only calm. Love always, Wendy."

Without judging motives or explanations, these words came from the tortured mind of someone who could not endure living and unlike the lyricist of 'Suicide Is Painless' earned the writer only posthumous sympathy.

The list of depressives is itself, depressing but the impact suicide can have on those left behind cannot be understood or quantified especially if the circumstances are inexplicable.

One suicide involved a fan of a musician rather than the actual artiste. The individual had developed an inferiority complex and became obsessed with fame and directly with the Icelandic singer Bjork.
Ricardo Lopez was infatuated by Bjork for a couple of years and when she began a relationship with the actor / drum and bass musician 'Goldie', Lopez's jealousy pushed him over the edge. The Uruguayan

born American began a video diary on his 21st birthday which portrayed him progressively losing control of reality and constructing a lethal letter bomb laced with sulphuric acid which he subsequently mailed to Bjork who was living in London at the time. The bomb was intercepted by the Metropolitan Police and did not reach its intended victim, but the sender had kept his video tape running as he recorded his ultimate scene.

While Bjork's song 'Remember Me' is playing in the background, Lopez is filmed shaving his head, painting his face and then fatally shooting himself.

This incident obviously affected the Icelandic musician and she decided to leave London and ensured increased security for her young son, but did express her grief for the stalker and acknowledged his death by sending flowers to his family.

This exemplifies the negative side to being a famous musician and highlights the increased threat level stalking victims can face. Although not all stalking incidents have such a terminal result, the fear and anxiety caused can still be traumatic.

Moving away from suicides, there are a few examples of stalking to highlight the problem.

Singer Janet Jackson was stalked for years by a man in his 40's and she eventually had a 3 year restraining order put on him and fellow singer Usher obtained a similar order against a female fan.

Former Red Hot Chilli Pepper's guitarist John Frusciante resorted to taking a female fan to court due to her stalking behaviour.

When Swedish pop sensations 'ABBA' called it a day in the early 1980's, the marriages between group members Benny Andersson and Anni-Frid Lyngstad as well as Bjorn Ulvaeus and Agnetha Faltskog were over. By this time the quartet had scaled the heights of stardom across the globe with their easy listening, catchy harmonious sound from the initial breakthrough 'Waterloo' through the dance floor favourite 'Dancing Queen' to the confessional 'Winner takes it All', ABBA had become one of the most successful pop acts ever.

Benny and Bjorn continued to write together but following solo success in various countries, the two girls took a break from music.
Anni-Frid, known as Frida was the only non-Swede out of the four, having been born in Norway to a Norwegian mother (who died at the age of 21) and a German, serving as a soldier when the two met. Frida had also been married prior to her nuptials with

Benny and following her stint as a pop princess in ABBA, she became a real Princess when she wed Prince Heinrich Ruzzo Reuss of Plauen (who died in 1999).

Agnetha withdrew from public life for almost a decade at the end of the eighties. She married and divorced again and then had a two year relationship which became problematic. The man in question was Dutch and when the romance ended, he began to stalk the singer who took the matter to court and a restraining order was issued banning him from entering Sweden. When the deportation order expired, the Dutchman again harassed the former ABBA singer and the Police were again called.

A former 'American Idol' contestant Paula Goodspeed became fixated by judge / dancer / singer Paula Abdul and she too took her own life by prescription pill overdose in a car near the musician's home. She had cd's and pictures of Abdul in the car and had written on a social media site that she had a secret crush on her namesake but sadly the torment of stalking turned into the tragedy of suicide.

Although these events are thankfully not common the controversial subject matter was the basis of a global hit by Eminem featuring Dido. The single 'Stan' about a fictional obsessive fan who eventually kills himself and his girlfriend, reached the top spot in more than 10 countries and charted in many others.

This example raises the question 'does art mirror reality or does real life provide material for artists'?

Murder On The Dancefloor

Although ending one's own life prematurely is tragic, in some cases it could be suggested that the individual is fulfilling their own destiny by their own hand but arguably more tragic is death by another's hand, as in murder.

Thankfully, not too many musicians have been murdered and where this has occurred, each situation has unique circumstances.

The most infamous name in rock music circles is Mark Chapman, not because he contributed anything positive to the genre, but because he murdered one of the most innovative, controversial, experimental, culture changing songwriters of the 20th Century.   As a member of the four piece group that changed rock and roll forever, spokesman for his generation, composer or co-composer of the most memorable songs in popular music and a genuine celebrity, John Winston Lennon was shot dead at point blank range as he left the safety of his apartment building.

It was hard to believe that someone would carry out an unprovoked attack on the man who sang, "All You Need Is Love", "Give Peace a Chance" and urged the world to "Imagine".

On 8 December 1980, everyone was stunned at the death of the 40 year old ex-Beatle but also at the blatant act of a lone gunman in broad daylight killing the dreams of so many. The murder of John Lennon was seen as epic and dramatic an event as the assassination of statesmen and world leaders. Sure, he had courted publicity with bizarre stunts, had been controversially outspoken on many topics and had rocked the establishment on many occasions but his message was always love, peace, harmony, expression, no war, freedom of speech and his art, writing, acting, playing and singing had educated and entertained an entire generation.

A cowardly act resulted in the incarceration for life of the man who pulled the trigger but the implications of Lennon's murder sent shockwaves and fear through the music industry and fellow musicians as well as the devastating loss for John's family, friends and legions of fans.

On 8 December 2004, exactly 24 years to the day that Mark Chapman killed one man and the dreams of many, another gunman, Nathan Gale attended a concert and committed another heinous murderous attack.

Gale was delusional, suffered from paranoid schizophrenia and took a handgun and at least 3 dozen rounds of ammunition to a live performance in Ohio by the metal band 'Damageplan'.

He aimed and shot 3 bullets into guitarist 'Dimebag' Darrell, killing him onstage, then shooting at others, killing another three innocent victims and wounding a further seven people, before Police arrived and ended the spree by shooting dead the killer.

Darrell had previously been guitarist with the band 'Pantera' and there have been numerous tributes since his untimely death at the age of 38.

A fan of the band 'Kiss', Dimebag Darrell had expressed a wish to be buried in a 'Kiss Kasket' – a bizarre piece of the group's merchandise, an actual coffin 'decorated' by pictures of the band – his wish was granted.

Another high profile musician's 'murder', had the hallmarks of fiction but again, tragically the facts are true.

A Minister from the 'House of God' Hebrew Pentecostal church raises eldest son in strict household, often using physical violence and bans him from listening to anything but Gospel music. Boy runs away from home and eventually joins the Air Force but drops out and becomes professional musician. Career starts slowly but eventually takes off and he becomes a major artist on the Tamla Motown label, marries the owner's sister who is 17 years older, has a child with her niece, his singing partner dies, he becomes depressed, argues with label boss about material and changes direction to record controversial album which becomes a big seller and crosses over to 'white market', becomes drug dependent, changes direction again and wins Grammy awards, moves back with his parents, threatens suicide, final argument with father results in parent shooting son dead.

This was a synopsis of the events that portrayed the life, career and death of Marvin Gaye.

He was signed to Motown and initially played drums on other artists' records, but when his own hits came, they were classics of the genre. 'How Sweet it is (to be loved by you)' and 'Aint that Peculiar' were followed by the Kim Weston duet 'It Takes Two' before Gaye began his string of successes with Tammi Terrell including 'Aint Nothing Like the Real Thing', 'You're All I Need to Get By' and 'The Onion Song'. Gaye was devastated when Tammi collapsed in his arms during a performance and was diagnosed with a brain tumour and despite numerous operations, she died in March 1970, aged only 24.
In the meantime Marvin Gaye had achieved major successes with his solo versions of 'I heard it Through

the Grapevine' and 'Too Busy Thinking About My Baby, but he became depressed and did not capitalise on his popularity.

However, in 1971, Gaye released 'What's Goin On' which spawned three major singles, the title song, 'Mercy Mercy Me' and 'Inner City Blues'. This successful move away from the 'pop' Tamla sound was followed by another acclaimed release 'Let's Get it On'.

Marvin Gaye was arguably the most popular 'black' artist of the time and although his life and career can be measured in peaks and troughs, following another dip during which time he would fail to turn up for performances, had allegations of owing vast amounts of back tax and was involved with drugs, in the early 1980's his popularity returned with the Grammy Award winning 'Sexual Healing'.

However, on 1 April 1984, the day before his 45 birthday, Marvin Gaye's father shot him dead with a gun given to him a few months earlier by the victim. Originally charged with murder, the verdict was given as voluntary manslaughter when it was revealed that the singer had beaten up his father and his drug fuelled depression and violence was becoming uncontrollable.

Another 'soul' artist was murdered 20 years previously.

Writer and singer of 'easy listening' pop standards 'Cupid', 'Chain Gang', 'Wonderful World' and 'Twistin' the Night Away', Sam Cooke was killed by a motel manager.

Cooke was only 33 and the events surrounding his death have been the subject of controversy and alleged conspiracy to murder.   However, the 'official' outcome was that the female motel manager acted in self-defence and the verdict was justifiable homicide.

Yet another talented musician was a victim of a violent death by the hands of another.

John Francis Anthony Pastorius III was an innovative 'jazz' bass player who was instrumental in popularising the sound of the fretless bass on his solo work, during his 6 year tenure with the jazz / rock ensemble 'Weather Report' and the many guest sessions specifically on four Joni Mitchell albums in the late 1970's.

Known by the nickname Jaco Pastorius, his initial instrument was the drums but following an injury to his wrist in his teens, he changed to his signature instrument and along with composing skills and performing flare, his talent augured a brilliant career. Unfortunately, behavioural difficulties, depression and eventual bipolar diagnosis resulted in periods of less productivity.

In September 1987, Pastorius was involved in a violent altercation with a club bouncer which left the 35 year old musician with multiple fractures and other injuries resulting in his death 10 days later.

The bouncer was initially charged with murder but was given a minimum sentence for manslaughter.

Peter Tosh was guitarist and one of the writers in the most influential Jamaican Reggae band, The Wailers. He also performed solo work and had a hit single 'Don't Look Back', as a duet with Mick Jagger. Following a musically uneventful period through the early 80's, in 1987, Tosh won a Grammy for best Reggae performance for his 'No Nuclear War'. Things appeared to be taking a turn for the better but later that year 42 year old Peter Tosh was shot dead during an attempt by crooks to extort money from him.   A number of people were injured in the crime and two disc jockeys as well as the guitarist were killed.

Saxophonist Don Myrick was a member of Earth, Wind & Fire and had played on other artists recordings most notably the sax solo on Phil Collins' single 'One More Night'. He was shot dead at the age of 53 in 1993, not intentionally murdered, but killed by a Police Officer during an investigation when he mistakenly thought the musician was armed.

Tupac Shakur was a controversial rapper with album sales in excess of 75 million.

During his short life, Tupac was the target of a shooting, sued the Police Department for brutality, was accused of shooting Police officers – but charges dropped, had been accused and found guilty of sexual assault, served a jail term and some of his associates were killed (along with an innocent child by a stray bullet) before he himself was eventually gunned down at the age of 25.

In addition to his controversial lifestyle, musically his subject matter covered subjects like racism, violence and social inequality and he was the only artist to have had a number one record whilst serving a jail sentence.

Tupac Shakur was murdered by members of a rival gang.

Tupac had sampled the track 'Let a Woman be a Woman, Let a Man be a Man' which had been a moderate hit for Dyke and the Blazers in 1969. Arlester Christian had fronted this 'funky' outfit before he too was gunned down in the street two years later, at the age of 27.

Houston rapper 'Fat Pat' was also 27 when he was shot dead in the street the same age as 'Lost Boyz' hip-hop artist Freaky Tah who was killed by a gunshot shot and Mexican singer Valentin Elizalde whose car was ambushed.

Mia Zapata was singer in the Seattle based punk band The Gits in the late eighties. They had just completed their second album in 1993 and not long after in the early hours of 7 July 1993, 27 year old Zapata was brutally assaulted, raped and murdered by an unknown assailant. The crime went unsolved for 10 years, but samples taken at the crime scene led to the conviction of a Cuban born fisherman.

Christian, Fat Pat and Zapata are another three names to add to the list of the mythical '27 Club '.

The Norwegian 'black metal band Mayhem' released albums with titles such as ' Pure Fucking Armageddon', 'Deathrehearsal', 'Deathcrush' and (translated) 'The mysteries of Satan'. Guitarist 'Euronymous' (demon) owned the record label Deathlike Silence Productions and record shop 'Helvete' (Hell) which specialised in this 'dark' genre. However, the morbid references were not merely marketing, anarchy prevailed in the scene.

Euronymous (Oystein Aarseth) was often at loggerheads with vocalist 'Dead' (Per Yngve Ohlin) and it was he who discovered Ohlin's remains following his suicide and reportedly took photographs prior to reporting the death.

Euronymous along with guitarist Varg Vikernes were rumoured to have been involved with the burning of churches and a plan to blow up a Cathedral.

In August 1993, Mayhem's 25 year old guitarist
Euronymous was killed by multiple stab wounds
inflicted by ex-Mayhem guitarist Vikernes who was
jailed for arson and murder.

This is not the only case of a musician being
institutionalised for committing manslaughter or
murder.

Jim Gordon was the most sought after session
drummer in the latter part of the sixties and into the
seventies.   He played with or on records by major acts
including, The Everly Brothers, The Beach Boys, The
Byrds, Steely Dan, Joe Cocker, Traffic and Alice
Cooper.

Gordon was also a member of Derek and the
Dominoes featuring on 'Layla and Other Assorted Love
Songs' and was responsible for the extended piano
section on the album's title single.

However, despite his ability, popularity and
unassuming character, the troubled mind of the
musician began to dominate and his behaviour
reached a critical impasse.

In 1983, the musician attacked his mother with a
hammer and then killed her by stabbing. Although it
was discovered that Jim Gordon was an undiagnosed
schizophrenic and had been hearing voices inside his
head, including his mother's, he was found guilty of
the murder and sentenced to 16 years in jail.

Huddie Ledbetter was born in 1888 and died in 1949. He became known as Leadbelly (although he emphasised the form Lead Belly) and is often cited as an influence on modern blues styled musicians.
The tenor voiced singer recorded his signature tune, the traditional folk number 'Goodnight Irene' in 1933 but the image of the classic romantic song was at odds with his temper and violent behaviour.

Lead Belly had been jailed for carrying a gun and was directed to work on the chain gang, from which he escaped, however, he was then found guilty of murdering a man in a fight over a woman and re-imprisoned.
Released after seven years, he was then convicted of attempted murder when he stabbed a man and back to jail where his talents were discovered and he recorded whilst incarcerated.
Lead Belly played twelve string guitar and accordion, sang well, was familiar with a wealth of material and his recorded legacy provided a fertile plundering ground for later musicians.

It has been suggested that his early release from prison was due to his musical ability but this has not been proven, nevertheless, a few years later he was charged with yet another assault by stabbing.

Another American singer of whom it was said, had a short temper was Little Willie John.   He had a number of hits in the fifties including 'Need Your Love So Bad' which was written by his older brother Merton, and was recorded more than ten years later by Fleetwood Mac. John was also responsible for showcasing the song 'Fever' which was then popularised by Peggy Lee, but unfortunately he was also infamous for an incident in which he fatally stabbed a man and was convicted of manslaughter and jailed where he died two years later in circumstances that have since been disputed.

Another fatal stabbing, another musician charged with murder and another disputed outcome was the well documented case of Sid and Nancy.

John Simon Richie (Beverley) became the iconic punk Sid Vicious, bass player of arguable ability of the Sex Pistols. His was the archetypal image of the genre, arrogant swaggering leering spitting scowling and potentially self-destructive.
Following the short lived career of the 'Pistols', Vicious was being managed by his then American girlfriend Nancy Spungen but during a confusing drug filled evening in which a knife bought by Sid was found in the body of Nancy, life became 'Pretty Vacant' with she dead and he the main suspect. Again there were conflicting stories but no conclusion as three months later, Vicious was dead from an overdose.

The highest profile musician charged and found guilty of murder has been described, prior to his conviction, using adjectives such as innovative, legendary, enigmatic, introverted, weird, frightening and by the noun genius.

He was a Teddy Bear (To Know Him is to Love Him), songwriter, record company owner, the husband of a Ronette, creator of the 'wall of sound', producer of the epic 'River Deep Mountain High' and 'You've Lost That Loving Feeling', collaborator on The Beatles 'Let it Be', producer of the Ramones biggest hit, arranger of Leonard Cohen's elaborate 'Death of a Ladies Man' and many more seminal moments in popular music. He is Phil Spector, currently serving a nineteen year sentence for murder, following a very public televised trial which resulted in a 'mistrial' verdict followed by a second less public but more decisive guilty result. Actress Lana Clarkson died in Spector's home and the musician claimed that it was accidental suicide, after she 'kissed the gun' but witnesses recounted Phil Spector's previous threatening behaviour with firearms and he was convicted of second degree murder.

These few manslaughter / murders of musicians can be backed up by facts and evidence but there are also conspiracy theories surrounding the deaths of two major stars, Elvis Presley and Michael Jackson.

Towards the end of his life Presley had gained considerable weight and he had also been prescribed numerous drugs and sedatives. His actual cause of death appeared to be from a heart problem but the details are conflicting with one doctor having identified the cause as cardiac arrhythmia which is an irregular heartbeat and although in some cases this can be fatal, the nature of it can only be detected when the patient is alive. Another of Elvis' doctors had been over-subscribing pills to the 'King' and although no action was taken at the time, his licence was eventually revoked for oversubscribing 13 years after Presley's death and he was no longer allowed to practice.

In Michael Jackson's case his physician had also been describing inappropriate drugs and in addition was accused of not reacting professionally when the singer was found close to death and perhaps could have been saved. He was also struck off and found guilty of manslaughter and jailed for four years.

These brief paragraphs do not do justice to the two legends of popular music but highlight how easily spectacular careers and human lives can end when fame overtakes reality and allows individuals to lose control of their own destiny.

42 year old Elvis Presley and 50 year old Michael Jackson gave so much, produced so much as a legacy but tragically left the stage before their acts were finished.

Chapter 10

Losing My Religion

"That's me in the corner, that's me in the spotlight, losing my religion, trying to keep a view and I don't know if I can do it, oh no I've said too much, I haven't said enough" (xx) by REM

In 1966, The Beatles were popular in most countries in the world following record breaking record sales, wonderful writing and innovative musicianship. However, that was the year that the group effectively played its final live concert in Candlestick Park, San Francisco (the 1969 Get Back / Let it Be performance on the roof of Apple was live but not a concert) and '66 was also the year that a controversial quote from John Lennon resulted in a backlash from many Americans which led to mass burning of Fab Four discs.

Lennon's comment was reported as stating that The Beatles were bigger than Jesus' and Christians objected to what they saw as arrogance at the very least but more so considered it a sacrilegious statement. Following the controversy, the song writing guitarist attempted to explain what he meant by the phrase which he maintained was taken out of context.

In fact, what John Lennon was highlighting, was the general popularity of rock ' n' roll as opposed to Christianity.

He did not maintain that he, the Beatles or popular music was superior to a belief system.

However, this event highlighted the link between modern popular musicians' public persona and their personal beliefs in relation to traditional religion. Prior to the rise of loquacious lyricists, articulate artists and spiritual sceptics, the private lives and views of performers was not publicised but as media interest in the political, moral and philosophical thoughts of musicians became more intrusive, those in the public eye were happy to oblige and divulge their personal beliefs.

The establishment had always been suspicious of the long haired, drug taking, peace loving, free loving attitude of sixties youth and were not slow in trying to make examples of celebrity musicians. One Sergeant from the Metropolitan Police Drug Squad gained an infamous reputation for apparently targeting high profile musicians in relation to drug possession. Norman Pilcher's drug raids led to the arrests of Mick Jagger, Keith Richards, Brian Jones, John Lennon, George Harrison, Donovan and various lady friends of these well- known 'law breakers'.

Pilcher was eventually discredited for his methods and jailed for four years for perjury.

San Quentin / Folsom Prison Blues

There have been numerous instances where musicians have been arrested and / or spent some time in jail as a result of their involvement with drugs but those incarcerated for other crimes are not of a high number. Before considering the religious views of some musicians, there are a few examples of those whose morals allowed them to get on the wrong side of the law.

As has been mentioned, Jim Gordon and Phil Spector are serving time for manslaughter and Sid Vicious was charged with the death of Nancy Spungen.

Other unsavoury acts leading to the imprisonment of musicians include 'outlaw country' singer and writer Johnny Paycheck who was sentenced to seven years in 1985 for shooting a man, in which he claimed was self-defence. The bullet scraped across the victim's head and did not seriously injure him and after serving nearly two years in jail, Paycheck was pardoned and released.

One of Johnny Paycheck's best known songs 'Take that Job and Shove it' was written by David Allen Coe, himself an outlaw country singer who also spent time behind bars.

Coe was frequently incarcerated throughout his teens and twenties and used the experiences as material for his songs.   His reputation has been mythologised with one story that he was on death row for killing a man who asked him for oral sex. There is no question that he is controversial, having performed wearing a mask and living in Nashville in the back of a hearse are just two examples but he made his mark in country music with artists such as Tanya Tucker, Billy Jo Spears and even Kid Rock covering his songs.

Away from strictly country music, Coe has toured with Neil Young and Grand Funk Railroad as well as recorded with Pantera but a clue to his musical roots can be found in the name of David Allen Coe's first album 'Penitentiary Blues'.

Although David Crosby's career has been dotted with drug incidents, his lowest ebb and perhaps the event that saved him was in 1982 when his exploits with drugs and firearms cost him almost a year in a Texas prison. Even inside, Crosby managed to upset the 'establishment' by joining the prison band and performing his rebellious anthem 'Almost Cut My Hair' much to the annoyance of the Governor.

Chuck Berry was jailed in 1962 under the Mann Act in the USA for transporting a minor across State borders – this referred to a 14 year old girl with whom it was claimed, Berry was having sex.

The CV of Peter Yarrow reads like a man with high ethical standards apart from one blemish. He graduated with a degree in Psychology, co-wrote and sang the children's favourite 'Puff the Magic Dragon, performed for years and had hit records as part of top folk trio Peter, Paul and Mary, was an activist for many good causes and created 'Operation Respect' which aims to help vulnerable children.

The blemish, for which he was eventually given a Presidential pardon by Jimmy Carter occurred in 1970 and Yarrow served three months in jail for the 'misdemeanour'.

At the age of 32, the singer had sex in a hotel room with a 14 year old 'fan'.   At the time, he maintains, 'the whole groupie thing was common practice' but he has since said his behaviour was reprehensible and his positive image was tarnished by a foolish action.

Writer, singer, producer, impresario and man of many aliases Jonathan King was sentenced for apparently having sex with underage boys. King always maintained his innocence and gained some support from established figures claiming that the case was unfair.

Known for being outspoken and opinionated, Jonathan King is both famous and infamous and despite his many critics, made his mark on popular music.

He wrote and sang his first international hit 'Everyone's Gone to the Moon' while still a student, discovered and initially produced Genesis, had involvement with 10CC and featured in the UK charts numerous times with novelty style material under his own name and in the guise of Sakkarin, Shag, Bubblerock, The Piglets and One Hundred Ton and a Feather. King is critical of the BBC and the UK Justice System, has spoken out about the need for prison reform and continues to have a major online following, including a best-selling e-book autobiography.

Glam-rock star Paul Gadd in the persona of Gary Glitter asked his fans in the early seventies if they 'wanted to be in his gang'. Many responded in the affirmative and Glitter was indeed the Leader of the Gang for a few years with his kitsch rock and roll show. However, he was convicted in the UK in 1999 for possession of child pornography and in 2005 Gadd was arrested in Vietnam for allegedly having sex with underage girls and subsequently jailed. Although he has always maintained his innocence, Gary Glitter is listed on the UK sex offenders register and in 2012 he was being investigated again as part of the evidence gathering for the case against the celebrity disc jockey and personality Jimmy Saville.

Writer, singer and record producer R Kelly has had many hits himself and in collaboration with others making him one of the best-selling R&B artists but outside his native USA he is best known for his 1996 ballad 'I Believe I Can Fly'. He has had a couple of run-ins with the law, one being for assault but in 2002 he was accused of having sex with an underage girl and in the next couple of years further charges in relation to pornography were made. Eventually court hearings were held in 2008, but he was found not guilty of 14 charges.

Back in the sixties, the Doors lead singer Jim Morrison was arrested for indecent exposure following an incident in Florida when a drunk Morrison simulated sex, asked the audience 'Do you want to see my cock' and briefly unzipped his trousers showing what was inside. Forty years later, the Florida Board of Executive Clemency' voted to posthumously pardon the dead vocalist.

In 1996, Green Day's Billie Joe Armstrong dropped his trousers in front of 6000 fans at a concert and was arrested for indecent exposure for baring his buttocks.

Country star Merle Haggard was often in trouble with the law as a teenager and found himself in San Quentin prison in 1958 following a botched robbery.

Having taken an interest in music, Haggard left the jail with the intention of pursuing country music and his gravel voice found acceptance in the genre, producing many hits over a long career, his best known being his co-written 'Okie from Muskogee'.

As a prisoner he witnessed a performance by the musician most associated with prison, Johnny Cash. The singer songwriter had a reputation as a jailbird although he was only ever locked up for the occasional overnight stay. Cash ran into trouble with the law a few times for possession of prescription drugs, vehicle offences and trespassing. One incident led to a major fine for burning down a forest but he did not get into trouble for any serious crime despite his image.

Johnny Cash, did however have an affinity with prisoners and recorded best-selling albums in jails with sentenced criminals as his live audience. The songs 'Folsom Prison Blues' and 'San Quentin' became two of the most popular in his repertoire.

Cash did overindulge in alcohol, was addicted for a time to amphetamines and frequently tried to kick his habits. He married singer June Carter in 1968 and although he termed himself a sinner, was always a Christian and around this time he re-affirmed his faith. Johnny Cash was known as 'the man in black' and he paraphrased this title for a controversial religious book he wrote about the apostle Paul calling it

'The Man in White'. He also has a song of the same name and throughout his career there are many religious references in his output.

I Believe

Some musicians have faith but keep their views separate from their careers while others use their celebrity to pass on the message of their beliefs.

UK popster Cliff Richard was always open about his Christianity and has managed to maintain parallel careers as a mainstream entertainer whilst releasing religious material. He has played a couple of times at 'Greenbelt' which is an annual Christian Festival in England that has grown from an audience of a couple of thousand in 1974 to approximately 20,000 and has attracted more of pop / rocks bigger names who are either Christian or sympathetic to the ethos.

In a career that has lasted more than 50 years, the Indian born Harry Webb adopted the stage name Cliff Richard and as the first 'pop singer' to be knighted, is so popular in the UK that he is often just referred to as Sir Cliff. His first hit was the rocker 'Move It' in 1958 and since then his style has tried to move with the times whilst trying to retain general popularity, which despite his many critics, Richard has managed to do. Single releases with and without his backing group The Shadows, are in excess of 150 with UK top 30 hits in almost every year of each decade, including 14 number ones and numerous chart placings in other countries but surprisingly few in the USA.

Cliff has also released approximately 70 albums, of which 7 were 'faith' albums and a few songs do nothing to disguise his beliefs.

Sir Cliff had once supported his Christian faith in a television debate against ex- Manfred Mann and solo vocalist Paul Jones, who would go on to be vocalist / harmonica player with the respected 'Blues Band' and coincidently also convert to Christianity.

Cliff Richard lived up to his 'Bachelor Boy' persona by never marrying but companions in his home have been 'religious' friends and managers, latterly a Catholic priest.

In 1989, Cliff sang a duet with Van Morrison on the latter's composition 'Whenever God Shines His Light'. Morrison is a prolific writer and his catalogue includes songs with the titles 'No Religion' and 'She gives me Religion'.   He had been raised in Northern Ireland at a time of conflict between Catholics and Protestants and for a time his mother was affiliated with Jehovah's Witnesses but Van reportedly read about various forms of spirituality, even toying with 'Scientology' which he later distanced himself from. Although there have been subtle references to meditation and spiritual themes throughout many of Van Morrison's albums, his 1986 release 'No Guru, No Method, No Teacher' proved that Van The Man is his own man.

Former topless model Samantha Fox moved into a pop career back in the mid-eighties with the single 'Touch Me (I want your body)' which reached the top of the charts in numerous countries and despite many sceptics Sam went on to sell in excess of 30 million albums.
By the mid-nineties, she had attended the 'Alpha' course exploring Christianity and renewed her belief in God. By the next decade her relationships had moved from male to female.

Early in the new millennium former 'Ginger Spice', Geri Halliwell reportedly attended the Alpha course.

Madonna (Louise Veronica Ciccone) was raised Catholic but early in the new millennium, she embraced 'Kabbalah'.

Roger McGuinn was responsible for the sound of The Byrds with his jangling guitar and slightly strained vocals as well as contributing to the song writing when the band weren't interpreting Dylan covers.
McGuinn has been committed to Christianity since the mid-seventies but ten years previous, the then Jim McGuinn was involved with the spiritual movement 'Subud' and changed his name to Roger.

This name apparently suited his 'vibrations', but although he quit the organisation after a decade, the ex-Byrd continues to be known as Roger McGuinn.

Contemporary songwriter Robert Zimmerman was born into the Jewish Faith and as Bob Dylan became the most influential songwriter of his generation. Dylan's songs have covered a variety of subjects and his music crossed styles.

The first transition from folk singer to electric music performer caused much consternation to 'traditional folkies', but following this progression in the 1960's, Bob Dylan treated music fans to pop, country, rock and rockabilly. He duetted with Joan Baez and collaborated with the Grateful Dead, The Band and Tom Petty along with The Heartbreakers and fellow Traveling Wilburys George Harrison, Roy Orbison and Jeff Lynne. Dylan also featured Emmylou Harris to provide harmony to his vocals and toured with various musicians in The Rolling Thunder Review, shared the bill with Mark Knopfler and Van Morrison, but eyebrows were raised and diehard fans questioned his decision when he became a 'born again Christian'. This phase was late 1979 into early 1980 and spawned the two religious album offerings 'Slow Train Coming' and 'Saved' along with the acclaimed single release 'Gotta Serve Somebody'. Dylan claims that he was never born again and has always been a believer, and although apparently not attached to any particular religion, he has been known to take part in Jewish religious ceremonies.

He is one of few people from the rock world to have performed for a Pope (in 1997 for Jean Paul II) and in 2009 surprised the music public by releasing a festive album 'Christmas in the Heart'. Bob Dylan's lyrics may have many interpretations but throughout his career he always appears to have been 'Knocking on Heaven's Door'.

Dylan co-composed the first song 'I'd Have You Anytime' with George Harrison on the ex-Beatle's first post group album 'All Things Must Pass'. This triple disc set contained a number of overtly religious, philosophical and spiritual songs such as 'Hear Me Lord', 'Beware of Darkness', 'Awaiting on You All' and 'What is Life'.

The record buying public was anything but put off by this blatant display of theological lyricizing and pushed the opus to the top of the charts. The single from the long player was a global smash reaching number 1 in many countries and it too had religious appeal in more ways than one and despite a melody similar to 'He's So Fine', Harrison's masterpiece 'My Sweet Lord' became one of the most played religious messages on the airwaves.

The guitarist already had a reputation as a deep thinker and was one of the first to embrace meditation and as far back as 1967 on the Beatles' seminal album 'Sgt. Pepper', Harrison's contribution was the eastern flavoured philosophical 'Within You Without You'.

George Harrison then used his influence to gather musician friends, play live, record / film and release the material for charitable purposes, in this case The Concert for Bangla Desh was for much needed funds for the war torn and starving nation.
However, this was the precursor of the pop/rock charity concerts epitomised by Bob Geldof's Live Aid & Live 8.

Harrison continued his spiritual outpouring with his follow up album 'Living in the Material World' and the single 'Give me Love Give me Peace on Earth'.

In addition to his own material, George Harrison championed the Hare Krishna cause and produced the Rhadha Krishna Temple's successful single urging the public to chant the 'Hare Krishna Mantra'.
For the remainder of George Harrison's career and life, he was a high profile follower of Hinduism and used his position to highlight the tenets of the religion.

A number of musicians are declared Buddhists including REM vocalist Michael Stipe, actress / singer Jennifer Lopez and 'punk poet' Patti Smith.
The late 'Beastie Boy' Adam Yauch, who died in 2012, converted to Buddhism in 1994 and became an

activist for Tibetan independence.

Singer and writer for Dream Academy, best known for 'Life in a Northern Town' Nick Laird Clowes spent some time in a Himalayan Monastery in the late nineties and returned with the adopted spiritual name 'Trashmonk'.

Although septuagenarian singer / songwriter Leonard Cohen is Jewish and continues to observe the faith, he also embraced Buddhism and in the 1990's he was ordained as a Buddhist monk.

Perhaps it is surprising to think that someone with a controversial background as an exotic dancer, drug addict and general wayward soul was drawn to Buddhism.

Then again, perhaps it is not so difficult to understand, when you consider the broken home, transient upbringing, fighting for child custody and suicide of infamous husband that Courtney Love endured. The 'Hole' writer and singer has been a practising Buddhist since 1989 and she maintains that this faith assisted her to overcome her drug dependent past.

I'm A Believer

The singing Jackson family were raised as Jehovah's Witnesses but Michael and his brothers as well as La Toya and Janet concentrated on music, only sister Rebbie continued as an active member.

The musician usually known as Prince and always known to keep his private life private, reportedly became a Jehovah's Witness on the advice of family friend Larry Graham ex bassist from soul funk outfit Sly and the Family Stone.

Musicians with previous involvement with the Watchtower Society include wannabe celebrity Peter Andre, tell her what you want what you really really want Ginger Spice Geri Halliwell and JaRule.

Two guitarists are still active in the movement, jazz/funk/soul player George Benson and one of the most influential wielders of an axe and large spectacles who came out of the Shadows Mr Hank Marvin.

There are a number of practising Mormons who are also practising musicians but few have achieved major popularity.

The best known act who were also members of the Church of the Latter Day Saints were the seventies pop sensation The Osmonds, a family that had hits as a group, solo success for youngest brother Jimmy and duo as well as individual success for Donny and Marie.

Another lead singer in a popular group is also a follower, Brandon Flowers from the best- selling Las Vegas band The Killers.
Arcade Fire brothers Win and Will Butler were raised as Mormons due to the conversion of their grandfather 'swing era guitarist' Alvino Rey and the influence of their mother.
Win graduated with a degree in Religious Studies.

The 'Religious Society of Friends' is the embracing term for the pacifist Christian movement of which members are commonly known as 'Quakers'.
Singer, songwriter, accomplished guitarist and anti-nuclear activist Bonnie Raitt was raised with Quaker principles as was folk 'protest' singer Joan Baez.
Other musicians with a leaning towards the 'Friends' are the '2, 4, 6, 8 Motorway' singer and now DJ Tom Robinson and 'Talking Head' on the road to somewhere, Scots born David Byrne.

Celtic based musician Mike Scott is also Scottish but much of his 'Waterboys' influence has Irish heritage not least much of the raw material that he hones into his act and many of the musicians who have graced the stage with the enigmatic frontman.

However, as a songwriter he also expresses personal content, his beliefs, historic and Scottish influence. Scott has always been a spiritual person and often cites God in his lyrics in an informative rather than a preaching way.
An association with the Findhorn Community in North East Scotland helped strengthen his spiritual path.

Singer, songwriter, producer and guitarist Lenny Kravitz is perhaps best known for his biggest hits 'It Aint Over 'til it's Over' and 'Fly Away' but he has also written for Vanessa Paradis, Steve Tyler and Madonna, worked Mick Jagger and Michael Jackson among others and been awarded Grammys.

The child of a mixed marriage, he is partly Jewish but is open about his Christian beliefs and in addition to acknowledging this in his lyrics, the much pierced Kravitz sports a tattoo stating, 'My Heart Belongs to Jesus Christ'.

One of George Harrison's observational songs, 'Isn't it a Pity' was covered by Dana, the Eurovision Song Contest winner for Ireland in 1970.

London born Dana Scallon's winning song was 'All Kinds of Everything' which was a hit in a few countries following the Contest. Although she has rarely troubled the charts outside Ireland since the early 1970's, Dana has released numerous Catholic albums with many of the religious themed songs written by herself.

Outside music and religion, she was at one time an Irish MEP and stood, unsuccessfully as a candidate for the Presidency of Ireland.

The flip side of musicians who have a taste for religion throws up an interesting Top 10 of pop/rock albums from none other than the Catholics with catholic taste.

An article in the Guardian newspaper (ib) quotes from the Vatican publication 'L'Osservatore Romano' listing the best albums in popular music and admitted that the choice was not "easy" and was "partial".

Nevertheless it is a list of perhaps surprising 'normal' rock artists without a hint of religion, apart from the occasional confessional song.

So, approved listening from the Vatican appears to be;

1) The Beatles - Revolver

2) David Crosby - If I Could Only Remember My Name

3) Pink Floyd - Dark Side of the Moon

4) Fleetwood Mac - Rumours

5) Donald Fagan - The Nightfly

6) Michael Jackson - Thriller

7) Paul Simon - Graceland

8) U2 - Achtung Baby

9) Oasis - (What's the Story) Morning Glory

10) Carlos Santana - Supernatural

Carlos Santana was a devotee of Guru Sri Chimnoy whose teachings were also promoted by jazz / rock guitarist John McLaughlin who even named his protégé's group as The Mahavishnu Orchestra.
The two guitarists collaborated on the inspired album 'Love, Devotion, Surrender' which despite its non-commercial jazz fusion style achieved top 20 in both Britain and America which proved that the musically appreciative public was not put-off by the spiritual content.

The 'High Numbers' changed their name to The Who and achieved high numbered chart placings with a reputation as 'mods' and wreckers of musical equipment. The majority of The Who's songs were written by guitarist Pete Townsend who progressed from pop material to the more mature rock opera format. Townsend also made reference in interviews and on albums to his 'guru – Meher Baba' whose metaphysical views had found increasing popularity in Western culture since the 1930's but contradictory to rock's marijuana generation, he was outspoken against the use of hallucinogenic drugs.

Don't Stop Believing

Acclaimed guitarist, songwriter and multi award winning musician Richard Thomson has had a long and distinguished career from his work with Fairport Convention, ex-wife Linda, various collaborations and solo performances. However, he has also maintained a dignified low profile, and does not seek false fame. Thomson also keeps his beliefs low key and does not preach or push his views to others but back in the mid-seventies he moved into a Sufi commune and embraced Islam.

He left the commune soon after but retained his faith and although now a lapsed Sufi, Richard Thomson still follows the tenets of Islam.

Danny Thomson is not related to Richard but the double bass player has often accompanied his namesake and played with many established and up and coming musicians, notably featuring on Nick Drake's albums and being a member of the jazz folk outfit Pentangle. Danny was also sideman for the unconventional John Martyn and stories of their outrageous exploits are as popular as their music and it is perhaps surprising that with that background, Danny Thomson converted to Islam in 1990.

The musical career of Cat Stevens has encompassed diverse images.
As a teenager, the London born of Greek heritage Steven Demetre Giorgiou adopted the stage name Cat Stevens and achieved chart success with a few records, most notably 'Mathew and Son'. He also found recognition as a songwriter with 'Here Comes My Baby' a hit for the Tremeloes and 'First Cut is the Deepest' for PP Arnold (and later Rod Stewart).

Serious illness kept him out of the business for a couple of years but he re-emerged in the early 1970's with a new image as a singer songwriter and had global album success with 'Tea For The Tillerman', 'Teaser and the Firecat' and 'Catch Bull at Four'. Popular singles included 'Lady D'Arbanville' ,'Wild World', 'Morning has Broken' and 'Moonshadow' and he continued making albums and performing through the seventies but in what appeared a dramatic decision, the singer / songwriter quit the music business and retired the name Cat Stevens.

Just before the age of 30, the 'Peace Train' composer converted to Islam and shortly after formally became known as Yusuf Islam, the pop star musician being resigned to history.

As a Muslim, he stopped performing his songs but his back catalogue brought in substantial royalties which he donated to worthy causes. Yusuf Islam occasionally appeared in news articles commenting on certain controversial events and some elements of the media tended to report unfavourably on his views but eventually he returned to music, initially concentrating on unaccompanied Islamic material but after an absence of 25 years the musician returned to performing in English and the Western journalists were more positive. A collaboration with Ronan Keating on a reworking of 'Father and Son' saw Yusuf Islam back in the pop charts, and in addition to writing and recording new material he also returned to performing other versions of his older songs live, although with some changes to lyrics to ensure compliance with religious standards. The old Cat Stevens hit 'I'm Gonna Get Me a Gun' was not included in the revamped repertoire but Yusuf Islam now appreciates the power of songs to portray positive messages to a new generation of music fans and has returned to touring.

Cat Stevens / Yusuf Islam has always maintained that his conversion was not sudden but a gradual progressive change of path.   One incident is often quoted as the catalyst that led Cat Stevens to 'work for God' and as Yusuf Islam he confirms that it was an impetus.

In the mid 1970's, Cat Stevens had a near death experience in which he almost drowned whilst in California but apparently shouted to God that if he was saved, he would work for the supreme being. A wave then carried him to safety on dry land and the already spiritual and theologically aware singer's destiny was set.

Another English born musician was converted to religion whilst in California but in this instance the decision was instantaneous.

Jeremy Spencer was one of three guitarists in the original blues version of Fleetwood Mac from 1967 but four years later whilst on tour in America he reportedly went for a walk one afternoon and did not return. The group's management searched for him but by the time they tracked him down, Spencer had joined the cult Children of God. The decision was on the spur of the moment but the guitarist had been disillusioned with the band and was looking for a new direction.   There was talk of brainwashing but Jeremy Spencer always maintained that he was not coerced and remained a member of the organisation, now called the Family International. Musically, Spencer continued to play within his religious setting and played at gospel based concerts but recently he has recorded material closer to his roots.

Exposure in the media can sometimes boost a serious artists profile but on occasion superlative praise can sometimes backfire.

A review by Robert Shelton in the New York Times in 1961 announced that Bob Dylan was "A bright new face in folk music......one of the most distinctive stylists....".
In the case of Bruce Springsteen, he and his band had been performing for a few years and had honed their live act to the exciting performance that many had yet to witness and they had also produced a couple of well-reviewed but commercially low selling albums. However, following a review of a concert in a Boston newspaper article, the career of the Boss along with the E Street Band really took off.
John Landau quoted in 22 May1974 edition of The Real Paper,

"I saw rock and roll's future and its name is Bruce Springsteen. And on a night when I needed to feel young, he made me feel that I was hearing music for the very first time."

This claim was a lot to live up to but 'Born to Run', 'Born in the USA' and a long career as one of rock's superstars proved the quote to be accurate.

Unfortunately for singer songwriter Andy Pratt, the prediction was not as accurate. Pratt had released some low key material and was making a name for himself in the Boston area when he had a breakthrough hit single with his opus 'Avenging Annie' which featured his piano skills and pre-Bee Gee falsetto.
A Review in Rolling Stone Magazine stated,

"By reviving the dream of rock as an art and then re-inventing it, Pratt has forever changed the face of rock".

 The prolific writer and talented musician has had a prodigious output since the early 1970's when success seemed likely but major recognition remained elusive. Andy Pratt converted to Christianity in 1978 and much of his work since has featured spiritual themes. He still writes, records and performs as well as being a faith healer because as one of his song titles profess, 'That's when Miracles Occur'.

Some musicians have taken their religious activities even further than Andy Pratt's working with the faith and become ordained preachers.

Faith

Bryan MacLean ex guitarist with American sixties innovative band 'Love' apparently 'saw the light' and released material with a Christian theme and toyed with the idea of becoming a full time preacher but relented and stayed in music.

Beach Boy Carl Wilson was a very spiritual person who organised communal prayers prior to live shows and even as he was weakened by cancer requiring him to sit while performing, he would stand reverentially to sing the classic 'God Only Knows'.
In the 1980's he was ordained as a Minister in the Movement of Spiritual Inner Awareness.

There is a direct link between Gospel music and soul music and many exponents of the latter learned the former in churches and progressed into mainstream singing while retaining their religious faiths.

Little Richard was a pioneer of rock and roll with his raucous renditions of 'Tutti Frutti', 'Lucille', 'Good Golly Miss Molly' and 'Long Tall Sally' to name a few. At his peak he had a flamboyant image and reputation as wild, participating in orgies with men and women as well as drinking and drug abuse. Despite this lifestyle, Richard Wayne Penniman was tortured by guilt and tried giving up his excesses and embracing Christianity.

For two periods in his career, Richards moved away from music and concentrated on his faith but even as Reverend Penniman he was never far from the limelight and other musicians. Reverend Little Richard officiated at the weddings of Cyndi Lauper, Tom Petty and Steve Van Zandt as well as preached at the funerals of Wilson Picket and Ike Turner.

The Reverend Al Green has been delivering sermons since 1976 when he became an ordained pastor. A few years previously, his soulful voice graced the airwaves and charts with renditions of 'Let's Stay Together', 'Tired of Being Alone' and 'I'm Still in Love with You'. Green also co-wrote the 'Talking Heads' hit 'Take me to the River' and recorded an emotive version of the Bee Gees' 'How can you Mend a Broken Heart' but he gave it all up to follow the evangelical route. However, in addition to continuing to record gospel music, Al Green has also recently returned to R&B.

Former Harold Melvin and the Blue Notes member Jerry Cummings also became an ordained minister.

Richey Furay was co-founder of the influential Buffalo Springfield along with Stephen Stills and Neil Young. When the group disbanded after three albums, Furay co-founded country rockers Poco while Stills and Young went on to superstardom.

Poco has had a long career with various line-ups and an element of success but not major sales during Richie's tenure. He left in the early seventies and joined American west coast stalwarts JD Souther (who had written for the Eagles among others) and Chris Hillman (ex Byrds, Flying Burrito Brothers and Manassas with Stephen Stills) and became the SHF band.

Around this time Furay became a Christian and in 1983 quit the music business and became a Christian pastor.

Over the years Richie Furay has released solo material, some of it with obvious religious themes, with moderate success and he still performs, appears at Poco reunions and more recently as per the album title, 'Buffalo Springfield Again' when he reunited with Stephen Stills and Neil Young for a benefit concert followed by a short tour.

The group known as 'America' began in 1970 as trio of Dewey Bunnell, Dan Peek and Gerry Beckley, who were the sons of American servicemen living in the UK. Peek left after seven years as he had renewed his faith and was drawn to the Christian music genre, Bunnell and Beckley continued successfully as writers and singers with backing musicians, as 'America'.

Coincidently, following their first eponymous album 'America', all albums released while the group was a

trio had titles commencing with the letter 'H' –
'Homecoming', 'Hat Trick', 'Holiday', 'Hearts',
'Hideaway', 'Harbor' and even a compilation simply
titled 'History'. When Peek left and the band moved
from Warner Brothers to Capital Records, the 'H'
trend ended, however when the Capital deal was
over, America's next releases were 'Hourglass',
'Human Nature' and 'Here and Now'.

Dan Peek passed away in 2011, aged 60 from fibrous
pericarditis.

Son Of A Preacher Man

Conversely, two of rocks 'darker' characters are the
sons of preachers.

The man who sang about dead babies, welcomed us
to his nightmare and played with guillotines and boa
constrictors onstage, Vincent Furnier aka Alice Cooper
was the son of a lay preacher from the Church of Jesus
Christ.

Collector of Nazi memorabilia, consumer of sex, drugs
and alcohol, Ian Kilminster has had a life in music that
is at odds with that of his father who was an ex-Royal
Air Force Chaplain. Kilminster is better known by his
nickname Lemmy and as lead singer on Hawkwind's
'Silver Machine' and Motorhead's 'Ace of Spades'.

Sympathy For The Devil

Even more sinister is the anti-religion of Satanism and there have been a few rumours of musicians with leanings in that direction.

Blues legend Robert John Johnson died in 1938 but has been listed as the major influence on modern rock acts from the Rolling Stones to Eric Clapton from Led Zeppelin to Fleetwood Mac. Comparing musicians from different eras or even different genres does not achieve anything but recognising influential talent is fair and Johnson did contribute to the catalogue of the acts mentioned as well as some of his recordings that surface in vinyl in the early sixties. The word legend is often used when talking about Johnson because of his contribution to the blues but also because of the stories surrounding his death and purported deal with the devil. Did he drink poison, was he murdered, did he accept the devil's assistance to help him play the blues are questions that give life to the word legend.

Rumours about satanic influences on Led Zeppelin, mainly guitarist Jimmy Page, gave certain factions of the press a theme to analyse in the seventies.
Page at one time owned an occult bookstore and was apparently fascinated with the dark arts of writer Aleister Crowley and even purchased the author's old house. His stage clothes sporting signs of the zodiac and his 'ZOSO' logo added to the image but there was

no evidence apart from interest on the part of Page to assume there was any connection to an anti-Christ.

Some Heavy metal rock bands and Goth musicians adopt the image of evil but much of this is public relations whereas in the heaviest of metal musical genres with names such as Death Metal, Black Metal and Grindcore, much of the image is based on anarchy but there are some bands who do actually follow Satanic views. American bands 'Acheron' and 'Angel Corpse' are from that background and England's 'Cradle of Filth' lean in that direction but the concentration of this style seems to be centered in Scandinavia.

Dark Side Of The Moon

Having descended the musical scale from the heights of heavenly believers to the depths of satanic sounds, we end at the dark side with Scientology and the on-going dispute that the Church of Scientology is fighting with the Governments of many countries for religious recognition.
While the US Government acknowledged the movement as having religious status in the early 1990's, with Sweden, Spain and Portugal following suit, other countries including Germany, France, UK and Canada reject its religious credentials.

John Travolta first found recognition as an actor in 1975 when he starred in the American television series 'Welcome Back Kotter'. The same year he recognised Scientology and has been a follower since. He has starred in many popular films from 'Look who's Talking' to 'Pulp Fiction' but his musical credential stretch from his dancing role in the much parodied 'Saturday Night Fever' and his singing role in the blockbuster 'Grease'. Travolta has released more than 20 singles and a few albums plus being included in compilations mainly for his biggest hits duetting with Olivia Newton John on 'You're the One that I Want' and 'Summer Nights'. During all the ups and downs in his career and personal life, John Travolta refers to his faith as keeping him positive.

Jazz musician keyboard player Chick Corea is a Scientologist as is rock keyboardist Edgar Winter and so was the late 'Shaft' composer Isaac Hayes.

Having had a successful career as an actress, Juliette Lewis branched out and became a 'rock chick' fronting a band, recording a few albums and giving credible live performances.
Lewis was born into Scientology and has progressed through the stages, even naming one of her albums "Terra Incognita" which is the title of an article written by the 'cult's founder L Ron Hubbard.

Ellvis Presley's daughter Lisa Marie followed her mother Priscilla into the Church of Scientology but appears to have renounced that path.

The other musical Presley, Reg from sixties outfit The Troggs found himself in the money in the 1990's, not so much from his recordings of 'Wild Thing' or 'With a Girl Like You' but from Wet Wet Wet's version of his song 'Love is all Around. He used the royalties to investigate a mystery that is not so much a religion, but the inexplicable phenomena known as 'Crop Circles'.

Needless to say his research was inconclusive and the enigma continues allowing conspiracy theories to perpetuate.

Twenty-seven

There have been many references throughout these pages to the '27 club' aka 'Forever 27 Club' and the many similarities and coincidences of those mentioned have also provided food for thought for conspiracy theorists.

Therefore to conclude on this enigmatic topic, I will reprise membership to date.

The initial 'members' of this fictitious institution were (note initial J);

Brian Jones   Jimi Hendrix   Jim Morrison   Janis Joplin

all of whom died between 1969 and 1971 at the age of 27.

When 27 year old Kurt Kobain shot himself in 1994, interest in the 'club' was resurrected and again with the passing of Amy Winehouse 17 years later at the same age, the story gained more interest.

There have been films using the theme, one starring Bono's daughter Eve Hewson, plays, books and articles throughout the last 40 years based on the phenomena, some merely for entertainment while others tending to build up the coincidence to near conspiracy level.   It is true that more musicians have terminated their careers and lives at this young age than any other, but then again, one age had to have the most former musicians leaving the stage and 27 came up trumps.

Not only were the initial four plus two in the club but going all the way back to 1938, legendary bluesman Robert Johnson was fatally poisoned at the ominous age and thirty years prior to that, ragtime musician Louis Chauvin was 27 when he passed on.

The list is extensive, including;

Badfinger's Pete Ham

Uriah Heep's Gary Thain

Stone the Crows' Les Harvey

Stooges Dave Alexander

Grateful Dead's Ron 'Pigpen' McKernan

Canned Heat's Alan 'Blind Owl' Wilson

Inner Circle's Jacob Miller

Echo and the Bunnymen's Pete De Freitas

Big Star's Chris Bell

Bloodstone's Roger Lee Durham

Drifter's Rudy Lewis

Friendly Fires' Richard Turner

Hole's Kristen Pfaffe

and many others with the common factor that they died at the age of 27 years.

.

What is also intriguing about a number of these deaths is that they were in suspicious or disputed circumstances.

Jones, Morrison, Hendrix and Johnson's were contentious, the suicides of Cobain, Ham, Wilson and Alexander Bashlachev raised questions.
There was the murder of 'Gits' vocalist Mia Zapata, Fat Pat, Freaky Tah, Valentin Elizalde, Arlester 'Dyke' Christian and obviously Richie Edward's 'disappearance – presumed dead' is confusing, but there are others.

The Argentenian singer Rodrigo Bueno died in a car crash when he was 27 and suspicions were raised as to the cause of the accident, with some alleging that another vehicle had caused the collision, and although not proven, could have been on purpose.

In 1960, parts of America were still very much racially divided and Little Rock, Arkansas was no exception. In February of that year, a concert was arranged featuring black artists Sam Cooke, Jackie Wilson, Marv Johnson and Jesse Belvin. This was the first concert of its type at the venue with an integrated audience and passions were running high.
27 year old Belvin had received death threats before his performance and on two occasions the music was halted due to racial taunts in the audience.
Following the gig, Belvin's car was involved in a head on collision which killed him and his wife. There was speculation that his vehicle had been tampered with but nothing was proven.

Perhaps 26 year old pop / rock musicians should be a little nervous as they near the fateful birthday but considering the variety of causes of death at this and any other age, there is no reason to be superstitious, or is there?

As has been shown, there are many unavoidable situations from accidents, illnesses and even murder that have caused the deaths of musicians, just like a cross section of society and in the cases of suicides and drug / alcohol abuse, again we are all susceptible to those pressures, musicians or otherwise.

The final word on the subject is taken from an article published in the British Medical Journal referring to a study carried out by an Australian team.   The piece is headed;

"Is 27 really a dangerous age for famous musicians? A retrospective cohort study"

Statistician Adrian Barnett and his team from the Institute of Health and Biomedical Innovation and School of Public Health, Queensland University of Technology, Brisbane, Australia concluded (ic) "the '27 club' is based on myth, but warn that musicians have a generally increased risk of dying throughout their 20's and 30's. This finding should be of international concern, as musicians contribute greatly to populations' quality of life, so there is immense value in keeping them alive (and working) as long as possible".

To sum up, musicians like everyone else are born, they live and they die – at various ages from a variety of causes.

During the middle section which is life, many of them live it to the full and in some cases beyond. They have relationships, they get illnesses, they consider their spirituality and they have flaws, most of which are played out in the media.

Admittedly some of them court publicity and controversy so why should we admire them?

Well, not because of the celebrity stories, nor the media headlines, but because they have talent as musicians and they produce the soundtracks that add to our lives but at the same time as we have just read, they are human (well most of them are).

APPENDIX

1) Partners

   Chapter 1 begins with a couple of lines from a
   Stephen Stills song called 'Change Partners'
   but another of his songs sums up the attitude
   towards sex and relationships as 'pop' music
   became embedded in popular culture and the
   young generation experimented with different
   sounds, ideas and stretched the boundaries of
   acceptance.

   "If you can't be with the one you love, love the
   one you're with" (xxi)

   The innocence and idealism of the sixties
   quickly took cognisance of reality as drug
   casualties mounted up and in the permissive
   society, as it was termed, loving the one you're
   with was a positive emotion but physically had
   repercussions with an increase in unplanned
   pregnancies, broken marriages and serious
   diseases.

   As the decade ended, the hippie dream also
   ended and the fantasy lifestyle was overtaken
   by reality. Many relationships did not survive,
   but the music did.

   In 2012 there was a public outcry in the UK
   about child abuse reportedly carried out by a

leading public figure, by then deceased, who had found fame as a disc jockey. Whilst there were serious allegations about Jimmy Savile taking advantage of his position as a celebrity with access to young and vulnerable persons and subsequently taking advantage of some of them, a number of musicians and others were worried that they could become implicated and some of them indicated the innocence of the times, apparent free love ethos and the 'groupie' effect as being the reasons for their behaviour. Many musicians enjoyed post gig pleasure with the company of someone or more than one, they had not previously met but were unaware of the ages of consenting partners.

While ignorance is not an alibi, there needs to be some perspective when considering alleged abuse to ensure that 'predators' are dealt with appropriately whilst acknowledging others may have committed what can now be seen as retrospective 'minor' crimes.

Loving the one you were with is not the same as abusing the one you can!

2) Children

Musical talent is not necessarily hereditary but for many children of musicians the exposure, interest and excitement rubs off and they follow the same path as their musical parent(s). In addition, they often have access to instruments, appropriate contacts and practical experience of living in the musician's lifestyle bubble.

3) Siblings

Like all families, musical families have competitive as well as intuitive attributes and although there are many examples of sibling rivalry in bands of brothers and sisters, there is a unique quality when their voices blend as singers.

4) Names

What's in a name? Amen(s)

5) Songs

Having acknowledged that artists may copy other work unintentionally, I was coincidently listening to Bob Dylan's 35th studio album 'Tempest' as I was writing this and the introduction to the first track 'Duquesne Whistle' (written in collaboration with Grateful Dead's some time lyricist Robert Hunter) was reminiscent of a song from back in the mid 1960's. Not from Mr Zimmerman, but one of his coffee house troubadour contemporaries Tom Paxton, whose melody from 'Last thing on my Mind' sounds similar. I suggest that this is not plagiarism, merely a grouping of notes to form a pleasant melody not unlike many other pleasant melodies.

When I hear Duqusne whistle, plagiarism will be the last thing on my mind.

I know many 'amateur' songwriters and have listened to many of their songs. They may not have the quality recordings afforded by major acts nor the marketing offered by major labels but occasionally even the non-professionals, the 'hobby' writers can come up with a gem and it is frustrating to hear songs on the radio that are below par when these well-crafted compositions go un-noticed, un-aired and unheard.

6) Disability

The examples exemplify that ability trumps disability in scaling the scales and opportunities for disabled musicians should be encouraged. In parallel with the 2012 Paralympics, the Paraorchestra were given prominence alongside Coldplay at the closing ceremony which was another encouraging step to recognition.

7) Death

As this publication shows, many talented musicians bowed out early through a variety of causes but musicians as a cross section of society do not have proportionately more deaths than other sectors.

On a slightly more personal note, I only met / knew two musicians who had any modicum of success in the fickle world of pop / rock. Bobby Paterson wrote, played and recorded with Sandy McLelland and the Backline, Set the Tone and the respected 'Love and Money'. Cha Burns was a member of Fingerprintz, Adam and the Ants band and The Silencers who had reasonable success in Europe in addition to their native Scottish fanbase.

I lived in the next street to Bobby, attended the same schools, played in the same school band and attempted writing songs along with him and some friends, but even then his ideas were in advance of the rest of our amateur efforts. We sarcastically referred to him as 'shovel hands' and his fingers were certainly formed to suit the bass guitar at which he became very proficient. Bobby would regale us with tales of recording in New York with members of Steely Dan or giving interviews in Japan in which teenagers wanted to know interesting facts like what is the band members favourite colour but despite the apparent 'high life' of rock and roll, he also confided that to an extent he envied the 'normality' of the lifestyle his old friends retained.

I met Cha through a mutual girlfriend just as he was beginning to make a name for himself in the music business and later on a visit to London, stayed in his flat for a few days. He was an interesting guy, at the time a bit intense and he kept moving his fingers as if thinking about playing guitar whilst having a conversation, we talked about various things and went to see some bands but apart from attending a Fingerprintz gig, I never saw him again.

However, what was apparent about both these guys, in addition to musical ability and talent, was a determined attitude to do what they enjoyed, play music.

There are many would be musicians, many competent players and many reluctant performers, but these two epitomised the final ingredient – not so much an end goal, but the desire to follow a path towards it.

I was born in 1955, Bobby in 1956 and Cha in 1957.

Sadly, Bobby died in 2006 and Cha in 2007, both in their 50th year.

As Bob Dylan sang in his song, 'Death is not the end' (xxii)

"oh the tree of life is growing where the spirit never dies and the bright light of salvation shines in dark and empty skies"

The legacy of musicians is in the music they made which does not die with them.

8) Eight Miles High

Many profess that certain drugs assist them to create and also to survive in the world of rock 'n ' roll, but what goes up must come down and the casualties are testament that as the Verve sing, 'The Drugs Don't Work'.(xxiii)

9) Suicide

Suicide isn't for everyone but once you've done it, there is no going back. The only suitable retort to the seriousness of this topic is to quote the old joke,
'I once tried to commit suicide but I nearly killed myself in the process so I'm not doing that again'.
Nothing that causes negative emotion is painless, anyone that causes positive emotion is worth listening to irrespective of how they came into the world or how they leave it.

10) Religion

Music is appreciated based on personal taste and religion is also appreciated from an individual perspective. Not everyone feels strongly about either and some are sceptical when musicians try to preach.
However, the impartiality of positive lyrics together with a melodic tune can induce a spirituality of its own.

One controversial musician from the rock world used music as a catalyst for humanitarian good and has been an outspoken critic of the establishment including politicians and religious leaders.

In an interview with a Jewish newspaper, Bob Geldof confirmed his religious credentials in his usual direct fashion (id)

"I was a quarter Catholic, a quarter Protestant, a quarter Jewish and a quarter nothing – the nothing won".

Perhaps he didn't like Mondays because that day was preceded by two Sabbath days.

Musicians eat cakes but coincidently bakers of cakes listen to music and there is a similarity in taking the ingredients and using talent to create the end product so there is a connection between the two.

I hope you enjoyed your slice of cake
musicianseatcakes@btinternet.com

Song and Album Answers

You're The One That I Want - Performed by
John Travolta & Olivia Newton- John, Written
by John Farrar   1978 Massive global hit
single taken from the film 'Grease' soundtrack

Famous Groupies - Performed by Wings,
Written by Paul McCartney & Denny Laine
1978 track taken from album 'London Town'
which was a minor hit

Summer The First Time - Written and
performed by Bobby Goldsboro 1973 hit single
taken from album of the same name.

Do It Again - Performed by The Beach Boys,
Written by Brian Wilson & Mike Love   1968
hit in many countries, number 1 in UK for 1
week, taken from album 20/20 but featured
on many compilations.

Together Again - A much used title for a
song and album by various artists. The two
most popular being the Buck Owens country
song which was successful for the writer in

1964 and has also been covered by numerous artists including hits for Ray Charles in 1966 and Emmylou Harris in 1975.

There is also a 1997 song of the same name that has sold over 6 million copies for Janet Jackson.

The Young Ones - Performed by Cliff Richard and The Shadows, Written by Sid Tepper & Roy C Bennett   1961 single, number 1 in UK, taken from album soundtrack to film of same name.

Meet On The Ledge - Performed by Fairport Convention, Written by Richard Thomson 1968 track from the album 'What We Did On Our Holidays'. Did not sell that well as a single but has become the unofficial anthem for the band and is the closing song each year at the Cropredy Festival.

Wasn't Born To Follow - Performed by The Byrds, Written by Carole King & Gerry Goffin 1968 recording features on the album and soundtrack to the film Easy Rider

Lullaby - Written and performed by Shawn Mullins 1998 single that was a major hit in the US, Canada and Australia taken from the album 'Souls Core'.

Join Together - Performed by The Who, Written by Pete Townsend 1972 single not taken from an album that was a reasonable hit in UK and USA

Two Of Us - Performed by The Beatles, Written by Lennon / McCartney (although really just Paul) 1969 track from 'Let It Be' The title 'Two Of Us'   is not preceded by 'The'

Brothers In Arms - Performed by Dire Straits, Written by Mark Knopfler   1985 moderate hit single on the back of the incredibly successful album of the same name which was one of the first to be manufactured for the CD market

Sisters Are Doing It For Themselves -
Performed by the Eurythmics and Aretha
Franklin, Written by Dave Stewart and Annie
Lennox 1985 top 10 single in many countries
which was included on both the Eurythmics
album 'Be Yourself Tonight' and Aretha's
'Who's Zoomin' Who'.

Family Affair - Performed by Sly and The
Family Stone, Written by Sly Stone 1971
number 1 US single is a much covered song.
Also a song by Mary J Blige et al which made
US number 1 in 2001 taken from her album
'No More Drama'.

Definitely Maybe - 1994 debut album by
English band 'Oasis'

X & Y - 2005 album by English band
'Coldplay' their third release

Nick Of Time - 1989 album by American
Bonnie Raitt, her tenth

For No One - Performed by The Beatles, Written by Lennon / McCartney (although really just Paul)   1966 album track taken from 'Revolver'.

Here There And Everywhere - Performed by The Beatles, Written by Lennon/ McCartney (although really just Paul) 1966 album track taken from 'Revolver'

Lucky Number - Performed by Lene Lovich, Written by Les Chappel & Lene Lovich   1978 UK hit single taken from the album 'Stateless'.

Colours - Written and performed by Donovan (Leitch) 1965 hit single

The Sound Of Silence - Performed by Simon and Garfunkel, Written by Paul Simon   1966 hit single taken from the album 'Sounds of Silence'

Someone Someone - Performed by Brian Poole and The Tremeloes, Written by Norman Petty & Edwin Greines Cohen   1964 UK hit single

Unchained Melody -   Written by Alex North and Hy Zaret in 1955, this song is one of the most covered ever in the history of music. Notable versions are by the Righteous Brothers from 1965 (although only Bobby Hatfield features) it became a major hit on its re-release in 1990. Other international hit versions include Al Hibbler and Baxter while in the UK the song has topped the charts by Jimmy Young, Gareth Gates as well as the duo of Robson Green and Jerome Flynn.

Word Up   -   Performed by Cameo, Written by Larry Blackmon & Tomi Jenkins Much covered 1986 hip-hop international hit single from album of the same name.   Alternative versions by Gun (1994) and Melanie C (1999) also charted in the UK.

I'd Like To Teach The World To Sing - Performed by The New Seekers, Written by Roger Cook, Roger Greenaway, Bill Backer & Billy Davis 1971 successful advertising jingle adapted into hit single in UK and USA.

We Sing We Dance We Steal Things -   2008 album by Jason Mraz

Lawyers Guns And Money   -   Written and performed by Warren Zevon   1978 track from the album 'Excitable Boy'

The Singer sang His Song   -   Written and performed by Barry, Robin & Maurice Gibb 1968 Bee Gees single not included on an album (except later compilations) double A side with 'Jumbo'

Eyes Without A Face   -   Performed by Billy Idol, Written by Billy Idol & Steve Stevens 1983 single taken from the album 'Rebel Yell'.

Putting On The Style   -   Performed by Lonnie Donegan, Written by Norman Cazden   1957 hit single in the 'skiffle' style, previously recorded by Vernon Dalhart in the 1920's

Fandango   -   1975 album by ZZ Top, their fourth – named after a dance

My Way   -   Performed by Frank Sinatra, Written by Claude Francois, Jacques Revaux & Paul Anka   1969 single became Sinatra's

signature tune although it has been covered by numerous artists in various styles.
Other chart versions Include Elvis Presley US hit in 1977 and UK positions for Dorothy Squires in 1970 and eight years later a punk rendition by Sex Pistols' Sid Vicious.

Doctor My Eyes - Written and performed by Jackson Browne 1972 top 10 US single for the composer taken from his eponymous first album. Also top 10 in the UK in the same year was a version by the Jackson 5.

I Can hear Music - Performed by The Beach Boys, Written by Jeff Barrie, Ellie Greenwich & Phil Spector 1969 international hit for the Beach Boys following an unsuccessful version by The Ronettes.

Behind The Mask - 1990 album by Fleetwood Mac their fifteenth release.
It is also the name of a song by the 'Yellow Magic Orchestra' written by Ryuichi Sakamoto and Chris Mosdell. With additional lyrics by Michael Jackson, who recorded a version as

well, it became a hit for Greg Phillinganes and Eric Clapton.

Move On Up - Written and performed by Curtis Mayfield 1970 UK hit single from debut solo album 'Curtis' following success with The Impressions.

Wreck On The Highway - Written and performed by Bruce Springsteen
1980 track from double album 'The River'

It's Getting Better - Performed by Cass Elliot, written by Barry Mann & Cynthia Weil   1969 hit single for the ex- Mamas and Papas' singer from her album 'Bubblegum, Lemonade and Something for Mama'
The Beatles track from Sgt Pepper's Lonely Hearts Club Band is called 'Getting Better'.

A Rush Of Blood To The Head - 2002 album by 'Coldplay', their second disc

White Ladder - 1998 album by David Gray, fourth release but breakthrough

Mellon Collie And The Infinite Sadness - 1995 double disc, 28 track release by the Smashing Pumpkins as a 'loose concept' product

Perfect Skin - Performed by Lloyd Cole and the Commotions, Written by Lloyd Cole 1984 track taken from debut album 'Rattlesnakes' moderate UK hit

Sugar Sugar - Performed by The Archies, Written by Ron Dante & Andy Kim 1969 Canadian, American and United Kingdom chart topper created using session singers and players to give voice to a fictional comic book group

I Want To See The Bright Lights Tonight - Performed by Richard and Linda Thomson, Written by Richard Thomson 1974 song from album of the same name, Thomson's second solo outing although shared credits with then wife

Too Close To Heaven - Performed by The Waterboys, Written by Mike Scott 2001 a lengthy track from album of same name, a collection of informal tracks recorded at the same sessions in late 1980's that produced Fisherman's Blues

Sea Of Madness - Performed by Crosby, Stills, Nash & Young, Written by Neil Young 1970 track from 'Woodstock' soundtrack album
Also a song by Iron Maiden written by Adrian Smith taken from 1986 album 'Somewhere in Time'.

Whiskey In The Jar - Performed by Thin Lizzy, Written by Trad. Arr Eric Bell, Brian Downey & Phil Lynott 1972 hit single building on the popularity brought to the traditional song by The Dubliners, Thin Lizzy's guitar driven version made it an Irish favourite where it topped the charts for four months. Grateful Dead gave it an American slant in 1999 and out of the many covers of the song, Metallica recorded a version that won them a Grammy in 1998

Streets Of Philadelphia - Written and performed by Bruce Springsteen 1994 Global hit and Oscar winning best original song from the movie 'Philadelphia'.

How Come - Performed by Ronnie Lane and Slim Chance, Written by Ronnie Lane & Clive Westlake 1973 top 20 single from ex-Small Faces/Faces musician Also a 2004 rap song by D12.

Heat Of The Moment - Performed by Asia, Written by John Wetton & Geoff Downes 1982 international hit single from the group's debut eponymous album

No More Tears (Enough Is Enough) - Performed by Donna Summer and Barbra Streisand, Written by Paul Jabara & Bruce Roberts 1979 international hit that appeared on Barbra's album 'Wet' and Donna's album 'On the Radio' a greatest hits compilation with this as a new track.

Flying On The Ground Is Wrong - Performed by Buffalo Springfield, Written by Neil Young

1966 track from Buffalo Springfield's debut eponymous album

<u>Drive</u> - Performed by The Cars, Written by Ric Ocasek   1984 international top 5 single taken from album 'Heartbeat City' which will forever be associated with the pre-live aid film portraying starving children

<u>Motor Biking</u> - Written and performed by Chris Spedding   1975 UK top 20 single

<u>Wasted Time</u> - performed by The Eagles, Written by Don Henley & Glen Frey   1976 track from 'Hotel California' album

<u>Anyone Who Had A Heart</u> - Performed by Dionne Warwick, Written by Burt Bacharach & Hal David   1963 hit single in US and various countries but not nearly as big in the UK as Cilla Black's chart topping version in 1964

<u>Slip Sliding Away</u> - Written and performed by Paul Simon   1977 hit single

<u>Silence Is Golden</u> - Performed by The Tremeloes, Written by Bob Gaudio & Bob Crewe   1967 UK chart topper and number 11 in the US where it had been at number 1 three years earlier as the B side of 'Rag Doll' by the group in which the composers sang, The Four Seasons

<u>Jagged Little Pill</u> - 1995 album by Alanis Morrisette which was international hit

   <u>21</u> - 2011 album by Adele which became global chart topper and best seller

<u>Bang Bang</u> - Performed by Cher, Written by Sonny Bono   1966 top 5 single

<u>Jumping Jack Flash</u> - Performed by The Rolling Stones, Written by Mick Jagger & Keith Richards   1968 top 5 single

<u>Hang On Sloopy</u> - Performed by the McCoys, Written by Wes Farrell & Bert Russell   1965 US number 1 single

<u>Hey, That's No Way To Say Goodbye</u> -
Written and performed by Leonard Cohen
1967 track from debut album The Songs of
Leonard Cohen

<u>The Last Farewell</u> - Performed by Roger
Whittaker, Written by Roger Whittaker & Ron
A Webster   1971 single which was not initially
a hit but eventually sold in excess of 10 million
copies globally

<u>Goodbye</u> -   Performed by Mary Hopkin,
Written by Lennon /McCartney (really just
Paul)   1969 hit single. Also a 1998 track by
the Spice Girls from their album 'Forever'
written by the girls plus Richard Stannard &
Matt Rowe

<u>Murder On The Dancefloor</u> - Performed by
Sophie-Ellis Bextor, Written by Sophie Ellis-
Bextor& Greg Alexander   2001 top 10 hit
throughout Europe

<u>San Quentin / Folsom Prison Blues</u> - Written
and performed by Johnny Cash   Although
Folsom Prison Blues was originally written in

1955, live versions of both of these songs were included on the 1969 release 'At San Quentin'.

I Believe - Performed by Frankie Laine, Written by Ervin Drake, Irvin Graham, Jimmy Shirl & Al Stillman   1953 top 3 hit in US & UK, much covered song which was again top 3 in the UK and Ireland in 1964 by The Bachelors

I'm A Believer - Performed by The Monkees, Written by Neil Diamond   1966 popular hit for the 'manufactured' group, UK top 30 in 1974 for Robert Wyatt and UK top 3 in 1995 for Vic reeves & Bob Mortimer

Don't Stop Believing - Performed by Journey, Written by Jonathan Cain, Steve Perry & Neal Schon   1981 US top 10 single which became UK to 10 in 2009 and become a major download favourite

Faith - Written and performed by George Michael   1987 international hit single taken from the equally successful album of the same name

<u>Son Of A Preacher Man</u>   -   Performed by Dusty Springfield, Written by John Hurley & Ronnie Wilkins   1968 international top 10 hit, much covered since

<u>Sympathy For The Devil</u>   -   Performed by The Rolling Stones, Written by Mick Jagger & Keith Richards   1968 track from 'Begger's Banquet' album that has proved popular and controversial, cover versions include a top 50 US hit single version by Guns ' n' Roses in 1994 and a remixed Stones' version in 2003

<u>Dark Side Of The Moon</u>   -   1973 album by Pink Floyd that has become one of the top sellers of all time, eighth album by the band that that catapulted them to legendary status

<u>Twenty-seven</u>   -   1992 album by The Adicts, the punk bands fifth

Song References

(i)   "1941" written by Harry Nilsson - 1967, RCA Victor

(ii)   "Without You" written by Pete Ham & Tom Evans - 1970, Apple Records

(iii) "Change Partners" written by Steven Stills - 1971, Atlantic Records   (Sony/ATV Music Publishing LLC)

(iv) "Teach Your Children" written by Graham Nash 1969, Atlantic Records (Giving Room Music)

(v)   "Brothers and Sisters" written by Guy Berryman, Jonny Buckland, Will Champion & Chris Martin - 1999, Fierce Panda

(vi)   "I've Got a Name" written by Jim Croce -

(vii) "I Write the Songs" written by Bruce Johnston - 1975, Arista (Universal Music Publishing Group)

(viii) "Bohemian Rhapsody" written by Freddie Mercury - 1975, EMI

(ix) "A Whiter Shade of Pale" written by Gary Brooker, Keith Reid & Mathew Fisher - 1967, Deram

(x) "Don't Let It Bring You Down" written by Neil Young - 1970, Reprise

(xi) "The Art of Dying" written by George Harrison - 1970, Apple Records

(xii) "Amelia" written by Joni Mitchell - 1976, Asylum

(xiii) "Dead Man's Curve" written by Jan Berry, Roger Christian, Brian Wilson and Artie Kornfield - 1964, Liberty Records

(xiv) "Terry" written by Lynn Ripley - 1964, Decca Records

(xv) "Why Me" written by Mary Cowan & Sharon Zigman - 2005, 'The Colour's Coming Back' – Zigman Creative Projects Foundation

(xvi) "Heart of Glass" written by Deborah Harry & Chris Stein - 1978, Chrysalis

(xvii) "Nursie" written by Ian Anderson - 1972, Chrysalis

(xviii) "Eight Miles High" written by Gene Clark, Jim McGuinn & David Crosby - 1966, Columbia

(xix) "Suicide Is Painless" written by Mike Altman & Johnny Mandel - 1969, Columbia/CBS

(xx) "Losing My Religion" written by Bill Berry, Peter Buck, Mike Mills & Michael Stipe - 1991, Warner Brothers

(xxi) "Love the One you're with" written by Stephen Stills, 1970, Atlantic

(xxii) "Death is not the End" written by Bob Dylan, 1988, Columbia

(xxiii) "The Drugs Don't Work" written by Richard Ashcroft, 1997, Hut

Liner Notes References

(a) 'Timespace : The Best of Stevie Nicks', 1991, Modern Records
Notes written by Stevie Nicks

(b) 'Decade', 1977, Reprise
Notes written by Neil Young

References

(1) Souness   2010, p.225

(2) Souness   2010, p.175

(3) Souness 2010, p.298

(4) Judd   2005, p.102

(5) Boyd (with Junor)   p.174

(6) Wood   2007, p.106

(7) Balfour   1986, p.15

(8) Balfour   1986, p.103

(9) Buckley   1999, p.110

(10) Balfour   1986, p.173

(11) Balfour   1986, p.174

(12) Balfour   1986, p.134

(13) Balfour   1986, p.132

(14) Wyman (with Coleman)   1990, p.26

(15) Wyman (with Coleman)   1990, p27

(16) Balfour   1986, p.28

(17) Balfour   1986, p.24

(18) Interview by Mikal Gilmore, Rolling Stone Magazine 12 September 2012

(19) Interviewees C. Martin & J. Buckland, Rolling Stone magazine, 2005

(20) Hewitt, P.   1995, p.

(21) Wall, M   2008, p.67

(22) Interviewee Olivia Newton-John, Australian Woman's Weekly magazine, November 2007

(23) Interviewee Stuart Goddard / Interviewer Matt Everett, 23 February 2011 BBC 6 Music

(24) Rich, Everitt   2004, p.

Internet Sources

(1A)   You Tube – Pamela Des Barres – Reading from "Let's Spend the Night Together – Backstage Secrets of Rock Muses and Supergroupies"

(2A)   www.evelyn.co.uk   1993, Hearing Essay

Newspaper & Magazine Articles

(ia)   Daily Mail, 3 November 2012, Daily Mail Reporter

(ib)   Guardian, 15 February 2010, article by Carrie Quinlan – 'Revealed: The Vatican's Favourite Bands'

(ic)   British Medical Journal, 20 December 2010, - 'Is 27 really a dangerous age for famous musicians?'

(id)   Manchester Jewish Telegraph, 22 March 2011 reprinted in Jerusalem Post Interviewee Bob Geldof

Bibliography

Balfour, V   Rock Wives   -   The Hard Lives and Good Times of the Wives, Girlfriends and Groupies of Rock and Roll,   1986,   Beech Tree Books, New York

Bockris, R   Keith Richards   -   The Unauthorised Biography,   2002, Omnibus Press, London

Boyd, P with Junor, P   Wonderful Today   - The Autobiography,   2007,   Headline Publishing Group, London

Buckley, D   Strange Fascination   -   David Bowie: The Definitive Story,   1999, Virgin Books, London

Clayson, A   The Quiet One   -   A Life of George Harrison,   1990, Sidgwick & Jackson, London

Coleman, R   Survivor   -   The Authorised Biography of Eric Clapton,   1985,   Sidgwick & Jackson, London

Crosby, D & Gottlieb, C   Long Time Gone - The Autobiography of David Crosby,   1989, William Heineman Ltd., London

Fleetwood, M with Davis, S   Fleetwood - My Life and Adventures in Fleetwood Mac,   1990, William Morrow & Company Inc., New York

George, B with Bright, S   Take it like a Man - The Autobiography of Boy George,   1995, Harper Collins, London

Giuliano, G   Dark Horse - The Secret Life of George Harrison,   1989,   Bloomsbury Publishing, London

Guralnick, P   Searching For Robert Johnson, 1989, Redwood Press, Wiltshire

Halliburton, S   Read Between My Lines - The Musical and Life Journey of Stevie Nicks, 2006, S K Halliburton Enterprises, USA

Halperin, I   Fire and Rain - The James Taylor Story,   2003, Citadel Press, New York

Harrison, G   I Me Mine,   1982,   W.H. Allen, London)

Hewitt, P   Small Faces: The Young Mods' Forgotten Story,   1995,   Acid Jazz Books, London

Judd, N   Al Stewart   - The True Life Adventures of a Folk Rock Troubadour,   2005, Helter Skelter Publishing, London

Leitch, D   The Hurdy Gurdy Man,   2005, Arrow Books, Random House, London

Parmer, S   Blue Jean Baby - One Girl's Trip Through The 1960's L A Music Scene,   2009, Booksurge, Los Angeles

Phillips, J with Jerome, J   Papa John - An Autobiography,   1986,   W.H. Allen, London

Rich, E   Falling Stars: Air Crashes that Filled Rock and Roll Heaven,   2004,   Harbor House, Michigan

Sachs, O   Musicophilia,   2008, Picador, London

Souness, H   FAB   -   An Intimate Life of Paul McCartney,   2010,   Harper Collins, London

Wall, M   When Giants Walked the Earth - A
Biography of Led Zeppelin,   2008, Orion
Books UK

Wood, R Ronnie, 2007, Pan McMillan,
London

Wyman, B with Coleman, R   Stone Alone -
The Story of a Rock 'N' Roll Band, 1990,
Viking (Penguin Books Ltd), London

About the Author

James Allan has been interested in musicians and the music they make since the year dot. Having been an amateur musical performer for many years, he thought, "Why not also be an amateur musical writer".
A graduate of both Glasgow University and Glasgow Caledonian University, James recently gave up the day job as a professional manager and is now managing to be a professional amateur at joining the dots.

2817088R00289

Printed in Great Britain
by Amazon.co.uk, Ltd.,
Marston Gate.